SACRED COMPLEX OF LUMBINĪ

SACRED COMPLEX OF LUMBINI

Dr Gitu Giri

ADROIT

Published by
ADROIT PUBLISHERS
4675/21, Ganpati Bhawan, Ansari Road,
Daryaganj, New Delhi-110 002
Phones : 011-23266030

Distributors
AKHIL BOOK DISTRIBUTORS
e-mail: akhilbooks@yahoo.com
akhilbooks@hotmail.com

ISBN: 978-81-87392-86-6

Printed in India on behalf of M/s Adroit Publishers
by Arpit Printographers • E-mail: arpitprinto@yahoo.com

Forewords

Lumbinī, the birthplace of Lord Buddha, is not only the Holy place of the Buddhists, but also the Fountain of World Peace for all human beings. As a *Tirthasthala* has played a vital role in the socio-cultural and religious life ways of the people. This study will play a definite role in relations of secrets of the sacred traditions of the Tirtha and in generation of love in the hearts of the people of the country to know the great glory of Lumbinī It will support in preserving their regular performances, conserving the sacred monuments, to develop the infrastructure of tourism, enhancing local arts and crafts to promote economic resources of the people. People of various faith, sects, traditions and language use to come to this place for their pilgrimage and the research made an effort to understand their spirit and mannerism, which creates unity in diversity in the domain of Buddhism. This book will support to know the local and regional complexities of this site and comprehend the process of modernisation and transformation because of general development of the area. It will help in strengthening the religious tolerance and respect among the people of different classes and castes of Lumbinī and adjoining areas on a common platform. Similarly, the sacred complexes of the site will work as a dominant balancing force between the traditional and modernised families as well as in the formulation of modern culture. This study has revealed that cultural and civilisation boundaries cut across the national boundaries.

The text throws light on sacred geography, history, master plan, art, architecture, pilgrims and pilgrimages, performances, specialists, fair and festivals, preservation, changes and modernisation, and tourism development of Lumbinī complex. The author, who is an intellectual luminary and a creative writer of

Lumbinī area, indeed combines a deep knowledge of Lumbinī, Kapilvastu and Devadaha. He has utilised his critical talents and experiences as an academic person to explore the obscure beginning the sacred value of Lumbinī. I hope that this book will be useful for the students, teachers, tourists, pilgrims as well as interested persons about the archaeological, anthropological and sociological aspects of the Sacred complex of Lumbinī. Finally, I wish the bright future in such academic work of Dr Giri.

(Prof. Dr Peshal Dahal)
Head of Department
Culture and Archaeology,
Tribhuwan Univfrsity, Nepal

LUMBINĪ INTERNATIONAL RESEARCH INSTITUTE
P.O. Box 39 Phone/Fax: 00977-71-58017 Bhairahawa, Dist. Rupandehi E-mail: liri@mos.com.np

Date: 12 Aug. 2007

Forewords

It is my pleasure to congratulate to Dr Gitu Giri, Bhairahawa Nepal, for the work on the SACRED COMPLEX OF LUMBINĪ, A Research Report submitted to the Tribhuwan University at Kirtipur, Kathmandu. I have read his draft with great interest and, I think, it is a valuable outline of the present status of Lumbinī in many of its inherent aspects. This book will be definitely an asset to the scholarly discussion on Lumbinī, particularly on its philosophical, archaeological and social aspects.

With best regards and wishes for your research.

Sincerely yours,
(Dr. Christoph Cueppers)
Director

Preface

Study on 'Sacred Complex of Lumbinī' is a milestone in the history of the Buddhist World. It is useful in understanding the cultural role of the traditions, tourism development and modernisation with the complexity of Buddhist civilisation. The researcher has brought to light certain facts of pilgrimage, for example, deserved to be studied carefully from different angles and in all its ramifications (Pandey, 2000 and Jha, 1971). The use of the places of pilgrimage as trade and manufacturing centres is the network of pilgrimage organisations. Methodologically, the study of Kāshi and Ruruksetra provided the first basic structure for such an appraisal of civilisation; the present study provides the complete superstructure in its details. The present study is based on the available Buddhist literature, foreign accounts and personal observation of the traditions of various kinds of facts with the help of five types of questionnaires in the random sample technique. Lumbinī being a mini Buddhist World and Fountain of World Peace various aspects have been studied in course of this research. This study involves the geographical, historical, sociological, archaeological, anthropological and observational methods. In the present study sacred geography, history, master plan of Lumbinī, art, architecture, pilgrims and pilgrimage, sacred functionaries, sacred performances, fair and festivals, conservation and preservation, development of tourism and changes and modernisation have been studied to bring to light the hidden knowledge of Lumbinī complex. This is a cultural-cum-anthropological study.

I would like to thank sincerely the Research Division Tribhuwan University which kindly made the present project available. I am grateful to Prof. Dr Peshal Dahal, Head of the

Department of Culture, Tribhuwan University, Kathmandu and Dr Christoph Cüppers, Director of Lumbini International Research Institute for their valuable suggestions and two words. I am particularly grateful to Dr Lam of the Vietnamese Monastery, Ven. Ashin Vivekananda and Ven. Bhadda Manika of the Panditarama Lumbini International Vipassana Meditation Centre, Phra Nirandorn Sihanam of the Thai Monastery, Ven. Thasuma of the Nipponzan Myohoji, Tasi Lama of the Mustang Vihar, Subas Sharma of Hokke, Ven. Maitra of the IBS of Lumbini complex. I would like to express my sincere thanks to Prof. Dr Tulsiram Vaidhya, Vice-Chancellor of Lumbini Intenational Buddhist University, Prof. Dr Prem Kumar Khatry, Dr Dinesh Chandra Regmi and Dr Nareshman Vajracharya, Head of Buddhist Studies T.U., for their affectionate encouragement and the help they rendered to me in various ways. In my endeavour all the members of my family, particulary my wife Basundhara and Son Ramesh, took attention and care. Thanks are also due to the people of Lumbinī area, monks, nuns and devotees who provided me great help in the collection of materials and to the writers whose writings have been utilised in this work. Finally, I thanks to Krishna Chandra Giri of World Vision who collected data from the study area and for the care, he has taken in faultless compute of this research work. Finally, I thanks to D.K. Sharma of Adroit Publisher of Delhi for this publication in proper time.

Dr. Gitu Giri

Content

List of Illustrations

List of Table

List of Abbreviations

APPA	Appreciative Participatory Planning Action.
CBO	Community Based Organization.
CDL	Committee for the Development of Lumbinī
CFNT	Cross Flow Nepal Trust.
CMC	Chairman Managers' Committee.
CO	Community Organization.
COS	Community Organization System
DDC	District Development Committee.
UKDID	United Kingdom's Department for International Development.
DNPWC	Department of National Parks and Wildlife Conservation.
DoA	Department of Archaeology.
DPP	District Participatory Programme.
FG	Functional Group.
HE	Health Education
IBS	Intenational Buddhist Society.
ICF	International Crane Foundation
JBF	Japanese Buddhist Federation.
JOVC	Japanese Overseas Voluntary Co-operation.
JRAS	Journal of Royal Asiatic Society.
LDC	Lumbinī Development Committee.
LDF	Local Development Fund.
LDT	Lumbinī Development Trust.
LGP	Local Governance Programme.
MoCTCA	Ministry of Culture, Tourism and Civil Aviation.
NBPW	Northern Black Polished ware
NfE	Non-formal Education
NRB	Nepal Rastra Bank

NTB	Nepāl Tourism Board.
PDDP	Participatory District Development Programme.
PGW	Painted Grey Ware
PPPP	Public Private Partnership Programme.
RK	Rupandehi and Kapilvastu
RWSSP	Rural Water Supply Support Programme.
RWSSSP	Rural Water Supply and Sanitation Support Programme.
SNVN	The Netherlands Development Organization.
SRT	Sustainable Rural Tourism.
STDC	Sustainable Tourism Development Committee.
STG	Special Target Group.
TEAP	Tourism Environment Awareness Problem.
TRPAP	Tourism for Rural Poverty Alleviation Programme.
UNDP	United Nations Development Programme.
VDC	Village Development Committee.
WB	World Bank.
WTPAP	Western Terai Poverty Alleviation Programme.

Scheme of Transliteration

The following table has been used for spelling of the place names and literary works except individual's names in the text.

c	a	9	dha
cf	ā	0f	ṇa
O	i	t	ta
O{	ī	y	tha
p	u	b	da
pm	ū	w	dha
P	e	g	na
P]	ai	k	pa
cf]	o	km	pha
cf}	au	a	ba
c+	am	e	bha
cM	ah	d	ma
s	ka	o	ya
v	kha	/	ra
u	ga	n	la
3	gha	j	va
ª	ńa	z	śa
r	cha	if	sha
5	chha	;	sa
h	ja	x	ha
em	jha	If	ksha or ksaṣ
~f	ńa	q	tra
6	ṭa	1	jńa
7	ṭha		
8	da		

CHAPTER 1

Introduction of Research

Statement of Problem

Lumbinī, the birthplace of Lord Buddha, is an important touristic as well as pilgrimage site. It is located at Rupandehi district of Lumbinī zone in the Western Terai region of Nepāl. Buddha had advised to visit Lumbinī, Varāṇasi, Bodha Gayā and Kushinagar to his disciples from his deathbed. Emperor Aśoka had visited these sacred-sites with his spiritual teacher Upagupta. In course of his visit, he kept a monolithic stone pillar in Lumbinī, which is inscribed in Brāhmī script. Chinese pilgrims Fa-hien and Hiuen-Tsing had also visited at Lumbinī in the fifth and seventh centuries AD respectively. They had described the location and monumental structures of Lumbinī and Kapilvastu in course of their visit. Their details have provided proper information to find out the exact point of Lumbinī and Kapilvastu in present situation. In the thirteenth century, Ripu Malla had also visited here from Karnāli Pradesh. In such a way, many pilgrims had contributed for Lumbinī during the Mauryan to the Medieval period.

The concept of pilgrims was deeply rooted in the society of Nepāl in the early Christian centuries in Hindu as well as Buddhist society. The holy *tirths* of Varāha ksetra, Mithilā ksetra, Muktināth ksetra, Ruruksetra, etc. are visited not only by the Hindus, but also by the Buddhist, Muslim and other sects without discrimination. Some of the Hindu sacred complexes of Nepāl and India, viz. Janakpur, Pasupatināth and Ruruksetra in Nepāl; Gayā, Kāshi, Bhuwaneshwar in India, etc. have been studied from the anthropological and cultural viewpoint. In the present situation, sacred complexes are not only the spiritual and religious sites, but also the source of income-generation in promoting tourism. Tourism is a main source of foreign exchange and an important factor in the promotion of industry and international trade. Beside it, foreign tourism encourages the understanding in social and cultural life ways of the people among them. Domestic tourism supports to travel their own country in order to familiarise themselves with their religion and cultural tradition and their own specific heritage. In course of industrialisation, Nepāl is deeply interested in developing its touristic activities due to favourable geographical situation, art, architecture, social–economic life ways of the people and cultural phenomena.

One of the cultural and pilgrimage sites of Nepāl, Lumbinī is enriched with potential heritages of tourism being the birthplace of Buddha. In the 19th Conference of World Federation of Buddhism held in Sydney (Austrailia) has declare that Lumbinī is the holiest pilgrimage shrine of the entire Buddhist and the peace loving people of the world. Mass tourism can contribute unique benefit in course of visiting the monumental structures, art, architecture, monastic zone, modern Lumbinī village, sacred specialists or functionaries of priest, monk and nuns in various complex and natural scenes of Lumbinī area. A large number of foreign tourists are interested to visit at Lumbinī. Tourist's facilities such as Hotel, Restaurant, facilated-transport, sport complex, guides and other proper information sources are not sufficient due to the unmanaged system. Sacred performances of Māyādevī temple are not publicly known. Performances as well as the role of the sacred specialists of the various monasteries and vihars have not studied. Many facts of the holy sites and their sacred traditions have mentioned in several *Jatak* stories and in other Buddhist texts. No systematic study was made in Nepāl until the beginning of the study of such tradition in India. However, these studies are incomplete, as they do not throw any light on the sacred specialists, sacred performances, art, architecture, sacred functionaries, preservation, modernisation and changing in the modern period.

Lumbinī was a pleasure garden in the territory of the Śākya of Kapilvastu in ancient period. The immigration and migration of the Tharu, Muslim and other hill people in this area have developed mixed culture. Due to the religious toleration of the area–Hindu, Buddhist and Muslim people are jointly conducting various social and cultural activities. Thus, the researcher is confronted with several problems: What are the sacred centres and performances? What is the role of the sacred specialists or functionaries? Is any national boundary of a civilisation, especially in Buddhism? What are the main elements of processing in modification and transformation because of general development in the large universe of Buddhist civilisation? How can we mobilise the cultural and natural heritage to alleviate poverty in Lumbinī area? How can we create peace and harmony through the process of compromise, combination and co-operation at the site among various faiths, sects and traditions? These are some of the questions that inspired the researcher to choose this topic for research and see it some of the viable answer can be found out.

Objectives of the Study

The main objectives of this study are:

(*a*) to find out tradition of sacred centres and performance of various monasteries, vihar, meditation centres and *gandhakuti;*

(*b*) to trace the role and position of the sacred specialists or functionaries;

(*c*) to examine the Buddhist civilisation at Lumbinī;

(*d*) to make a critical study of the process of modernization and transformation;

(*e*) to find out the general process of mobilising cultural and natural resource to alleviate poverty;

(*f*) to highlight the components of peace, harmony and non-violence through co-operation and compromise among various sects.

Statement of Purpose

Lumbinī, the birthplace of Lord Buddha, is an important pilgrimage site of the Buddhist society. Buddha had advised with feeling of holy reverence and awe that these sites, viz. where the *Tathagata* was born (Lumbinī), the place where he had reached perfect enlightenment (Bodha Gaya), the place where for the first time he had proclaimed the law (deer park near Varāṇasi), and the place of his final extinction (Kusinagar). Known as the sacred spot to the pilgrims hence the nobles, royalties, devotees and scholars from all over the world visited it. Aśoka, Chinese pilgrims Fa-hien and Hiuen–Tsiang, Khas kings as well as other devotees had visited at Lumbinī. At the last decade of the nineteenth century, Führer and Khadga Shumsher J.B. Rana discovered it. From the beginning to recent years, only archaeological activities were performed by the authority there. In the present study, a modest attempt has been made to study the sacred complex of Lumbinī, particularly the sacred geography, history, temple and monasteries, various aspects of pilgrims and pilgrimages. In such a way performance, specialist, various fair and festivals, conservation and preservation of the monuments, development of tourism, modernisation and changes in the behaviours of the people are also contained here. This study throws light on the hidden knowledge of the people and will support to prepare the plans and programmes to the government of Nepāl. It supports to find out the basic elements of preservation and promotion of cultural tourism for the enhancement of economic status of the people in the region.

Tirthasthala has played a vital role in the socio-cultural and religious life of the people. This study will play a definite role in relations of secrets of the sacred traditions of the *Tirtha* and in generation of love in the hearts of the people of the country to know the great glory of Lumbinī. The consciousness of the people, particularly the inhabitants of the ksetra, is being instrumental not only in reviving the prevalent sacred traditions, but also in preserving their regular performances and conserving the sacred monuments built by various agencies in Lumbinī. It will support to develop the infrastructure of tourism in Lumbinī enhancing local arts and crafts to promote economic resources of the people. At the academic level, it will help to understand the origin, development and functions of various traditions through the process of compromise and co-operation. People of various faith, sects, traditions and language use to come to this place for their pilgrimage and the research made an effort to understand their spirit and mannerism, which creates unity in diversity in the domain of Buddhism. It is helpful to know the local and regional complexities of this site and comprehend the process of modernisation and transformation because of general development of this site.

The study of the sacred complex of Lumbinī will play a significant role in unity and bring the people of different classes and castes of Lumbinī and adjoining areas on a common platform. It will help in strengthening the religious tolerance and respect among them. Similarly, the sacred complexes of the site will work as a dominant balancing force between the traditional and modernised families as well as in the formulation of modern culture. The belief which lies at the root of cultural differences, especially Buddhist, Hindus and Muslims, is also the potent factor integrity the heterogeneous cultures. M. Jha (1971) has adequately described the pattern and process of the territorial extensions of culture. According to him, the sacred complexes of Nepāl are undoubtedly an integral part of Indian culture and civilisation. Thus, the cultural and civilisation boundaries cut across the national boundaries. In brief, the solidarous elements in sacred complex function as the linchpins in the Indian Modes of Cultural integration. Thus, this study will bring to light on a lot of hidden knowledge and given a new dimension to the social, religious, pilgrimage, sacred specialists, sacred performances, modernisation and changes of this area. In the light of this study, government may be able to make plans and programmes of the conservation, preservation of important historical and archaeological monuments to promote tourism at this complex.

Review of Literature

Lumbinī, the birthplace of Lord Buddha, is situated about 22 km from Bhairahawā (Siddharthanagar), below the churia range, the foothills of the Himalayas, on the western bank of the Telār River in Rupāndehi district of Lumbinī zone in Nepāl. It is about 34 km from Naugard Railway station on the North-Eastern Railway of India. Buddha, known as the Lord of Asia, was born in Lumbinī during the full moon day in the month of Vaiśākha in 563 BC.

He was born under a *sal* (shorea robusta) tree when Māyādevi was going to her maternal town on delivery.

Suttanipata has mentioned the earliest description of the birth of Buddha in Lumbinī. After the birth of Buddha he took seven steps towards north and, looking in all directions, he declared that, 'I am the foremost of all creatures to cross the riddle of the ocean of the existence, this is my last birth and here after, I will not be born again.' The site is spelt as Rummindei or Rupāndei (beautiful woman), the perverted form of *Rupā Devi*, the queen Anjana of the king of Devadah which was situated to the east of Kapilvastu in ancient time. In Buddhist literature, it is known as *pradimoksa vana* blessed with various trees and flowers, which is compared to the *chittalata* grove of Indra's paradise in heaven. The earliest Pāli text *suttanipata* has mentioned that, 'The wisdom–child that Jewel so precious, that cannot be matched, has been born at Lumbinī, in the Śākya land for well being and joy in the world of men'. A Muslim historian of India named Abul Fazal has called *Mokta*. It is also known as Paderiya (Parariya) where the Aśokan pillar is located in the Nepalese Terai. The name of the site is spelt Lumbinī game and Lumbinī vana in the Aśokan Pillar Edict still standing at the same place. The location of Lumbinī is pointed out in the Buddhist literature as well as, in the Chinese pilgrims who visited India and Nepāl in the fifth and seventh centuries AD.

According to *Jataka S*tory this *sal* garden was in joint possession of the Śākyas and Koliya during the lifetime of Buddha. It was linked through popular *Uttara path* to Kapilvastu, Ramagrama and other important cities during the Buddhist period. The present location of Lumbinī, the exact birthplace of Lord Buddha, is clear. The Buddhist texts *Lalitavistara, Jatak Nidankatha*, *Divya vadana* and *Mahavamsa* have mentioned Lumbinī as the birthplace of Lord Buddha. When Buddha was lying down on the deathbed at the age of eighty in Kusinagar his disciples, monks and nuns surrounded him. On this occasion, he advised with feeling of holy reverence and awe, viz. the place where the *Tathagata* was born (Lumbinī grove), the place where he had reached perfect enlighten (Budha-Gaya), the place where the first time he had proclaimed the law (Deer park near Varāṇasi), and the place of his final extinction (Kusinagar).

Thus, Lumbinī was declared as the sacred spot to the pilgrims and was visited by the scholars, nobles, royalties and devotees from all over the world. According to *Kundala vadana* of *Divyavadana* having led king Aśoka into the Lumbinī jungle, venerable Upagupta indicated with his and said, '*Asmin Maharaja Pradase bhagavan jatah*', meaning–'oh great king! Here the Blessed one was born!'. King Aśoka made an offer of one hundred thousand gold coins and established the first *cetiya* or pagoda. In the Aśokan pillar of Lumbinī it is inscribed that, 'Here *Bhagvan Śākyamuni* was at the Lumbinī village'. King Aśoka installed the stone column with a clear legend inscribed on it that it is the spot of Lumbinī where the Blessed one was born. After the visit of Emperor, many monks and nuns had started visiting at the place. A large number of monasteries and Vihars most have been built for their stay in this sacred complex. A large number artifact of the Mauryan, Sunga, Kushana and Gupta periods were recovered in course of various excavations. It is thus clear that it continued to birthplace of pilgrimage since the third century BC till to date.

Chinese pilgrims have given a more accurate and authentic description of Lumbinī. Shui-ching-chu describes that at Lumbinī the Aśokan tree, which was gripped by Māyādevi at the time of Siddhartha's birth, was still in a living condition and an image of Māyādevi was placed there where devotees used to offer *Puja* articles. The spot where Siddhartha's feet touched the earth first, Aśoka got the Siddhartha's footprints shielded with stones. His description has been ratified by the noticeable findings discovered during the joint excavation of the Department of Archaeology, Lumbinī Development Trust and Japanese Buddhist Federation from 1993 to 1997. It is clearly seen that Aśoka had shielded the Siddhartha's footprints with stone in order to secure it. The then Honourable Prime Minister Sher Bahadur Deuba publicly declared this significant news of the findings of the excavation on February 4, 1996. According to Fa-hien in Lumbinī the queen (Māyādevi) having entered the pool to bathe, came out on the north side, and after walking twenty paces, raised her hands and grasped the branch of a tree. He has stated that tank was used to take both of Siddhartha by two dragon kings. In this context, Hiuen-Tsiang had stated that there was the bathing tank of the Śākyas, the water of which was clear as a mirror and the surface to which was covered with a mixture of flowers. He had seen fallen Aśokan tree, Stūpa and water tank. He has mentioned the detail of the site. After Hiuen-Tsiang, many other pilgrims had visited this place from time to time. One of them was Wu-kung who came in 764 AD. Due to the absence of records very little is known about the condition of the area.

The monumental and habitational structures, stone sculptures, terracotta human and animal figurines, fragments of pottery belonging from Mauryan to Pala-Sena periods, found here reveal that Lumbinī was well-populated till the early-medieval period and was frequently visited by the monks, nuns and other devotees from time to time. Khasa kings of Karnāli Pradesh named Jitari Malla and Ripu Malla had also visited at this sacred complex in the fourteenth century in course of their pilgrimage. After their visited at Lumbinī, its existence was unknown until nineteenth century. Bhuwan Lal Pradhan has claimed that Sikandar Lodi (1489-1517AD) and Aurangzeb (1668-1707AD) were mainly responsible for the destruction of cultural heritage and property of the Lumbinī, Kapilvastu and Devadaha region.

In search of Aśokan pillar A. Führer found two broken pieces of an inscribed Aśokan pillar on the bank of Nigli Sagar at Taulihawa on 1895. At the end of November 1896, Führer had gone to Niglihawa to supervise the contemplated excavations there. In course of his visit, Führer saw the Aśokan pillar at Lumbinī on the 1st December, 1896, which was dug by Khadaga Shamsher J.B. Rana. The importance of the Rummindei pillar inscription for understanding the history of ancient Śākya of Kapilvastu in general and the sacred history of the Buddhism in particular was published on 23 December 1896. When the sensational news of the discovery of the Lumbinī pillar was published, British Government of India sent Mukherji to fix the exact location of Kapilvastu. He published the structural plan of Lumbinī for the first time in his monumental archaeological report in 1901. Kesher Shamsher J.B. Rana had conducted excavation work during the years 1933-39. Debala Mitra had also excavated a small trench at the base of the Aśokan pillar to identify the nature of brick enclosure described by Mukherji and to know the nature of the pillar foundation. N.R. Banerjee (1966-72), B.K. Rijal (1975-83) T.N. Mishra (1984-85), Japanese Buddhist Federation, Lumbinī Development Trust and Department of Archaeology had conducted archaeological activities at Lumbinī.

After the visit to Lumbinī in 1967 U–Thant, the then General secretary of the UNO, had suggested to H.M.G. of Nepāl that Lumbinī should be developed as a place of pilgrimage and a tourist centre equipped with accommodations. A three-member team of UNO Mission had specific instructions to advise the Government on the infrastructural requirements, viz. transportation facilities, drinking water, energy and appropriate accommodation for the visitors from the 10th December to 9th January 1967-68. In 1970 International Lumbinī Development Committee was formed by the representatives of Pakistan, Śri Laṅkā, India, Myanmar, Afghanistan, Thāiland, Cambodia, Indonesia, Laos, Malaysia, Japan, Singapore, and Nepāl. Bhutan and South Korea later joined the committee.

The Master Plan of Lumbinī Development was prepared by Kenzo Tange, a renowned Japanese Prof. and Architect. An area of Lumbinī about three-square miles divided into Sacred Garden, Monastic Enclave and New Lumbinī village have been restored. In order to monitor the Development Committee was constituted in 1971. Late King Mahendra had shown keen interest in developing Lumbinī as a sacred complex for all the human being. Then His Royal Highness Prince and present king of Nepāl Sri 5 Gyanendra Bir Bikram Shah Dev, then Chairman of Lumbinī Development Committee, paid a visit to the United Nations and addressed the International Committee for the Development of Lumbinī in 1986. Javier Perer De Cueller, then Secretary General to the UNO, had also formally addressed the committee. At that time present king Gyanendra had visited Japan and Korea to promote awareness and to develop friendly relationship with each other. King Gyanendra lit a torch of eternal peace in Lumbinī in commemoration of the International year of peace in 1986. The eternal peace flame in Lumbinī is still burning as a Symbol of World Peace.

According to Master Plan New Lumbinī Village area is developing as a community centre providing facilities of comfortable lodges, restaurants, and other facilities. International monastery Zone is developing as a sacred complex to the pilgrims and devotees. In these complex forty-two plots of land is a side. In the complex, the monasteries of Japan, South-Korea, Myanmar, France, Vietnam, Thāiland, China, India and Nepāl have been operating regular worship to the general public. In the process, International Research Institute (Liri and Museum have been operating and providing facilities for meeting, seminar and study to the concerned. The circular sacred garden contains the Aśokan pillar, Māyādevi temple, sacred pond, ruined structures of Stūpas and vihars and other objects within barbed area. In the complex ornamental flower and hedge, Japanese overseas co-operative volunteers (JOCV) to create a reverent atmosphere conducive to remembering and exercising Lord Buddha's, universal message of peace and harmony do plantation.

Almost all the previous activities of the sacred complex of Lumbinī have been concentrated to excavate monumental structure and build Buddhist monasteries, vihars and, meditation centres by LDT and donor agencies. As a whole sacred complex including peace land, pilgrims and pilgrimages, sacred performances, sacred specialists or functionaries, art, architecture, tourism development, etc. components have not carried out in course of study like Hindu sacred complexes, viz. Gaya, Kāshi, Janakpur, Ruruksetra, etc. The American Anthropoligists Prof. Milton Singer and Redfield first started mainly the concept of sacred complex in 1951–53. Among these few attempts, mention may be made of Prof. Cora Dubois (Bhubanseshwar), Dr. Baidyanath Saraswati (Varāṇasi), Dr Surjit Singh (Kali temple), Dr N. Pattanaik (Puri temple), L.P. Vidyarthi (Kāshi), M. Jha (Janakapur) and R.N. Pandey (Ruruksetra), who studied some aspects of certain sacred complexes in India and Nepāl. This study will bring out the structure of the sacred complex that served the entire Buddhist world without any discrimination of national, linguistic, ethnic and sectarian considerations. This study like other studies on this subject is of both academic and applied value. It helps us to understand problems relating to Buddhist civilisation as well as the question of changes in traditional Buddhist culture and for that matter the changing lifestyle in Nepalese and Indian society.

At the applied level, it reflects the fundamental unity of Buddhist and Hindu society and thus unfolds the traditional channels of integration at the level of civilisation. The boundary of a nation is not necessary the boundary of a civilisation. Thus, this study will reveal that the sacred complex is in process of change and integral part of the civilisation. To sum up, it appears that, in terms of general changes, the sacred complex is in the process of re-organisation. It provides a kind of institutional and inspirational continuity and this creates feeling of solidarity which unit the members of a religious group, and will ever remain in the hearts of the followers.

Definition of Concepts

After the second global war and independence of India, a number of American anthropologists like Morris Opler (1948, 1950), Oscar Lewis (1951), David Mandelbaum (1949), Robert Red field (1955, 56, 57) and Mitlan Singer (1955, 58) were stimulated to take up study of theoretically sophisticated problems in the field of social anthropology. Under the influence of the scholars of Chicago School of Anthropology Vidyarthi (1961) studied the sacred city of Gaya and Kashi (1979). Jha (1971) and Pandey (2000) had followed the concepts of cultural specialist, cultural performances and cultural stages. On the basis of these concepts, a new model is developed in the study of the Buddhist civilization of Lumbinī in Nepāl. The concepts of Vidyarathi, Jha and Pandey have been followed in this empirical work. Proper concepts are defined as follows:

1. *The Sacred Complex* : The sacred centres, the sacred performances and sacred specialists of a Buddhist place of pilgrimage reflects the level of continuity, compromise and combination of the traditions.

2. *The Sacred specialists* : Performance great tradition, to the rural population by popularizing certain texts, by organizing pilgrimage and by officiating as the ritual and monastic priests is known Sacred specialist.

3. *Civilization* : Social structure of traditions, value system and cultural personality define civilization.

4. *Modernization* : The sacred Complex and sacred specialist's development leads in the process of modernization and transmission.

5. *Consumers of Sacred* : Citizen and pilgrims, involved their routine, specifying their activities related to sacred performances, and the distribution of time devoted to sacred secular activities.

Location of Study Site

Lumbinī, the birthplace of Lord Buddha, is located in the western Terai Region Rupāndehi district and Lumbinī zone of Nepāl. It is situated abut 22 km. from Bhairahawā (Siddharthnagar) below the churia range, the foothills of the Himalayas, on the western bank of Telār river and 34 km. from Naugarh Railway station on the North eastern Railway of India. 780 hector area of Lumbinī complex is divided into three sectors viz. sacred archaeological garden, monastic zone and modern Lumbinī village on the basis of Master Plan prepared by Prof. Kenzo Tange. Being the land of peace and harmony not only the Buddhists, but also all the human beings are motivated to visit at this sacred complex. Thousands of pilgrims come here in each year for their pilgrimage.

Test Hypothesis

Some of the hypothesis, which has been tested in the study of sacred complex in Lumbinī, are the following :

1. That the sacred complex developed as the sacred centres, the sacred performances and the sacred specialists' combination and continuity of Buddhism;
2. Role of the sacred specialists (monk and nuns) and their position to mobilize social awareness through sacred centres;

3. Process of modernization and transformation of Buddhist civilization in Lumbinī;
4. Mobilization of cultural and natural resources to alleviate poverty by tourism.
5. Continuity, compromise and combination of various sects and groups are needed to create peace and harmony.

Methodology

The data and information required for the study has obtained mainly from the field study. These became supplemented by secondary sources of data from various reports, papers, maps and photographs. In course of this study mainly direct observation, interview, questionnaire and literary methods and techniques have adopted. Stages of the study are as follows:

(i) Pre-field Study

Literature review and preliminary activities have studied during this stage.

1. Data collection: The traditional as well as all the activities that exist there have been personally observed since 1987 AD. The researcher had been involved as Assistant Researcher in course of 'Sacred Complex of Ruruksetra' Project sponsored by UNESCO to Pandey. Processing and techniques of this study have adopted from Kāshi, Janakpur, Ruru, Pasupathinath and other Sacred Complexes of Asia. Consulted Buddhist texts, i.e. Jatak stories, Lalitavistar, Tripitaka etc., as well as research reports of Lumbinī complex.

2. Data Interpretation: Relevant data interpreted in a proper way to fulfil the objectives, giving attention to the proper collection, logging, interpretation and evaluation of available data.

3. Questionnaire and formats: Observational checklist, rating scale, structured – questionnaires, structured interview, scheduled and other relevant field formats have been prepared so that all the required information did not omit during field study.

4. Desk study Report: On the basis of desk study required information and proper data for the programme of field study, a comprehensive report has prepared.

(ii) Field Study

During the field survey, information on vocational characteristics has been obtained through participant observation, interview and questionnaires. In this stage, following activities have been carried out:

1. Data collection: Field data have been collected from Lumbinī Development Trust, Monasteries, Vihars, Museum, Archaeology Department, Lumbinī International Research Institute, Hotels, Guest House, etc. of Lumbinī, Taulihawa, Siddharthanagar and peripheral VDCS' of Lumbinī Sacred complex. Field survey and exploration have been carried out.

2. Interview and questionnaire: The observation was followed by interviews using structured questionnaires separated for pilgrimage, monks and nuns, citizens and pilgrims. During the field work, functionaries, sacred specialists, service providers and local agents were involved in course of interview programmes. In particular, projective tests, observation, open-ended questionnaires and opinionnaires and interviews have used in quantitative research. In order to understand different dimensions of the pilgrimage programmes, interdisciplinary and holistic approach have been appropriately strategy of the study.

3. Sampling: The sample size composed of citizen; pilgrim, monk and nun are determined on random and judgmental sampling principal and adequate to fulfil the survey requirements. In the citizen's questionnaire survey, mainly their visit and sacred performances at the complex, conducted by them, were required (Appendix-1). In the pilgrim's questionnaire survey their aim, residence along or with companies, staying-time, their knowledge about the sacred-site and influence has generated proper information (Appendix-2). Life history of monks and nuns has provided their religious beliefs, concerned monastery or Vihar, cultural knowledge and actual behaviours (Appendix-3).

Additional information, discussion and informal talks were held with the local people, intellectuals, politicians, administrators, and other related person in the area to obtain more information concerning various issues. Useful information arising during the field study has been recorded precisely to understand and interpret the response of person in their real context. Records of all the shrines have been collected (Appendix-4). The position of tourism has also studied (Appendix-5)

(iii) Post-field study

During the period of post-field study, following activities have been conducted:

1. Computerisation of Data: All technical and statistical data have been computerized in proper order.

2. Up-dating the desk data: The desk data have been up-dated and new field data is added. Necessary changed is made in the desk study report to make it more comprehensive and relevant. Essential comments on desk report have mentioned in proper order.

3. Interpretation and evaluation: Proper information of field study has re-evaluated and an aspect like comparative study is prepared. A system's approach has adopted for analyzing the quantities and qualitative data. A careful effort has been make to ensure accuracy in noting down from the records. The information from the community, pilgrims, sacred specialists, functionaries and local informants collected schedules; interviews and case studies have been coded. A key is prepared far each questions indication the number of code for which a response understand for its perspective. The simple statistical method as percentage, mean and ratio has been applied in the data analysis.

(a) Draft report: After the tabulation of required data and information, first draft is prepared on the basis of chapter organisation.

(b) Final report: Incorporating comments on the draft report a final report is prepared to submit.

Limitation of Method

Desk research was carried out at Lumbinī International Research Institute, Tribhuwan University Central Library, Kathmandu, National Library, Harihar Bhawan, Lalitapur, and other enriched-libraries of Buddhist literature in India. Review of published materials, proper data collection, interpretation and development of formats were completed in required time. Desk information was up to dated.

In course of field study direct observation has been conducted in Lumbinī Complex as well as seven Village Development Committees, viz. Lumbinī Adarsa, Madhuvani, Tenuhawa, Akala, Khudabagar, Bhagawanpur and Ama. 10 per cent of total population has been taken through judgemental sampling to fill up citizen questionnaires. Pilgrimage questionnaires were used to the pilgrims at the sites of monasteries, vihar, meditation centre and Lumbinī Development Trust. Sacred specialists, i.e. monks, priests and nuns have involved filling up required questionnaires to them. Rating scale and checklist is used for quantitative research through participant observation. It has become useful to measure their behavioural changes and modernisation through religious activities and performances.

Pilgrims consisting internal and foreigners were participated to express their attitude and skill through structured interviews. This is used in study period. The researcher was engaged as assistant researcher to study the project on 'Sacred Complex of Ruruksetra' sponsored by UNESCO to Pandey in 1996-98. Doctorial degree is also obtained on the topic of Archaeology and Art of the western Terai Region of Nepāl, especially Lumbinī, Kapilvastu and Ramagrama areas. Thus, the researcher has been involving in research activities, which has supported to complete this work with in a short span of time and limited.

Organisation of the Study

Introduction of research, Sacred Geography, History, Master Plan and Development, Art, Architecture, Pilgrims and pilgrimages, Sacred performances, Fair and Festivals, Sacred specialists, Conservation and Preservation of the Monuments, Development of Tourism, Changes and Modernisation and Conclusions are its main chapters.

CHAPTER **2**

Sacred Geography

Location and Physical Features

Lumbinī, the birthplace of Lord Buddha, is situated about 22 km from Bhairahawā (Siddharthanagar), below the Churiā range, on the western bank of Telār River in Rupāndehi district of Lumbinī zone in Nepāl. 28 km west of Lumbinī lies Tilaurakot, the capital town of the Śākyas and 38 km east of Lumbinī is Devadaha, the capital of Koliyas. It is about 34 km from Naugarh Railway Station on the North Eastern Railway of India. It is about 100 MSL. Buddha, known as the Lord of Asia, was born in Lumbinī during the full moon day in the month of Vaiśākha in 563 BC. He was born under an *Asoka* or sal (Shorea robusta) tree when Māyādev? was going to her maternal town on delivery.

Suttanipata has mentioned the earliest description of the birth of Buddha in Lumbinī. After the birth of Buddha he took seven steps towards north and, looking in all directions, he declared that 'I am the foremost of all creatures to cross the riddle of the ocean of the existence, this is my last birth and here after, I will not be born again. The site is spelt as Rummindei or Rupāndei (beautiful woman), the perverted form of Rupā devi, the queen Anjana of the king of Devadaha which was situated to the east of Kapilvastu in ancient time. The site is called Lun-min and La-Fa-Ni by the Chinese pilgrims Fa-Hien and Hiuen-Tsiang respectively. In course of exploration of the ancient Buddhist sites General Cunningham has mentioned La-Fa-Ni is Sanskrit Lavani, a beautiful woman (Cunnigham, 1990:350). In Buddhist literature, it is known as *Pradimokṣa vana* blessed with various trees and flowers, which is compared to the *Chittalata* grove of Indri's paradise in heaven

(Führer, 1972:4). The earliest Pali text *Suttanipata* has mentioned that 'The wisdom-child that Jewel so precious, that cannot be matched, has been born at Lumbinī, in the Śākya land for well being and joy in the world of men'. A Muslim historian of India named *Abul Fazal* has called Mokta (*Cunnigham*, 1990:351). It is also known as Paderiya (*Parariya*) where the Aśokan pillar is located in the Nepalese Terai. The name of the site is spelt Lumminigāme in the Aśokan pilllar edict still standing at the same place (*Führer*, 1972:31-33). *Mukherji* has also mentioned the name Rummin-dei in his report. In the Magadhi language, being used in the north-eastern pillar edicts in India and Nepāl, 'la' is invariable substituted for 'ra'. The location of Lumbinī is pointed out in the Buddhist literature, as well as, in the records of the Chinese pilgrims who visited India in the fifth and seventh centuries AD. As mentioned in *Jātaka* story this *sāl* garden was in joint possession of the Śākyas and Koliyas during the lifetime of Buddha. The *Mahāvamsa*, a Ceylones chronicle, and *Nidāna kathā* have also located it between Kapilvastu and Devadaha. During the reign of the Śākyas of Kapilvastu and the Koliyas, Lumbinī was a small dwelling site from where the visitors of two states use to walk through there. Due to the use of bullock carts for the common people and horse chariots with palanquin for the richer people and royalties, they traveled about 20 km in a single day. In this situation, they might have spent a night in Lumbinī (*Bidari*, 2003:6). The s*āl* garden was the place of recreation during the reign of the Śākyas and Koliyas. *Buddha charita* of Aśvaghosa describes Lumbinī as 'gay like the garden of *caitra ratha* with trees of every kind. According to *Fa-Hien* it was located about 50 *li* east of Kapilvastu (Giles, 1981:38). *Hiuen-Tsiang* had also pointed out that it was about 80 or 90 *li*. (21.729 or 24.445 km) north-east of arrow-well (*Beal*, 1994:24). It was linked through the popular 'Uttara path' to Kapilvastu, Rāmagrāma and other important cities during the Buddhist period. The present location of Lumbinī, the exact birthplace of Lord Buddha, is clear in the western Terai region of Nepāl. The narrow ridge of the Churiā range runs parallel to the *Mahābhārat* Mountain range from east to west.

The Siwālika Range

The *Mahābhārat* range is composed of loose non-metamorphic rocks in the western Nepāl (Hashimoto, 1973: 286). Almost the Neocene rocks in Nepāl are the molasses deposits of the Siwālika group, which forms the Churiā hills. The lower Siwālika, regarded as late Miocene in age, is the Chinji formation consisting of reddish clay stones with minor sand stone. According to *Hagen* most of the exposed Siwālika ranges in this region belong to the middle Siwālika of mio-Pliocene era (Hagen, 1961:3-48). Due to rapid increase in human activities in this region rather gently inclined bad land areas had developed, especially along the southern side of Dāṅg valley between Butwal to Nepālguñj. It is formed of grey to pale-brown medium to coarse-grained sandstone and pale-brown mudstone. A thick bed of ill-sorted conglomerate of more than fifty metres forms its basement in thickness (*Yoshida*, 1982:64). This belt shows a few scattered houses made of wooden pillars and dry-grass as a protection-tower against wild animals. Sandy soil with boulders of the region is not so fertile for regular cultivation.

The Terai Zone

On the south of the Siwālika range the Indo-Gaṅgetic plain named the Terai is distributed with an elevation lower than two hundred metres MSL from Nārāyaṇī to Rāpti River in the region. The Terai is composed of gravels and sands and of the late Pleistocene to Holocene age (Ibid). The great river system, viz. Rohiṇī, Telār, Tināu, Koṭhī, Bāṇagaṅgā and their tributaries form the fertile and sandy alluvial soil in the region. In course of his pilgrimage *Hiuen-Tsiang* has pointed out that, the soil of the region was fertile and farming operations were regular in suitable weather (*Watters*, 1961:1).

The Forest and Weather

In this region thick forest contains *Shorea robusta* (*sal, sakhuwa*) *pinus longifolia (chir)*, elephant grass, *acacia catechu* (khair), *Salmalia mala boica* (simal), *Dal bergia Sissa (Sisau)*, *Zyiphus Jujuba (Bair)* even now, especially in the northern belt from east to west in the region (*Sharma*, 1973:2-3). In the sixth century BC *plaksha* tree (*Ficus lacor*), mango tree (*Mangifera indica*), pipal tree (*Ficus religiosa*), *sal* tree (*Shorea robusta*) and Aśoka tree (*Saraca indico*) were associated with the indigenous trees of the area (Bidari, 1996:11-24). According to *Bhadda-Sala Jataka* there were trees in the park for making columns of the palace; but transportation was impossible due to rough road (*Cowell*, 1901:91-97). This evidence reveals that natural forests as well as parks had been developed in the Buddhists period. *Mahavana* and *Lumbinīvana* were associated with this region (*Upadhyaya*, 2018: 293-99).

This region has hot and humid climate. Lumbinī (elevation 100 m) has a tropical monsoon climate characterised by a cold season, hot season, monsoon and transitional periods. The core of the cold season extends from the beginning of December to the end of January with temperature occasionally dropping to +6°C. Rainfall is minimal and relative humidity may reach 89 per cent. There tends to be a spell of 7-10 days of foggy weather in December and another such spell in January otherwise sunshine prevails. The hot season lasts from the beginning of March until June. During the peak of the hot season (May), temperatures may rise to + 39 °C with a low relative humidity and minimal rain fall. Some times strong winds blow across Lumbinī. HMG Department of Meteorology cites June 12 to September 23 as the period of the annual monsoon in Nepāl. The highest rainfall (approximately 300 mm.) is recorded in July and August. The maximum temperature in June (Approximate + 37°C) gradually comes down to slightly above + 30 °C doing July, August and September. Minimum Temperature was 8°C and maximum 40°C in Junaury and May 2004 respectively. The monsoon remains active between June and September. Being alluvial and fertile area, it is known as the granary of the western Nepāl.

The Rivers

The rivers flow southwards and meet Gańges in India forming wide beds (Sharma, 1977:39-40). During the Miocene the Churiā range was under the shallow sea and its river system was responsible for the deposition of the present. Due to the deposition of sediments from the rivers, flowing from north to south, Indo-Gańgetic plain was created. The rivers related with Himālayan, Mahābhārata and Churiā ranges, were responsible for the formation of the Terai region. The level of the plain land rose due to the sedimentation of Indo-Gańgetic through forming new river channels in this area for the drainage. Rivers flow from the north to the south slope in this area· The Tināu, Dāno, Tilār, Bāṇagańgā (Bhāgirathi) and Koṭhi have their origin in the Himālayan and northern hills. The position of the Rohiṇi, Tilār, Bāṇagańgā (Bhāgirathi) and Anomā is more precisely indicated by the Chinese pilgrims and Ċeylonese chronicle.

During the modern period, after the eradication of malaria, many people of the hills have migrated in this Terai region. The present population of the region included the aboriginal Thāru, Indian imigrants, viz. Muslim, Yādav, Pasi, Mallahā, Dhobi, Kalwār and hill migrants, viz. Brāhmaṇ, Kshettri, Sanyāsi, Magar, Guruṅg, Kāmi, Damāi, Sunār etc.

Ancient Pilgrimage and Trade Routes

Due to the open border between India and Nepal, cultural activities and social norms are similar at the site of the present study and Uttar Pradesh. The trade routes between India and this region of Nepāl pass through western hills and the Himālayas. During the lifetime of Siddhartha Gautam his followers, especially monks and nuns, used to pass through these routes (Rhys Davids, 1971:44). As stated in the ancient Buddhists literature the Brāhamaṇ and ascetics used to travel from Kausambi to Vaiśāli passing through Sāketa, Śrāvasti, Setabhya, Kapilvastu, Kuśinagar, Pāvā. *Vinaya piṭaka* refers to a direct road from Kapilvastu to Vaiśāli (Regmi, 1982:39). Buddhist monks and followers used to travel in Tibet and Mangoliā passing through the route of Kapilvastu, Butawal, Pālpā, Ridi, Kāga-beni and Muktinātha in ancient period. On 21-30 September 1995 Buddhist Route Expedition Team of UNESCO had conducted a meeting in Lumbini to survey the ancient route in this area (Pandey, 1985:2). The team was agreed that the Buddhist pilgrims through the Terai frequently traveled it to the Himālayan region, particularly Muktinātha, Tibet and Mongoliā.

The other important route was Surāhi-nākā, at the north-west corner of Kapilvastu district, from where the traders as well as pilgrims frequently travelled to Surkheta, Dailekha, Rukuma and other sites to the western Nepāl.

Emperor Aśoka had come to Lumbinī and Kapilvastu with his spiritual teacher Upagupta in the twentieth year of his reign. Chinese pilgrims Fa-Hien and Hiuen-Tsiang had entered in Lumbinī, Kapilvastu and its vicinity during the fifth and seventh centuries AD respectively through Śrāvasti. They have mentioned the direction and distances of the places, viz. circuit of the capital town of Kapilvastu, various Budhhist monuments and images of Kapilvastu, Royal field, Arrow-Fountain , Lumbinī, the birthplace of Lord Buddha, and Rāmagrāma which help us to identify the ancient ruins of those places today. It is being identified with some ancient sites of the western Terai region of Nepāl, whose geographical feature and situation is known by the account of the Chinese pilgrims as well as Buddhist literature.

In the eighteenth century, Prithvi Nārāyaṇ Shah had also come through Varāṇāsi, Gorakhpur, Nautanawā and Butwal to Gorkhā from time to time. The pilgrims and traders regularily follow these routes even now. The region is plain and fertile and is known as the granary of the western Nepāl. The northern portion of Rupāndehi district is formed mainly by sandstone and pale-brown mudstones of the Siwālika range, as such, is not fertile. To the south of Siwālika range, the fertile and alluvial soil is also covered with *Chara kose jhadi* [about thirteen kms. deep]. Tiger, leopard, lion, elephant and rhinos live in the dense jungle. The people in the fertile lands cultivate rice, wheat, corn and mustard crops. Bāṇagañgā, Telār, Ghāgharā, Rohiṇi and Koṭhī are ancient rivers as mentioned in Buddhist period. All the commercial goods are taken to the hill region of the western Nepāl from the southern Terai region as well as from India. Thus, these ancient routes are still important to the traders and pilgrims as it was in the past.

CHAPTER **3**

Sacred History

A brief historical survey of the region is mentioned in order to follow the chronological framework of the study of sacred complex. Preliminary stages of the history of Śākyas and Koliyas are categorised under proto-history. Thereafter, the historical age begins in the area as we start getting evidences in the form of inscription, seals and sealing. The history of the area is divided into ancient, medieval and modern periods. The purpose of this short description is to delineate the cultural history, the life-style of the people in the area, and to trace the dynamic cultural process of Lumbinī.

Pre-history

On the basis of variation in shape, size, polish and their usage of stone tools, the period is divided into traditional three ages.

Palaeolithic Age

Pre-historic men used to live in the foothills of the Siwālika ranges in this area. Most of the valleys of this range are formed of the sedimentary rocks of the Miocene and Pleistocene era containing shale, sand and pebble beds. Due to deforestation and landslides, the range has no human habitation and is naked at present. River terraces are composed of gravels. Stone tool industries found in the gravels are of considerable importance to the pre-historian. A river cuts away its banks and carries the material along with it up to the sea where it is deposited. However, all this depends on the velocity and volume of the flow. Some of the material is left only on the way. In this context, the rivers sites of Koṭhi, Ghāgharā,

Tināu, Rohiṇi, etc. are very important as the pre-historic dwelling sites in the region. In December 1980, a team of scholars from USA and Nepāl, under the leadership of Dr J.H. Hutchison consisting James Munthe, K. Munthe, R.M. West and Vishṇu Dāṅgol, found the remains of *Ramapithecus* at Butawal on the bank of the river Tināu attached to the rocks cliff. A piece of the upper left jaw, which is 1 cm in width and more than 1 cm in length, is kept in the Natural Museum in Kathmandu. It was dated approximately eleven million years old on the basis of palaeomagnetic dating method. This hominoid finding is the oldest in Asia and the second oldest in the world. Cultural lifestyle and remains of *Butwalpithecus* was similar to the *Kenyapithecus* of Africa and *Brahmapithecus* of Asia. Having been great forest area the pre-historic men used to live by hunting and gathering wild fruits in the neighbourhood of Lumbinī.

Mesolithic Age

The stone tools of the Mesolithic age are found in limited number in Nepāl. However, some evidences of this phase have become known in the region. In course of excavation and exploration to the north-west of Kapilvastu district, Surāhi-nākā area, G. Corvinus, a German scholar, has discovered many prehistoric sites in the beds of the Surāi kholā. There were workshop sites, camping sites, simple flaking and small activity spots. A lot of plant fossils of leaf impressions, fossilised carbonised wood and leaf material were found in the fine classic deposits of clay stones and mudstones in the older period. In course of rock-cutting, a large bedding plane of a mudstone was exposed, on which a set of animal footprints of some smaller artiodactyl animals were seen. In course of the examination of these findings, a profile column of 5,500 m of Siwalik deposits was recorded with all the details of palaeontological and sedimentological data. Palaeontological and magnetostratigraphical studies along the Surāi kholā, north-west of Kapilvastu district, suggests dates on the basis of major lithological units that it is not so different from those found in Pākistan by Johnson, et al. and in western India by Ranga Rao. Above-mentioned evidences reveal that the prehistoric man immediately on the northwest side of Lumbinī had used microlithic industries as will as Mesolithic tools.

Neolithic Age

The Neolithic culture of the Terai region is presented by surface collection. The warmer climates of the sheltered valleys of the Terai region were ideally suited for the habitat of the prehistoric man. The Neolithic culture presents a change. Permanent habitation, start of agricultural activities, animal husbandry, industries of pottery and polished microlithic stone tools were the main features of the Neolithic man. The culture associated with food-production and self-dependence was developed in the western Terai region of Nepāl. Unique tools have reported from Dandakottadi and Parvas.

Proto-history

Lumbinī was a part of Kapilvastu of the Śākyas in the western Terai region of Nepāl. The banished sons and daughters of the Kosala king Okkaka formed the Śākya kingdom here. According to the *Divyadana,* the town of Kapilvastu was situated by the side of Bhāgirathi (Gańges), close to the *āshrama* of Rishi Kapilmuni. According to the *Lalitavistār* during the long time, it was organised into a big town as other people came from other sites to dwell in the new settlement. Two theories have been propounded regarding the origin of the tribal name Śākya–the first is based on the name of the *sāl* forest (*Shorea robusta*), where Kapila used to live, and the second theory is based upon the legend of the banished sons and daughters who married each other to protect the purity of their blood. The four brothers married to the four younger sisters and appointed the eldest sister as queen mother (Rockhill, 1972:11). When the father of the children came to know about them, it is said, he delightedly exclaimed: *Śākya vata-bho-kumara-parama Śākya-vata-bho kumara* (Aha! smart men indeed, Śākya indeed are the princes, very smart men). So the endogamous tribe is known as Śākya. Different sources have incorporated different names of the Śākya kings. According to *Lalitavistara*, Opura was the first king of Kapilvastu and Suddhodhana belonged to this dynasty. He became the king in the seventh generation (descent) after him (Oldenburg, 1971:94-99). *Mahāvamsa* has mentioned that Ulkamukha was the first king of Kapilvastu and after several generations, Jayasena became the king of Kapilvastu. He was succeeded by his son Simhahanu, father of Suddhodana. Simhahanu had five sons namely Suddhodana, Dhautodana, Shakradana, Sulkodana and Amṣitodan and two daughters named Amrita and Pramita. Princess Amṣita was married to Prince Suprabuddha of Devadaha, the father of Yasodhāra. *Mahāvamsa* refers that Māyādev? and Prajāpati were the daughter of Anjana, Śākya chief of Devadaha (Rockhill, 1972:19-21).

Suffering from leprosy the queen mother, Priya, resided in a cave in the forest, where the king of Varāṇāsi, Ram, also resided as he was suffering from the same disease. After sitting under a Kolan *(nauclea Cordifalia)* tree they were cured and both of them were married. To the east of Kapilvastu they organised the town named Devadaha and procreated the race of Koliyas. It is known as Devadaha, Vyāghrapur, Kolinagara or Rāmagrāma.

The Śākyas of Kapilvastu and the Koliyas of Devadaha had established matrimonal relations in future as well. King Suddhodana of Kapilvastu had married Māyādev? and Gautami, the princess of Devadaha. Siddhartha Gautam was born from the womb of Māyādev? in Lumbinī. Thus, the ancient Buddhist literature reveals that the present study area was inhabitated by the Śākyas.

In course of exploration and excavation of the region, a lot of art remains, structural remains as well as habitational depositions are found. In 1964, S.B. Deo has discovered a few rammed-up clay walls of plain huts from the low flattish heavily eroded mounds of Baṇjarāhi, near Lumbinī. A habitational deposit on the opposite bank of the Dāno river has yielded similar evidences indicating that the ancient habitational deposits were bifurcated by the river. According to the excavator, it is dated from 700 to 600 BC. The pottery of P.G.W., Red ware and N.B.P. ware are also found in course of excavation from the site (Deo, 1968:3-7).

In the sixth century BC, Siddhartha was born in Lumbinī garden under a sāl or Aśoka or *pipal* tree, which is comparable to the

Chittalata grove of Indra's paradise in heaven in the Śākya land. Lord Buddha himself had advised the monks and followers from his deathbed at Kusinagar to visit the four places, viz. Lumbinī, Bodha Gayā, Sāranātha and Kusinagar. Therefore, Lumbinī remained not only as a pleasure garden, but it also developed as a place of pilgrimage after the birth of Lord Buddha (Führer, 1972:63). Structural remains as well as artifacts found from Lumbinī reveal that monks and his followers used to stay here from the beginning of the Buddha's enlighten. The excavation conducted in 1970-71 has indicated that the earliest human habitation in ancient Lumbinī *grāma* must have started in N.B.P. period (Rijal, 1975-77:30). The site seems to have been occupied from the time of Lord Buddha, i.e. the sixth century BC. The successive human deposit in the southern mound of Lumbinī dates from sixth century BC to the Gupta period on the basic of its antiquities.

King Vidudhabha of Kosala had attacked Kapilvastu at four times. Buddha saved three times from the attack; but, at last, Buddha did not interfere. During the period of invasion, several Śākyas were massacred and stone slabes of the mote hall was washed with their blood. The Śākyas, who saved their lives, fled in different directions, some to Nepāl (Kathmandu), some to Rājgṣiha and Vaiśāli, some to Vedi, some to Pippalivan. Thus, the city of Kapilvastu became ruin and rack during the lifetime of Buddha, i.e. 500 BC (Upadhyaya, 2018:291).

The Mauryan Period

According to the *Kundavadana* of *Divyavadana,* having led King Aśoka into the Lumbinī jungle, the Venerable Upagupta pointed out with his right hand and said, 'Oh! Great king here the Buddha was born'. Thereafter king Aśoka made an offering of one hundred thousand gold coins and established the first pagodas (*ceitiya*) in the twentieth year of his reign· Thus, the abovementioned documentary and circumstantial evidences reveal that Lumbinī region was absolutely developed as the Buddhist pilgrimage site during the Mauryan period. Mauryan terracotta human and animal figurines, stone sculptures and structural remains, viz. vihār, temple foundation, stūpas and bricks are found here (Giri, 2003:206-232).

Condition after Aśoka

Almost all the habitational sites had been deserted, but the religious complex and some portion of the region had been actively mobilised during the Suṅga, Kushāna and the Gupta periods. During these periods terracotta human and animal figurines, stone sculptures, beads, bangles, seals, sealing as well as architectural monuments, viz. vihār, stūpa Buddhist temples and loose bricks are found. Various art remains of the region are assignable, on the basis of comparative study with the Magadha antiquities, to fourth century AD.

Accounts of the Chinese Pilgrims

In the fifth century AD Fa-Hien had seen some monks and a few families of the common people living at Kapilvastu. He mentions, 'Fifty li to the east of the city (Kapilvastu) is the royal garden called "Lum-min" (Lumbinī). It was here the queen entered the bath to wash herself, and, having come out on the northern side, advanced twenty paces, and then holding a branch of the tree in her hand, as she looked to the east, brought fourth the prince. When born he walked seven steps; two dragon kings washed the prince's body, the place where this occurred was afterwards converted into a well, and, here, as likewise at the pool, the water of which came down from above for washing (the child), the priests draw their drinking water (Beal, 1983).' About 80 or 90 *li* (21.729 or 24.445 km) to the north-east of the Arrow Fountain there were bathing tank, Aśoka flower tree, two stūpas, a great stone pillar surmounted with a horse figure on the top and river of oil were seen in Lumbinī by Hiuen-Tsiang in the seventh century AD at the birthplace of Lord Buddha (Watters, 1961:15). Lumbinī can be clearly identified with the site near present Bhagawānpur in Rupāndehi district. 300 *li* (81.486 km) to the east of Lumbinī, he reached to the ruined town named Lan-mo (Rāmagrāma) where the accounts of these pilgrims are reliable excepting some events mentioned by them. There are a few differences in the details of the descriptions, such as the direction and distance of it; but such discrepancies are very negligible.

Lumbinī, which is the main key to identify other ancient sites in the region, has been identified on the support of Chinese accounts. In addition, the details given in the accounts entitled Shui-Ching-Chu describes Aśoka tree, Siddhartha's birth under the tree, sweet-smelling flowers and Aśoka had shielded the imprint of Siddhartha's feet on long slab of lapis lazuli (Petch, 1950:34-35). With the help of this description, it was possible to prove the real position of the conglomerate stone, discovered in the foundation of the old Māyādev? temple in Lumbinī (Uesaka, 1997:15).

Early Medieval Period

In the early medieval period, the older convention of art began to be replaced by new conceptions in the ninth century AD. After the rise of the Rajput states in different parts of India colossal creation and cosmic conception were refined in the field of art (Agrawal, 1965:257). A lot of stone sculptures belonging to the Pāla-Sena school of art of eastern India, are found from the surface of the region, and are dated in ninth and tenth century AD. King Ripu Malla, Saṅgrāma Malla, Nagarāj's descendant of Karṇāli region had visited in 1312 AD and got engraved their inscriptions on the Aśokan pillars in Lumbinī (Führer, 1972:33). The visit indicates that this region was under the sovereignty of this dynasty and that this region was still widely known as holy place of pilgrimage. In this context, various antiquities and monuments reveal that Lumbinī was continuously inhabited from the sixth century BC to the fourteenth century AD. The surface collections of the site include some beads of terracotta and semi-precious stones, fragments of iron nails and small bits of bronze objects.

In the fourteenth century AD after the termination of the Nāga dynasty, the region was ruled by Malebom and his successors. During the period of Chaubisi it was under Tanahu principality of Magar rulers, in the fifteenth-sixteenth century (1489-1517AD). Sikandar Lodi, then the Sultan of Delhi, might have conquered the weak Magar kings of Tanahu. In this connection, Lodi Sultan might have destroyed the stone sculptures as well as monuments at Lumbinī and Kapilvastu in the process of propagation of Muslim movement in the region (Pradhan, 1979:30-35). A number of stone sculptures are found without leg, hand, nose, mouth, cheek, forehead, shoulder, etc. It seems that they were broken by force. Muslim rulers may have been instrumental in this destructive activity in the area as it has been a case in the Northern portion of India in this period. The king of Pālpā had conquered the Magar principality of Tanahu during the period of Mukunda Sen I. After the partition of the Sen kingdom, Vināyaka Sen became the king of the Terai region of Pālpā, the areas of Butwal, Lumbinī, Parasi and Kapilvastu. Mukunda Sen I had built a seasonal palace *Rańga Mahala* at Butawal *Phūlabāri* area. In the reign of Mukunda Sen II [1750-82 AD], a conflict arose with the Nawab Vazier of Oudh. However, the king of Pālpā had got some terrain lands, to the west of Gaṇdak? river, on lease due to their friendship with them later. Mahadatta Sen, son of Mukunda Sen, had also received more terrain lands including its peripheral area. The rate of the lease was cheap because it was an unhealthy, unproductive and swampy area. In 1801, the British Government of India and Nawab Vazier of Oudh had imposed a treaty under which Gorakhpur, Rohilakhaṇd and the area under study became a part of the British rule. In 1804, the Government of Nepāl conquered Pālpā, including the Terai region. Thus, Nepāl Government became the lessee and the British Government was a lessor of the region.

Modern period

After the unification of the region the Government of Nepāl had established the administrative Headquarter of the region at Pālpā from where all the disputes were decided and creative activities for the welfare of the people were undertaken (Mishra, 1999:129-35). The Terai region of Kapilvastu and Rupāndehi, including Butwal area, became the issue of debate between Nepāl and British Government of India for suzerainty over it. This led to the Company–Nepāl war in 1814-16. At last, the Treaty of Sugauli was signed in March 1816, which provided the ownership of the region to the Nepāl Government. This region was under the jurisdiction of Butwal, Seorāj and Khajahni districts under the overall charge of the Governor of Pālpā before 1962. In rearrangement of the administrative districts, this area was mentioned in Rupāndehi district of the Lumbinī zone.

Some monuments and sculptures are also seen in the region built under the dynamic leadership of the Sena kings of Pālpā principality. Being far from the capital, a Governor from Kathmandu was appointed for the regional administration during reign of the Rāṇās. During all these periods' kings, nobles as well as people of the area had contributed to make artifacts for the purpose of their domestic and religious life, which provide us a glimpse of the social activities of the region.

CHAPTER **4**

Master Plan and Development

Lumbinī, being the birthplace of Gautam Buddha, is being visited by many VVIP, VIP, monks, nuns and general devotees from ancient period to modern period. On the occasion of the Fourth World Buddhist Summit, king Mahendra had visited at Limbinī in 1956 (7 phagun 2012). He had shown keen interest in developing Lumbinī as a sacred complex for all the human beings. After the visit to Lumbinī in 1967 U-Thant, then Secretary General of United Nations had suggested to Nepāl Government that Lumbinī should be developed as a place of pilgrimage and tourist centre equipped with accommodations. A three-member team of UNO Mission had specific instructions to advise the Government on the infrastructural requirements, viz. transportation facilities, drinking water, energy and appropriate accommodation for the visitors from 10 December to 9 January 1968. In 1970, an International Committee was constituted with the support of the United Nations known as 'International Lumbinī Development Committee' under the chairmanship of the permanent representative of Nepāl (CDL, 1970: Introduction). The committee constituted of the representatives of Śri Laṅkā, Pākistan, India, Myanmar, Thāiland, Afghānistān, Cambodiā, Indonesiā, Loas, Malayasiā, Jāpan, Siṅgāpore and Nepāl. Bhutān and South Koreā later joined the committee. The committee has the representatives of 15 nations under the chairmanship of UNO. UNDP had contributed through them one million dollars in order to prepare the Master Plan for the development of Lumbinī including archaeological and engineering activities.

The Master Plan was prepared by Kenzo Tange. The first

phase of the outline design for Lumbinī development was completed and the report was circulated in September 1972. The basic orientation and the functional layout of the project were designed in the 'Final Outline Design for Lumbinī' compiled by Tange and Urtec. For the implementation of the project necessary technical data of the site has been assembled by Nippon Koei through the sponsorship of the Japan EXPO Foundation in 1974. In 1975 Phase II of the Master Plan was engaged with Tange and Urtec. Chapter one of this report contains basic premises in developing the preliminary of the Master Plan. Chapter second and third constitute final proposals and detail site plan. Fourth and fifth chapters contain a preliminary cost estimation and implementation schedule. This proposal was based on figures and practices of domestic standards. The United Nations provided comments on the preliminary Master Plan, Phase II, Stage I, suggesting design improvements to be incorporated into the final scheme of the Preliminary Master Plan on 20 July 1977. During this period tourist accommodation, cultural centre, central link, monastic zone, sacred garden and archaeological sites were slightly revised in practical way. Lumbinī Development Committee had provided seventeen components as the requirements for Lumbinī Development Project in July 1877 (Tange, 1977 : Introduction). The plan was completed in 1978. With a total area of 25 sq. miles, only 3 sq. miles is main core area of Lumbinī plan. One sq. mile in each sector from south to north is separated as restricted area. After the restricted area one sq. mile on east, one sq. mile on west and two sq. mile on south is planned Agriculture Zone (Buffer zone.)

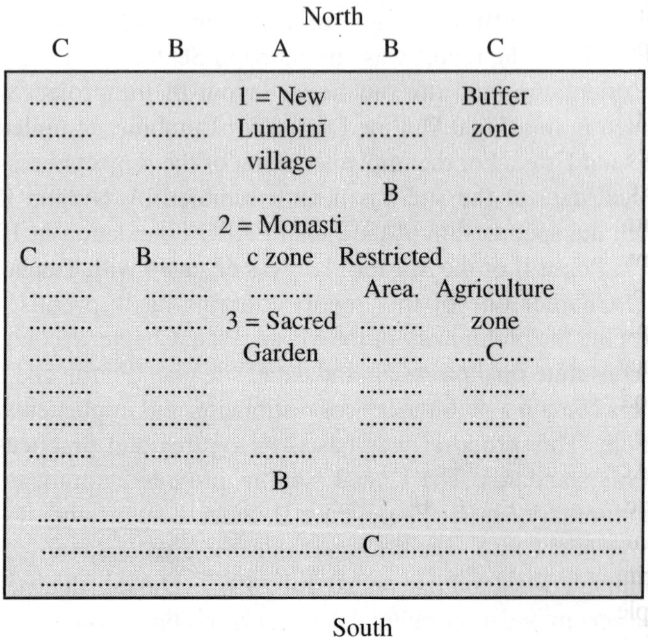

Note:

A = Project Area
B = Restricted Area
C = Buffer zone (Agriculture zone)

1 = New Lumbinī village
2 = Monastic zone
3 = Sacred Garden

Project Area is divided into three zones (1 sq. mile each), viz. New Lumbinī village, Monastic zone and Sacred Garden. To start with, the first phase of Master Plan was land acquisition because earlier only the area of Māyādevi temple belonged to the Master Plan.

New Lumbinī Village

Division of project area into three zones is symbolic and based on philosophical concept. Components of settlement, education and culture, religious and *nirvāṇa* have managed from north to south from philosophical point of view respectively. In course of this planning four types of resting houses, viz. luxurious hotel of 100 beds, middle-class hotel of 150 beds, pilgrimage rest house of 200 beds and camping-grounds for general visitors are proposed at this zone. Two hundred residential-houses for two hundred households, high school, electricty, drinking water, communication, drainage system, etc. have stated on plan. Asian Highway is also proposed from the north of this zone. The village will be the location of the administrative offices of the Lumbinī complex. Architecturally, the village is divided into eight blocks aligned with two parallel arcades. The buildings on the north of the road will be utilised as the administrative centre. On the south of the road will be occupied by the tourist centre.

At this complex standard hotel like Hokke has been operating after completion in 1990. As stated in Master Plan middle-class accommodation, i.e. Mikasha hotel is going to be operate. Cheapest pilgrimage rest house, viz. Śri Laṅkān pilgrimage rest house is completed in 1986. It is also operating for pilgrimages. Foundation of high school is also completed. International Crane Foundation has operating the project to protect cranes in Lumbinī. Bird watching tower is also completed with the suport of TRPAP and ICF. Construction of high school, camping ground, administrative blocks and water tank are incomplete. The three major buildings, viz. museum, library and research institute have completed in 1989, 1989 and 1996 in respectively and in operation (Figs. 7 and 8). The construction of auditorium is not started until 2007. The world peace stūpa named Niponzan Myohoji of 156 feet in height is completed in November 2001, which was not mentioned in the Master Plan (Figs. 1-6).

Monastic Zone

Monastic zone is situated in the centre within the forest area, north of the Sacred Garden complex which is divided into two halves East and West Monastic zone, with a canal originating from the Eternal Peace Flame, a symbol of peace and prosperity of human existence (Fig.10). There are 43 plots for Hinayān and Mahāyān monasteries, stūpa and meditation centres on east and west respectively. According to Master Plan central canal should be constructed in beautification with water-lily flowers on its bank, soundless leg-boating system to the interested visitors, green-field on both sites and resting chairs. Facilities of public-toilets, cold-drinks, etc. are also proposed in Master Plan. Evergreen varieties of plantation in 16 lines of 14 types of plants have proposed. Eastern zone is for Theravadi (Hinayān) (Figs. 11-17) and Western zone is separated for Mahāyan and Vajrayān stūpa, vihār, monaseries and bahāls (Figs. 18-21). Central bride for adjoining the eastern and western complex is also mentioned in plan.

Monastic zone is also divided into three parts on the basis of their shape and size consisting 80, 120 and 160 meter in area.

TABLE 4.1 : Plot-Division

S.N.	*Area of plots*	*Western (Mahayan) Zone, No. of plots.*	*Eastern (Hinayān) Zone, No. of plots.*	*Total of Plots*
1.	160 × 160 m.	2	–	2
2.	120 × 120 m.	6	3	9
3.	80 × 80 m.	20	10	30
4.	Meditation centre	1	1	2
	Total	29	14	43

The governmental and non-governmental organisations of 15 nations have been allotted for the construction of monasteries in the international monastic zone. The eastern monastic zone has 13 plots and contains one meditation centre. The western monastic zone has 28 plots and one meditation centre. Eleven eastern plots are assigned to six countries, viz. India, Myanmār, Nepāl, Śri Lankā, Thāiland each with two and one plot to Cambodia. Myanmār and Nepāl have taken plots in eastern as well as western zone. The government of China and Myanmār, the Mahābodhi Society of India, the International Nun's Association, the Manāng Sewā Samāja, the Tāra Foundation of Germany, Royal Monastery of Thāiland and the Lama Monastery of Dharmodaya Sabhā, Nepāl have completed the construction and are operating to the visitors.

The governments of Śri Laṅkā, Cambodia, the Linhson of France, the temple of Vietnam, the Mahābodhi Society of South Korea, the Sokyo of Japān and the Geden International of Austria have been constructing proper monasteries, stūpa and meditation centres in their assigned plots. The governments of Bhutān and Mongoliā as well as various organisations of Nepāl have also shown keen interest to construct vihar, stūpa and monasteries in this sacred complex of Lumbinī.

The east and west monastic zones set a side for the two major sects of Buddhism. Theravada (Hinayān) and Mahāyan (*Mahāsanghika*) have witnessed a number of developments by friendly states and institutions. These stūpa, vihār and monasteries have been developing the Lumbinī as 'A Mini World of Buddhism'. Each of them has constructed their building own their national architectural design, tradition, techniques and religious trends. Some of them have been providing accommodation to pilgrims as well as visitors upon payment in different forms. Korean, Myanmār, Vietnamese and International Bhikshuni Sangh have providing such services to the visitors at present.

Peace Flame

Then Prince and present king Gyanendra Bir Bikram Shah Dev lit a torch of Eternal Peace in Lumbinī in commemoration of the International Year of Peace in 1986. The Eternal Peace Flame in Lumbinī, immediately south of the central link canal and north of circular leeve, is still burning as a Symbol of World Peace.

Peace Bell

Immediately east of Peace Flame, on the east bank of central link canal, is hung a huge metal Peace Bell donated by Nyigma Meditation Centre of USA. Its weight is 2.5 ton. Donors' list and details is engraved on it.

Central Link Canal

Central link canal is 1.464 km from north to south and 16 meter wide between the Eastern Hinayān and Western Mahāyan Monastic zone. This central link establishes the sanctity of the

Sacred Garden. It will be used for boating to disables, old visitors as well as foreign pilgrims to feel peace and harmony. Four boat-stations are proposed in Master Plan.

Monastery Zone

Monastery zone is divided into two sectors, viz. Eastern *Theravadi* (Hinayān) and Western Mahāyan (*Mahasanghika*) complex.

Eastern complex

In this area Nepal, Mynamār, Śri Laŋka, India, Cambodia and Thailand Government and non-governmental organisations have built monasteries and mediation centres on eleven plots out of thirteen. Their outline is mentioned below in brief.

Myanmār

Assigned on: 11–2–1993
Party: Government
Plot No.: EC-3 and WA- 2
Plot size: 120 × 120 m & 80 × 80 m
Project: Monastery and Stupa
Position: Completed.
Cost Estimate: NRS. 42.6 million.

Nepāl

Assigned on: 13–9–1994
Party: International Bhikshuni Sangha
Plot No.: EC-6
Plot Size: 120 × 120 m.
Project: Monastery
Position: Completed.
Cost Estimate: NRS.10 million.

Nepāl

Assigned on: 1–1–1995
Party: Vipassana Centre.
Plot: Mediate Centre
Plot size: 70 × 160 m.
Project: Meditation Centre.

Position: Under construction.
Cost Estimate: N.A.

Śrilaṅkă

Assigned on: 3–5–1996
Party: Srilanka Government
Plot No.: EC-1 & 2.
Plot size: 80 × 80 and m & 80 × 80 m
Project: Monastery
Position: Under construction.
Cost estimate: N.A.

India

Assigned on: 1994
Party: Bauddha Dharmakar Sabha.
Plot: EC-9

Plot size:

Project: Monastery, Guest House
Position:
Cost Estimate: IRS. 40 million.

India

Assigned on: 19– 7–1994
Party: Mahabobhi Society
Plot No.: EC-8
Plot size: 80 × 80 m.
Project: Monastery
Position: Completed.
Cost Estimate: NRS. 20 million.

Thailand

Assigned on: 14–9–1994
Party: Thailand Government
Plot: EB- 2 & EC- 7
Plot size: 120 × 120 m. & 80 × 80 m.
Project: Monastery
Position: Under construction.
Cost Estimate: NRS. 200 million

Cambodia

Assigned on: 20 October, 2006.
Party: Kingdom of Cambodia.
Plot No.: EB-1
Plot size: 120 × 120 m.
Project: Monastery.
Position: Under construction.

Western complex

Seventeen plots have been assigned to build monasteries out of thirty plots by the government and organisations of Nepal, Korea, China, Vietnam, France, Germany, Japan and Austria. India, Nepal and Myanmār have assigned in both complex. Mongolia, Bhutan and two Nepalese parties are interested to assign for monastery construction in this complex. Their brief introduction is mentioned here.

Myanmār:

Assigned on: 1–7–1995
Party: Panditarama
Plot: Meditation Centre
Plot size: 80 × 200 m.
Project: Meditation Centre
Position: First phase completed.
Cost Estimate: N.A.

Nepāl

Assigned on: 24–2–2000.
Party: Manang Sewa Samāj.
Plot No: WC-10.
Plot size: 80 × 80 m.
Project: Stupa
Position: Completed.
Budget Estimate: N.A.

Nepāl

Assigned on: 11–2–1993
Party: Dharmodaya Sabha

Plot No: WB-3
Plot size: 120 × 120 m.
Project: Vahāl, Gompā, Stūpa
Position: Under construction
Cost Estimate: NRS. 83.6 million.

Nepāl

Assigned on: 11–12–1996
Party: Ka-Nying Shedrup Ling.
Plot: WB-1
Plot size: 120 × 120 m
Project: Monastery
Position: No started.
Cost Estimate: N.A.

S. Korea

Assigned on: 27–2–1995 & 20–8–1997.
Party: Mahābodhi Society
(Chogye order)
Plot No: WA-3, WC–14 & WC–18.
Plot size: 160 × 160 m, 80 × 80 m & 80 × 80 m
Project: Monastery
Position: Guest house completed and monastery under construction.
Cost Estimate: N.A.

S. Korea

Assigned on: 22–11–1993
Party: Yong Do Society
Plot: WB-5
Plot size: 120 × 120 m.
Project: Monastery
Position: No started.
Cost Estimate: US$ 282.500.

China

Assigned on: 29–11–1996
Party: Buddhist Association
Plot No: WA-1

Plot size: 160 × 160 m.
Project: Monastery
Position: completed.
Cost Estimate: N.A.

Vietnam

Assigned on: 9–4–1993
Party: Phat Quoc Tu
Plot No: WB-2
Plot size: 120 × 120 m.
Project: Monastery, Stūpa
Position: Under construction.
Cost Estimate: NRS. 1.1 million.

Austria

Assigned on: 13–1–2003.
Party: Geden International.
Plot No: WC-9.
Plot size: 80 × 80 m.
Project: Monastery.
Position: Under construction
Budget Estimate: N.A.

France

Assigned on: 23–3–1993
Party: W. Linh Son Buddhist
Plot No.: WB-6
Plot size: 120 × 120 m.
Project: Monastery & Guest House.
Position: Under construction.
Cost Estimate: US$500,00.

Germany

Assigned on: 15-12-1999.
Party: Tara Foundation Düsseldorf.
Plot No.: WB-4
Plot size: 120 × 120 m.
Project: Monastery
Position: Completed.

Budget Estimate: N.A.

Germany

Assigned on: 22–3–1994
Party: Karma Kagyo Dachverband
Plot No.: WC-2
Plot size: 80 × 80 m.
Project: Monastery
Position: No started.
Cost Estimate: NRS. 20 million

Japan

Assigned on: 21–2–1993
Party: Sokyo organisation
Plot No.: WA-2
Plot size: 160 × 160 m.
Project: Monastery.
Position: Under construction.
Cost Estimate: Yen 420 million.

India

Assigned on: February 2000.
Party: Drigung Kagyud
Plot No.: WC-16.
Plot size: 80 × 80 m.
Project: Meditation Centre Ladakh.
Position: Under construction.
Budget Estimate: N.A.

Mongolia

Assigned on:
Party: Republic Mongolia.
Plot No.: WC-4.
Plot size: 80 × 80 m.
Project:
Position: No started.
Budget Estimate: N.A.

Bhutan

Assigned on:
Party: Royal Government of Bhutan.
Plot No: WC-3 & WC-8.
Plot size: 80 × 80 m & 80 × 80 m.
Project:
Position: No started.
Budget Estimate:

Nepāl

Assigned on:
Party: Zanrong Tgupten Medol Dogna Choling.
Plot No: WC-1.
Plot size: 80 × 80 m.
Project:
Position:
Budget Estimate:

Nepāl

Assigned on:
Party : Karma Lekshey Ling Institue.
Plot No: WC-5.
Plot size: 80 × 80 m.
Project:
Position:
Budget Estimate:

Russia

Assigned on:
Party: Buddhist Traditional Sangh of Russia.
Plot No: WC-15
Plot size: 120 × 120 m.
Project:
Position:

Circular Levee

Circular Levee link to protect the sacred site from flooding and to preserve the archaeological (sites) structural remains. There are four ponds around the sacred garden. Ponds are 3.25 m deep, bottom level 96 m and water level 97 m from the sea level.

Other nations as well as institutes have also allotted remaining plots to build monasteries in proper sites. Six lakh trees were planted in monastic and New Lumbinī area. Hedge plantation is done along the central canal, internal road, around Bus Park, Car Park as proposed in the Master plan. Many *kadamba* trees and bottlebrush trees along the central canal are missing. Various types of trees should be planted there.

Sacred Garden

The Sacred Garden is the focal point of Lumbinī due to the exact birthplace of Lord Buddha. Its form of a circle enclosing squares is a universal symbol of purity, peace and simplicity. The squares have proposed by a network of raised walkways between the landscaping and archaeological areas. The Garden is going to be surrounded by a pond and a circular levee as mentioned in plan. In order to preserve the historical integrity and combination of the location, new construction is strictly prohibited. Philosophically and symbolically, when the visitors will cross a bridge over the circular levee from the Monastic zone to Sacred Garden, they will feel the spirit and simple approach of Buddhism after entering there. According to Master Plan, there should be no temple or monument, but a simple garden kept much as it was when Gautam Siddhartha was born.

Aśoka pillar, Māyādevi temple, Puskarini pond, ruined structures of ancient vihar and stūpas have been exposed in course of excavations. JBF, DOA and LDT have obtained important findings, i.e. marker stone, stone fragments, seals, coins, pottery fragments and Siddhartha Yasodhara terracotta panel, in course of restoration of Māyādevi temple. It is to be remarked that 21 meeting of World Conservation Society held during 1–6 December 1997 has mentioned Lumbinī as one of the World Heritage Sites. According to the provision of Master Plan, a circular levee link to protect the sacred site from flooding on north-west side of this zone and to preserve the archaeological sites.... The plan has designed four ponds around the circular levee. Earthworks, retaining structure and slope turning for the pond in the north-east quadrant have been completed. The depth of the pond is 3.25 m, the bottom level is 96 cm and the water level is 97 cm from the sea level (LDT, 2007). The four ponds will maintain the perennial source of at least 1 m water level to enhance the beauty of the entire holy site as per the Master Plan.

Many components of infrastructure have been running and some of these are not yet started due to the lack of proper fund. Major Pedestrian space, road service, staff-colony, meditation centres and school building are partially completed. Boundary wall of the Master Plan is going to be completed. Telecommunication system is underground. Due to the open boundary, the animals are grazing in project area and the property of the Trust is stolen day to day. The security of the monasteries, monks and nuns is also poor because of open complex. Secondary pedestrian, water management, water supply system, sewerage system, electrical power system, tourist information building, administrative building, medical centre, retails and service facilities, colonnade, auditorium, south-pond and footbridge project components have not yet started (LMP project components, 2004).

In order to monitor the development programmes in Lumbinī complex the Lumbinī Development Committee was constituted in 1971 and since 1974, it was given the change of the total area with all the activities working under different departments of Nepal Government to be co-ordinated in consultation with it. (LDC, 1975:17-18). In 1985, Lumbinī Development Trust was created as an autonomous and non-governmental organisation for the creative and concrete action in the region instead of LDC. Lumbinī Development Trust Act, 1985 was amended according to the interest of the working team. The trust had focused on to develop and mobilize the physical facilities, viz. water supply, communication, electrification, transportation, road construction, land acquisition, land scaping, afforestation, as well as to promote academic and archaeological activities from time to time. According to the condition of Master Plan besides these infrastructures, Bhairahawā airport extension and plantation on roadside from Bhairahawā to Lumbinī were also completed in preliminary base. UNO had taken the responsibility to prepare the Master Plan with the technical support of Nepāl Government. Governmental and non-governmental agencies of various nations were requested to build their monasteries, stūpa and vihars in their interest. LDT has been conducting world summit and conference declaration to provide valuable guidelines and financial supports to complete the Master Plan as soon as possible. Then His Royal Highness Prince Gyanendra Bir Bikram Shah Dev, Chairman of LDT, paid a visit to the United Nations and addressed the International Committee for the Development of Lumbinī in 1986. Present King Gyanendra had also visited Japan and Korea to promote awareness and to develop friendly relationship with each other. He lit a torch of eternal peace of Lumbinī in commemoration of International year of peace in 1986. The eternal peace flame in Lumbinī is still burning as a symbol of World Peace.

Kenzo Tange's Master Plan was designed between 1970 and 1976 and adopted by Nepāl Government in 1978. It is the main asset for the development of Lumbinī. However, some of its items are outdated and need to be reconsidered in the light of recent development. LDT has succeeded in implementing some components of the Master Plan and some remain to be implemented. Outdated components of Master Plan seem not feasible. Thus, certain components should be reviewed. Lumbinī Institutions as well as Lumbinī Development Review Mission have suggested reviewing certain components of Master Plan on the basis of needs and utility. Lumbinī Development Review Mission, organised under the leadership of Dr Ananda Guruge, a renowned Buddhist scholar of ŚriLaṅkā, has suggested that Lumbinī should be developed as a centre of World Fountain of Peace, as well as pilgrimage centre (Khatry and Vaidhya, 2002:7). Trebor Sophida of Murdoch University has also advised to prepare Master Plan for Tourism in Lumbinī. Vision and Scoping Mission has also suggested promoting Lumbinī as the World Fountain of Peace. Lumbinī city development programme was proposed to submit in National planning and its area should be extended at 100 square mile.

Lumbinī Institutions (2004) have also suggested revising the certain components of Master Plan. The Federation of Lumbinī Institutions has recommended the following suggestions to revise in the Master Plan:

- Allow the construction of religious structures within the monasteries according to individual needs.
- Change the present location for the water-tower in the New Lumbinī Village as it aesthetically interferes with the *Shanti* Stūpa.
- Do not tear down the Royal Nepāl Buddha Vihara and the Dharma Swami Maharaja Vihara unless these monasteries collapse naturally.
- Revise pedestrian path along the central canal, i.e. now dirty road.
- The new bus park is feasible only if all secondary facilities in Lumbinī have been accomplished, such as complete service roads, enough rickshaws, Safa-tempos, facility of drinking water, benches and garbage bins.
- Give up the idea of having gondolas on the central canal as the water dries up during the hot season.
- Revise design of garbage bins.
- Increase the number of public toilets on the Master Plan.
- Include trails across the Master Plan.
- Revise and improve tree planting.
- Outdated items of Master Plan should be revised.
- Control cutting trees and cattle grazing.
- Land charge should be increased only after consulting with the concerned monasteries and institutes, which is 150,200 and 300 $ of 80,120 and 160 sq. m. in area per year respectively at present.

Apart from these suggestions, other conferences and meetings have also recommended certain components to revise in Master Plan on the basis of synchronous times. About 35 per cent of the total works of Master Plan have been completed in two and half decades. Political instability of the country has been on obstacle to the progress of the plan. Lumbinī International Development Committee should be activated to mobilise in proper direction. The authority should be free, fair and unbiased to implement and offer the components of Master Plan. The total cast of Master Plan was ascertained US $ 55 million. Donor agencies should be encouraged to provide cash and materials to develop Lumbinī. At the preceding ratio of development indicates that the plan is going to take another four to five decades to complete it. If it is so late, the first developed part will already reach a state of restoration. In this critical situation, the authority should be active to complete Master Plan as soon as possible.

CHAPTER 5

Art

Art specimens reflect the socio-cultural, economic and religious modes and thoughts of contemporary societies. Lumbinī is also an important area in the region from where a number of art remains have been brought to light, viz. stone sculptures, terracotta figurines, beads, bangles, etc. These art remains help us in understanding the past life ways of the people from Mauryan to modern period. These art remains have been classified into stone sculptures, stone objects, terracotta figurines and other objects, seal and sealing, beads, bangles, coins, metal objects and pottery.

Stone sculpture

Brahmanical and Buddhist icons in stone have been found all around the present study area datable from the Gupta to the modern period. These are either kept in the courtyard of the shrines or enshrined in the sanctum of the temples. Stone sculptures include Vishnu, Devi, Śiva, Bodhisattva and Buddha. These specimens provide a glimpse of the religious movement and artistic ability of the contemporary society.

Buddha

Before the representation of Buddha in human form, he was represented through one or more symbols with decorative themes in the Buddhist art tradition. He was represented by *Chaitya-vṛiksha, Bodhi-druma*, stūpa, *Dharmachakra*, deer park, lion, bull, cow, halo, footprints, coffin, riderless horse and turban associated with a story in the life of Buddha, his message and events connected with this history of Buddhism. According to Buddhist tradition a *Bodhi* tree, a wheel, a stūpa and a *sāl* tree symbolic the memory of holy places connected with the life of Buddha, viz. Bodha Gayā, Sāranāth, Kuśinagar and Lumbinī. Nativity sculptures of the region may be representation of Kapilvastu. *Dharmachakra* is also available from Lumbinī. The sculptures of Buddha in various forms were executed first during the Kushāṇa period at Mathura, dominating the northern part of the country, and influenced as well as inspired other subsequent schools of art. Stone sculptures of Buddha used to be brought back from the holy places as a small material souvenir of what they had there seen. Thus, stone sculptures of Buddha from Mathura are distributed over all the holy sites, including Lumbinī and Kapilvastu. Various wall paintings have been executed on the walls and ceilings of the Buddhist shrines of Lumbinī (Figs. 23 & 24).

Buddha Images

A head of Buddha, measuring 7.5 cm high and 5 cm wide, is executed with a plain bump like the one *ushnisha* and *urna* marked on the forehead, open eyes and smiling face (Mitra, 1972:199). The sculpture is of red sandstone, which came from the atelier of Mathura. On the basis of style, it is ascribable to the Kushāṇa period. One other Buddha sculpture of chlorite from Lumbinī, measuring 17cm.x 12 cm, is in *bhumi-sparsa-mudrā*. He is seated in *vajra-parayaṅkāśana* on a damaged *visvapadama* below the *Bodhi* tree. Another fragment of Buddha of chlorite measuring 11.5 cm high in *bhumi-sparsa mudrā* is seated in *vajra-parayaṅkāśana* on a fully blossomed lotus. Two badly defaced figures including a hooded-*naga* are supporting the lotus. On the basis of art style the figure representing the Miracle of Śrāvasti, belong to the Gupta period. The sculpture from Sainā mainā, now placed in the courtyard of Lumbinī Development Trust office in Lumbinī, measuring 78 × 65 cm, is seated on lotus in *bhumi-sparsa mudrā* (Giri, 2003:205). A portion of the head is broken. The deity seated crossed-legged in *dhyāna-mudrā.* The right hand is displaying in earth-touching pose and the left hand is broken. Buddha wears usual dress and ornaments ascribable to the Gupta period. It is similar to the two Buddha images found from Yamunā river area and kept presently in the Mathura museum (Sharma, 1995: Nos.110 & 111). The head of Buddha executed in black-brown stone represents ovalish face, pendant ear-lobe, narrow temple, vertical incised-lines to indicate locked hair as a knot, big eyes, encircled-eyebrows, prominent nose, thin lips and precisely hewn chin in the figure. The appearance of the deity reveals that it is a broken piece of *dhyani-Buddha*, which is kept in the Kapilvastu museum. The head of Buddha is similar to a head from Mathura, now kept in the Boston museum and dated in the fifth century AD. This head may also be ascribable to the Gupta period on the basis of style. An image of Buddha from Sainā mainā, now in Lumbinī, measures 33.5 × 40 cm and is in *dhyāna mudrā*. In course of excavation, Mishra has also noticed a stone Buddha image in *bhumispara mudrā* belonging to the Gupta period, details of which are not mentioned.

A sculpture of eight great miracles presents the figure of Buddha in *vajra-parayankāśana* on a double petalled lotus and his damaged right hand shows *bhumisparsa-mudrā*. The deity wears *dhoti* and a scarf; the latter with ends tucked on the left shoulder has left the right chest and shoulder bare. Around the figure of Buddha are represented the seven other great incidents of Buddha's life. In the birth scene, Buddha is seen on the right side of his mother, holding a branch of Aśoka tree and left hand resting on her hip. Above the birth scène of Buddha is seated in *Vajarparyankāśana* on a double lotus displaying hands in *dharma-chakra-pravartana-mudrā*. The sculpture measuring 18 cm × 17.5 cm from Lumbinī is made of greyish sandstone (Mitra, 1972 : 200). Remaining figures of the birth and the first sermon are offering of honey of the sinister.

The Nativity Image of Buddha

A nativity image of Buddha from the Lumbinī measuring 167 × 106 cm shows Māyādevi giving birth to Buddha from her right side under the *sāl* tree and grasping its branch with her right hand while the left hand is resting on her waist (*katyavalambita*). The deity (she) wears a solid earlobe (*ratnakuṇdala or mukta-phala kuṇdala*), armlet in her right hand, and one piece of heavy anklet

(*Tulākoṭi or Hansaka*). Curly hairs on both sides of her head are visible in the relief. Prajāpatī (Gautamī) holds her waist from her right side as is usual during delivery. Her oval face and curly hairs are depicted in a beautiful manner. On extreme right in the relief is executed a figure of Brahmā, wearing *karaṇdaka mukuṭa* catching the body, perhaps on a cloth, having been delivered by Māyādevi. Behind Brahmā, Indra (Sakra) is depicted wearing a *kiriṭa mukuṭa* and watching the birth scene. Down the centre of the panel is executed the figure of prince Siddhartha probably standing on a lotus flower with a circular halo (*prabhāmaṇdala)* behind his head. Broken into three parts the panel has been divided into three horizontal sections on which the latest figure of Māyādevi is executed in the first line in the upper part. In the second and the third lines figures of Prajāpatī (Gautamī), Brahmā, Indra and Siddhartha Gautam are depicted. Scholars have dated of the panel on the basis of its style. Führer was first to inform this sculpture. However, he did not mention the details of this panel. Mukherji is of the opinion that the sculpture may be associated with the time of Aśoka as he found similarity in material and workmanship of Yaksha with the door-keepers of Pātaliputra belonging to the Mauryan period. Agrawal is of the view that it may belong to the Kushāṇa period as the style of the *dhoti* of Māyādevi, wavy flowing locks of hair of Gautami, projecting high crown of Indra and *mukuṭa* of a male figure seems to be in a style of that period. Mitra however placed the sculpture in the Gupta period. Krishṇadeva, an eminent scholar of art history of India, says that this sculptural panel may be dated in 400 AD. Mishra places this panel in about 300 AD. Pandey agrees with the opinion of Mukherji who placed it in the Aśokan period. *Silā vigadabhicha* on the Aśokan pillar of third century BC may be interpreted as referring to the making of this panel. Venerable Bhikkshu Sudarsan is of the view that the term *silā vigadabhica kālāpita* in Aśokan pillar refers to this Māyādevi image. Execution of Buddhist images, including the nativity sculptures of Buddha, began in first century AD at two art centres-Mathurā and Gandhara. Sculptures originating in Mathurā were sent to sacred places at Saranātha, Kuśinagar (Kasiā), Śrāvasti and Lumbinī from where the present

Nativity groups of sculptures are available (Agrawal, 1965:163). Chinese Yech-Chi monk Shengtsai saw it in course of his visit during 250-375 AD in Lumbni (Petech, 1950:35). It proves that the sculpture was established there before his pilgrimage of the site. Thus, the present sculpture belonging to the second-third century AD is the earliest and the best of all the Nativity panels so far discovered from the sub-continent.

Bodhisattva

Images of paṇch dhyāni Buddha and Bodhisattva have been obtained from here. Two-armed images of Bodhisattva of buff-coloured stone from Lumbinī is 7 cm in height and 4.8 cm in width. It is seated in *lalitaśana* pose. It is shown resting with one leg on a double lotus pedestal and the other one is placed on a two-tiered pedestal. The deity is wearing a long *dhoti* a girdle diaphanous scarf like object in *upavita* fashion, an *upavita* and a tall *jatā-mukuṭa*. The Bodhisattva in *vyākhyana-mudrā* is shown with half-closed eyes, graceful flexion and sensitively modelled limbs. The stalks of the flower pass through both the armpits. On the top of the relief, the corner is encircled with a row of petals. The panel belonging to the eighth-ninth century is in the *mudrā* of *Manjushri* and *Maitreya.*

Maitreya

22 × 14 cm high greyish sandstone sculpture of Maitreya from Lumbinī is crudely executed in *lalitāśana mudrā* (Mitra,1972:200). Bodhisattva depicted in *vyākhyana-mudrā* wears an *hāra* and a *jatā mukuṭa* with, possibly, a stūpa in it. The branch of an *nāgakesara* with three leaves and a flower passes through the left armpit. Another branch with four leaves and a flower is also shown on the right side of the figure. Thus, Maitreya is shown in traditional *āśana mudrā* with a stūpa figure on the *mukuṭa*. The image agrees with the description of the *Sādana mālā* as well.

Ratnasambhava

A head of Bodhisattva measuring 12 cm high exhibits the features of Ratna sambhava (Ibid.). The figure of *dhyani*-Buddha is executed with half-closed eyes and a short crown with a decked triangular piece at the bottom of the long *jatāmukuṭa*. On the basis of the features of the fragment its right hand seems to be in *varada-mudrā*.

Stone sculptures are executed on the basis of the Mathurā and Gandhara art tradition during the Suṅga-Kushāṇa period. Pāla-Sena art tradition has influenced the art of the region from the eighth century to the fourteenth century AD. However, between the middle of the fourteenth century up to seventeenth centuries the influence of art traditions of India decreased due to the Muslim invasion in this region. Sculptures as well as shrines were disturbed by the Muslims. Thus, fragments of the deity with missing eye, nose, head, hand, leg and other parts are found in course of exploration.

Padmapāṇi Avalokiteśvar

Other fragment of a sculpture of Padmapāṇi Avalokiteśvar from Lumbinī, measures 8 cm high and 14.2 cm wide. It is made of greenish black stone belonging to the tenth century AD. The deity holds a full-blossomed lotus stalk in his left hand and the other one is missing. The high jata-*mukuṭa* is decked with a tiny figure of Amitaba, a fan-shaped projection and a stūpa on the head.

Vishṇu

Vishṇu, one of the supreme deities in Hindu pantheon, is known as Urugaya, Urukrama and Trivikrama in the Ṛigveda. With the passage of time, his portion changed as in reflected in the Brāhmaṇas, Āraṇyaka and Upanisadic literature as well as in the Epics and Purāṇas. Vishṇu is associated first with the Vedic god Urugaya, Urukram, thereafter with Nārāyaṇa of the Brāhmaṇas and the Āraṇyakas and finally with Vasudeva–Krishṇa. In the early period, his symbolic representations are found in the region in the forms of Sāligrams and in the form of worship of *Tulsi, Bar* and *Pipal* trees. Representations of wheels on the coins found in the region may be taken as the depiction of his Sudarśan Chakra. A standing figure of Vishṇu from Sainā mainā, now on the ground in front of Lumbinī Development Trust Office in Lumbinī, in *samabhańga* pose measures 33 × 16 cm. It is wearing *kiriṭa mukuṭa*, heavy pendant earrings and *dhoti*. It holds a discus in the left hand and the right hand is broken. Its physical features are fine from the artistic point of view. Another sculpture from the same site, measures 27 × 14.5 cm. Two–armed Vishṇu holds mace in the right and discus in the left hand. The deity is shown wearing a loin-cloth, girdle, a long garland up to the knee. A portion of the head is missing. Its pronounced chest and thin waist are in usual form as of other sculptures in the region. Its back portion is rough and unfinished. Both the sculptures are ascribable to the medieval period on the basis of style and quality of brown-sandstone. These deities are defaced and broken due to negligence and lack of preservation.

Simple form of Vishṇu

The images of Vishṇu are divided on the basis of their standing, sitting and reclining position, called s*thānaka, āsana mūrti* and *śayana–mūrti*, respectively. These are again sub-divided into *yoga, bhoga, vira* and *abhichārika* as well as each having *uttama, madhyama* and *adhama* categories. The devotees use to worship different forms, viz. *yogi* to *yoga* form*, bhogi* to *bhoga*, strong ones to *vira* and for conquering enemies the *abhicharika* form.

Vyūha Images

Different incarnations of Vishṇu are supposed to have taken place to destroy the wicked and safeguard the virtuous. In *Taittiriya Samhita* and *Satapath Brāhmaṇa* the form of *Matsya, Kurma* and *Varāha* forms of Vishṇu are mentioned. However, in other *Purānas* ten *avatars* of Vishṇu, viz. Matsya, Kurma and Varāha, Nṛsimha, Vāmana, Paraśurāma, Rāghava-rāma, Krishṇa, Buddha and Kalki are mentioned. The sculpture of *Varāha* is found in the area of Lumbinī.

Varāha

According to the *Rigveda* it is known as *Emusha Varāha* who was the god of fertility and symbol of truth. In this incarnation, he killed the demon *Hiraṇyākshap* and lifted the earth. According to the *Agni-Purāṇa,* Vishṇu had taken the form of *Varāha* to kill the demon. As stated by V.S. Agrawal the icons of Ādivarāha, Yajñvarāha, Śvetavarāha Brahmavarāha and Emusha-vārāha are executed at different sites. The form of *Emusha* or *Prithivi* is associated with Lakshmi. As stated in the Matsya-Purāṇa Mahāvarāha keeps a leg on the *kurma* and another on Ādiśesha with a mace and a lotus in his hands. *Prithvi* should be seated either on his snout or on the elbow with *nilotpala* flower in one of her hand and the other hand resting on the hip. *Agni-Purāṇa* and *Vishṇudharmottara* give similar descriptions except with slight variation. In this region, only one type of *Bhuvarāha* image is found in anthropomorphic form with a boar-face.

The sculpture of *Bhuvarāha* measuring 42 × 25 cm was found from Masinā village Rupāndehi, now placed in the Kapilvastu Regional Museum. It shows four-armed boar in anthropomorphic form. He is standing with his right leg stretched and the left are slightly turned. On the front left elbow of the deity is seated *Prithivi*, probably, carrying a lotus in her hand. He keeps his back right hand near the hips and holds mace in the front right hand. He holds discus in the front left hand and a lotus in the back left. The deity wears neck-ornaments, armlets, anklets, waist-band, loin-cloth and *vanamālā*. A dagger is also noticed. The deity is gazing at *Prithivi* with admiration in usual style. Two legs are placed, probably, on *Kurma* and *Ādisesha* as mentioned in the *Matsya-Purāṇa*. On the basis of style the image may be placed in Pāla-Sen art tradition of the region.

Devī

Goddess in the Hindu pantheon is the representation of the universal energy, pure knowledge, absolute truth and fertility. The figurines of mother-goddess were made in the Mohanjodaro and Harppan culture. In the early Vedic period goddess Aditi, mother of Varuṇa, Sarasvatī, Hotrā, Bhārati, Ilādevī, Prishṇi, Vāk and Rātri were known. In the later Vedic period, goddess Umā-Haimavati, Bhavāni, Isāni, Rudrāṇi, Durgā, Mahākāli and *Bhāgavati* were worshipped as the representative of *śakti*. In the *Mahābhārata* Arjun prayed Durgā for victory in the forthcoming battle. The concept of the composite goddess such as mother, daughter and sister and other forms are available in the Vedic Aryan society. In *Devī-mahātamya* of the *Mārkandeya-Purāṇa*, other forms, such as, Raktachandikā, Satākshi, Pārvati, Śākambhari, Durgā, Devī, Bhimā and Bhramāni forms are also mentioned. Devī is known in three forms of Lakshmi, Mahākāli and Sarasvatī representing the *Rajasa,* the *Tamasa* and the *Sattvika gunas*. In course of time, she became an independent deity. Mahālakshmi is worshipped as the representative of the creator, protector, and annihilator of the universe.

Ancient stone sculptures of devi from Sainā mainā, at present fixed in the courtyard of Lumbinī Development Trust, belong to the Gupta period and are in much dilapidated condition. One of them measuring 40 cm in height is wearing usual earrings with plain halo. Miniature figurines of Devī discovered in this region belonged to the third-second century BC to fourteenth-fifteenth centuries AD.

Images of Divine-mothers

Stone images of *sapta-mātrikas* are found from the Gupta period in the region. Among them Vajravārāhi, Chāmuṇdā, Lakshmi, Sarasvatī and Gańgā-Yamunā images are available here.

Vajravārāhi (Tara)

Vajravārāhi image from Lumbinī in s*thānaka* pose, measuring 122 × 55 cm, belongs to the Gupta period (Pandey, 1985 : 58). Two-armed deity holds a discus in the right hand and the left one is broken. The deity wears waist-band, *sādi* upto the heel and other usual ornaments. Two circular lines are executed at the back of the head. Halo of the panel is decorated with floral and geometrical designs. The relief is broken into two halves across the breast (Mukherji, 1969 : 36). It is also called Tara. Other parts are not clearly visible and cannot identify to Tara due to its damaged-condition. It is similar to the image of Vārahi from Kumbheśvara and Balkhu in Kathmandu (Bandel, 2039 : Figs. 14 & 18) dated in second-third century AD. The panel partially agrees with the descriptions of *Sādhanāmālā*.

Śiva

The anionic and anthropomorphic forms of Śiva are known from Mohenjodaro, Harappa and other sites connected with the Indus culture in the forms of phallus and *yoni.* It is considered as the prototype of later Pasupati-Śiva. In the *Ṛigveda,* Rudra is known as the deity of destruction and benevolence. In the *Yajurveda* and later *Samhita* god Rudra is regarded as the protector and guardian of the children. In the *Atharvaveda,* Rudra is known as *Nilasikhandin* and medicine. In the *Upanishadic* period, he achieved the highest position of Māheśvar, Śiva, Iśāna and Iśa. In the *Grihasutras,* he is frequently known as Śiva and Śaṅkar. Image worship tradition had started in this period. Pāṇini and Kauṭilya have also mentioned Śiva as Bhava and Sarva. He further refers to the existence of the Śivālaya. He is called Maheśvara, Isāna, *Mahādeva*, *Bhagawān* and Śiva in the *Mahābhārata*. In the *Purāṇas,* he is regarded as *Chaṇda-Bhairava* and Mahākāla, and is described with different *gaṇas,* viz. *Rākshasas, Dānavas, Gandharvas, Daityas* and *Yakshas*. Having been popular deity in the Hindu pantheon, *liṅgas* represent of the two great generative principles of the universe, Śiva and Sakti, or *Purusa* and *Prakriti*, the father and the mother of all creation or the energy and matter. *Liṅgas* are found from very ancient period. Idols of Śiva and his representatives were executed in various styles and techniques in this region.

Śiva, among other deities, viz. Skanda, Nārāyaṇa, Kuber, Sūrya, Vishṇu, was also known as a god during the Śākya period in the region of Nepāl. The *Makuṭāgama* classifies the *sthira Liṅgas* (*acala or dhruva*, i.e. immovable or permanently fixed) into four classes viz. the Daivika, the Arsaka, the Gānapa, and Mānusa. Bānaliṇgas, according to one of the *Kāmikāgama*, are natural objects like the *Śāligrāmas*, which are mostly picked-up from the bed of the Gaṇdakī river, a tributary of the Gaṅges in north India. These emblems are carried by Saivites and offered to the god. Many monolithic stone pillars are also found in the region. Figures of this deity are also available on the Kushāṇa coins, viz. Wema Kadphises, Kaniska, Huvishka and others.

In the sanctum of *Mahādeva* temple at Prakateśvar a brown–sand stone *lińga* and *yoni*, measuring 3 m high and 5 m in diameter, are installed. Its Rudra-*bhāga* is round and is about 91 cm. high, Vishṇu-*bhāga* is octagonal and *Brahma-bhāga* is in round. Its structure agrees with the description of *Vishṇudharmottara*. This *lings* must have been broken and disturbed during the Muslim invasion of the region from the fourteenth to seventeenth centuries.

Umā-Maheśvar Mūrti

The figures of Umā-Maheśvara, executed on the terracotta seals and coins in Lumbinī found in course of the excavation of the sites. However, their features are not clearly identifiable as they are in defaced condition. The sculpture of *Umā*-Maheśvara in *samapāda-sthānaka mudrā from* Lumbinī, measures 72 cm in height and 39 cm in width shows Umā on the left of Mahādev. Umā's earring and other ornaments are not clearly visible. Oval face, small forehead, short neck, breast and thin waist reveal the size and shape of the body. On the basis of iconographic features, it is known as *Umā sahita Chandraśekhar*. However, the mark of Chandra is not seen on the forehead of the deity. It is similar to the Umā-Maheśvara image of Kirtipur in Kathmandu, which is dated in the fourth century AD.

Seated image of Maheśvar on the wall of Prakateśvar Mahādev temple measures 70 × 43 cm. and is in embracing pose. The deity has four arms holding a lotus flower in the front right hand and rest three hands are broken. Umā wears an elaborate coiffure diadem, earrings, single necklace and other usual ornaments. She is seated on his left lap embracing Maheśvara with her right hand. Other features are not clearly seen as it is in defaced condition. Her features partly agree with the description in the *Śilparatna, Suprabedagama* and are comparable to Ellora panel of Umā Maheśvara in the eighth century. On stylic grounds, it seems to belong to the Pāla-Sena art tradition of the region. It is partially similar to Umā-Maheśvara panel of Dailekha.

Stone objects

Besides beads, bangles and stone sculptures many other stone objects, viz. prehistoric stone tools, disc, balls, slate pencils, querns, mullers, ear ornaments, bowl and lids of casket, etc. have been found at Lumbinī. The study reveals that stone, though within an easy reach, was not a common medium of any domestic article of daily use, except querns and mullers. Some of them are highly polished and decorated. We are not clear about their usage.

Ear Ornaments

Besides the beads and bangles in semi-precious stones, ear ornaments have also been obtained from Lumbinī. Ear-stud and earring are the principal ornaments for the ear. One specimen of ear-stud from Lumbinī is made of Jasper and is like a short cylinder. This is dated in second-third centuries AD.

Terracotta Figurines

Terracotta, being a cheap and most popular medium and within the reach of poor and common man, has been used not only as the medium for artistic expression but also for personal ornaments like beads, bangles and rings, seal and sealing, children's toys and objects of domestic and ritualistic needs. A large number of terracotta animals and bird figurines were undoubtedly children's toys. Terracotta plaques with holes at the top were suspended against the walls. Some of them were kept as decorating objects on the mantel-pieces or niches made on or in the walls of the houses. Flat, rectangular, oval or round plaques could be made out of clay without any difficult. Being a cheap and tractable medium it was highly demanded in contemporary society. It is largely concerned itself with the representation of the scenes of everyday life, and, as such, its social imports appear to be immense. Terracotta, in its varied uses and applications, gives us an idea for constructing the social, cultural, political and religious life of the contemporary people. Terracotta human and animal figurines give us a clear picture of the life-ways during the ancient period. Increase in communication between Northern-India and the western Terai region of Nepāl resulted in the introduction of many classical elements of Indian art in the pattern of Nepalese culture and art tradition. Terracotta figurines from Lumbinī have brought to light a large variety of terracotta remains, which throw considerable light on the trends of plastic art and nature of Nepāli artists during the pre-Christian and early Christian centuries.

As far as the dating of the human figurines is concerned, scholars generally believe that hand-made figurines were made earlier than those produced with the help of a mould were. However, this common belief does not find any favour in this region because practice of both modelling and moulding went hand in hand at the same time in some cases. However, many of the significant terracotta figurines, relevant for a study of this art, are simply accidental finds and no accurate data with regard to the level of their discovery are available. These specimens seem to have been disturbed from their original level due to some actions of men or of nature. Some terracotta figurines of different dates have been discovered in the same Pit. In the study of the terracotta art of this area, special attention has been taken to spell out its date, even if it could be ascribed to a particular piece on the basis of its context. Many of the excavating teams have not published their detailed excavation reports. Terracotta figurines have been classified on the basis of the variations in use, style, model, shape and types.

Human Figurines

Both human and divine figurines reflect not only the socio-cultural, economic and religious modes and thoughts of a community, but also delineate its artistic tradition. In the primitive stage of human civilisation, many symbols as well as anthromorphic forms had been used to express human emotions, spiritual feelings, e.g. snake, and mother goddess associated with the ritual of fertility or agriculture, a phenomenon common to all cultures. In the study of human figurines many specimens as well as fragments are included which were found in course of excavation from Lumbinī. These figurines hardly reflect any characteristics peculiar to this region alone. Bearing the impress of the trends, tastes and fashions of the artistic movements of the Mauryan, Suṅga and Kushāṇa periods, most of them throw light on the common features of the contemporary terracotta art-tradition of northern and eastern India. Latter among them were intended for house-decoration, a presumption substantiated by the suspension holes made in plaques found here.

Suńga Figurines

The Mauryan and the Suńga art do not appear to have any relation with each other so far as stone sculptures are concerned. However, in terracotta art there appears to be some relationships between the two. There was a sudden increase in the manufacture of terracotta art due to an important change in the technique and tradition of its production. Modelling was given up during this period. It was replaced by the mould technique, which was extensively used for the depiction of a variety of subjects. This change of technique was probably due to heavy demand for terracotta art in contemporary society. Stone was a hard and scarce material. Therefore, it was not a convenient medium for mass production. It was not available in plenty in most regions. Due to its dexterous quality, it could not be easily converted into figurines or plaques. However, it was easy to display sensitive features of body in clay by subtle modelling. The plaques were produced from a single mould, and are, therefore, entirely flat without any decoration at the back. Some are produced in low flattened relief, while others come out with the background in fairly high relief. Some plaques are provided with holes at the top for hanging on the wall. In course of time, the Suńga artist produced fine pieces modelled in bold relief displaying disciplined sensitive modelling. They are of extremely fine fabric and are uniformly baked. They have light darkish red colour, though some of them do have a red-slip on them. They have an elaborate headdress, beaded bands on the head, studs or discs shaped earrings in their ears and with elaborate flat necklaces. Apart from these, they are heavily decorated with bangles anklets armlets and broad bejewelled girdles on the waist. As a rule, the figures have heavy coiffure and wear elaborate apparel and jewellery concealing, to a certain extent, the beauty of the delicatly-modelled body. The female wears an extremely elaborate headdress and is loaded with jewellery, while the male wears a turban round his head. The plaques have decorative borders and the background is stamped with floral and rosette pattern. The treatment of the drapery is also varied.

Suńga figurines have been found at Banjarahi, Nipania and Lumbinī in course of excavation and exploration. Most of the excavated figurines from here have clear features and the evidence of fine modelling on it.

Human Figurines

Indeterminate human figurines, as well as fragments, are included here, especially male specimens. Head of an old man with prominent nose is highly individualistic and speaks of the hands of a skilled artist in its making. It was found at Lumbinī (Mitra 1972 : 201). One figurine of a young boy is available. It is with parrot, the favourite bird. Two other specimens are also remarkable. One of them is a figurine of a toy without head and feet. It is holding a long tailed parrot on the right fore-arm.

Kushāṇa Figurines

A large number of big-size male and female heads, busts and figures, which usually betray crude workmanship, have been found in Banjarahi, Nipania and Lumbinī. The specimens reflect that the artist did not use the mould, which was so commonly employed by the Suńga artists. In some cases, a mould was occasionally used, particularly for producing large figures of which the busts were hand modelled and only the heads were pressed out of moulds. The inferior qualities of clay, mixed with grit, husk and other impurities, have been used to execute these Kushāṇa figurines. The eyes and mouth are wide open and the nose is long, pinched out by hand. The workmanship of this group is poorer than other Suńga figurines found at the site.

The return of modelling forms does not seem to have been successful. According to Agrawal available specimens from the datable layers at Ahichchhatra are of crude workmanship, showing neglect in the use of mould and a reversal to hand-made form. A large quantity of the figurnines made in same tradition of manufacturing is found in this region. Deterioration in terracotta figurines may have been due to the mass production of stone sculptures in contemporary society. Eyes, mouth and nose are made with either incised lines or punched-dots made with the help of bamboo or wooden pins. The female figurines have been bedecked with heavy ornaments, especially earrings, necklaces and fan-like headgear. Mishra has classified these specimens into three groups: round and carved up to the feet, figures with oil lamps and *Negam* type. However, his classification is not attested in this region probably due to lack of sufficient specimens.

Kushāṇa figurines have been modelled in inordinate large size and are in the round. Life-size terracotta statues had also been produced during this period. Various figurines with religious affiliations are far more interesting. A large number of gods and goddess of different pantheons, especially Buddhism and Hinduism, came to be represented in terracotta for the first time. Due to the religious eclecticism of the Kushāṇa rulers and popularity of *Bhakti cult,* a lot of Brāhmaṇical and Buddhist deities have been represented in terracotta forms. The most important contribution of the Kushāṇa artists was the representation of Buddha in the anthropomorphic form in both stone and clay. Unfortunately, it is difficult to know out the real position due to lack of complete plaque. Heads, torso and other fragments are separately obtained at Banjarahi, Nipania and Lumbinī.

Gupta Figurines

Gupta art objects are the glorious heritage of humanity evidence of which is found over a large part of India. Its influence on the terracotta figurines in this area is apparent. The Kushān elements had gradually disappeared in the early Gupta period. The clay used in the Gupta period was extremely fine without any impurities, i.e. grit, husks and sand. Moulding technique was again revived which was commonly practiced during the Suńga period, but was neglected in the Kushāṇa period. Both modelled and moulded figurines have been found. Gupta artists were capable of using single or double mould. They were also capable of partly moulding and partly modelling the figurine as and when required. Some figurines are also completely hand-made. These figurines are well-baked. The artists paid special attention in making of the face. However, they neglected the human body. The specimens are treated with a deep red slip and red only in some cases. The lips are full and the fingers tender. Entirely hand-made figurines are not refined.

The artist handled both the religious and secular subjects with equal ease. Buddhist images fashioned by the artists of this period are of great iconographical interest. Among these are the images of Bodhisattva, Siddhartha with Yasodhara, Buddha in earth touching and *Dharmachakra* pose found in this region, especially from Lumbinī. Secular art objects like female and male figurines as well as animal figurines like elephant and horse have also been reported from this area. Every terracotta object in the Gupta age was done in a perfect manner and style.

A bust of Bodhisattva from Lumbinī is endowed with real grace and elegance of the Gupta Period. Its slim right hand is raised in *abhaya mudrā*. It is dressed in transparent cloth. The face is elongated with a straight nose, smooth cheeks and thick lips, having depressions at the corners. The two sides of the chin are separated in the middle. The crown is bedecked with crest with dotted design on it in oblique technique. It is a beautiful terracotta piece of art of this area (Rijal, 1979:20). A leaf-shaped plaque impressed with the figure of Bodhisattva (Manjusri) is reported from the preceding site (Mitra, 1972:203). It is seated in *maharājalilā* pose on a double petalled lotus. It carries a long sword in the right hand and the left hand is hanging down towards the lotus. The hair appears to be in three locks and a square-based stūpa is executed on the dexter of the head. On the basis of Buddhist characters, especially three lines on the dexter and one line on the sinister of the figure, it seems to belong to the late Gupta period.

A terracotta figure from Lumbinī depicting Prince Siddhartha with Yasodhara is the most valuable and very rare type of image in this region. It was discovered at the south east corner of the Māyādev? temple. It measures 68 × 37 cm in size (R.L. 102.759)

(Rijal, 1996:10). This panel is square in lower base and round at the top. Yasodharā is shown in the background as lying in the Royal bed with folded legs. Her left hand is holding her nipple to feed her son Rāhula and the right one is kept below her head. Legs are folded and rested on the pillow. She is bedecked with beaded necklace, armlets, beaded, bangle and anklets. The image of Siddhartha is also in full royal attire, sitting at ease on the royal bed with his left hand pressing the knee of Yasodharā, probably to check whether she is in sound sleep or not in order to leave the palace and renounce the world. His right hand is broken below the elbow. He is bedecked with a turban with lion-faced crest on the head, heavy circular earrings, single necklace, armlets, beaded bangles and well-elaborated anklets. Rijal has claimed that it is influenced by Gandhara art and dated it between fourth to sixth centuries AD. Mishra has dated it in the Kushāṇa period. Some main features of this piece are similar to the Gupta images from Ahichchhatra, as such; it seems to belong to the fifth–sixth centuries AD.

A moulded terracotta plaque representing Lord Buddha in the earth touching posture has been reported from Lumbinī (Rijal, 1979:16). Fragment of an architectural member with the head of Buddha is also reported from the previous site. The halo around the head is plain. It is possibly elliptical at the bottom. It has open eyes, prominently arched eyebrows, *ushinsha* and stylised *dakshinavarta* curls covering his head. The lips are made in full as in usual in the Gupta tradition. It is comparable to those found in temple 3 of Nalanda and *Kachchi kuṭi* of Śrāvasti. These plaques were probably inserted into the sunken panels between two sets of moulding.

Terracotta *Dharmachakra* with 32 spokes is reported from the excavations of Lumbinī in the eastern side of Māyādevi temple. The relief is a part of a big panel of *Dharmachakara* sculpture, which might have been worshipped at the site by the devotees. Two other animal figurines, possibly of bull and a deer, are depicted in this panel. It belongs to fifth century AD.

Apart from Buddhist images, heads of standing men and women, and bricks with animal and floral motifs are also found.

The face including eyes, eyeballs, nose, nostrils, mouth, cheeks, chin and ears are carefully executed. These are quite artistic and beautiful. Most of these display open eyes and partly open mouth showing the upper row of teeth. In some case rice husk have been mixed in the clay. Cast busts of well-burnt buff fabric with deep red-slip are also reported.

A fine head from Lumbinī has half closed meditative eyes and a peculiar crown on its head. Its modelling is reminiscent of the Gupta style. Rijal has reported two terracotta heads from the same site. One of them is having well-dressed hair in the style of deep curls called *dhupika kuntala*. Its thick lips without bold depressions at corners and in the middle of the chin provide an evidence of the transitional phase. Facial details of the second one are worn out. Hair dressed up in the style of turba is, however, noticeable. A solid head, which is a flat at the backside from Lumbinī, has its hair arranged in the form of three knots. This crude specimen has large open eyes. Three defaced-heads, the first possible of a woman, the second well modelled with a top knot and the third well-modelled, are reported from the preceding site. All of them exhibit fairly good workmanship.

A head from Lumbinī with spiral curls and open eyes displaying pupils is also known. Partly open mouth exhibits the upper row of teeth. A large quantity of rice husk has been mixed with clay to form it in chocolate-red. Two heads from the same site have been beautifully modelled with open eyes.The back portion of their head is hollow. A head with a crown on the extremely narrow forehead is crudely marked by incised lines. Its torque, eyes and lips appear to have been made in applique technique.

Lower part of the figurines made in Gupta art tradition and techniques are also reported from this area. One of them from Lumbinī is adorned with frilled skirt or *antravesaka* and a scarf or *sanghati*. One leg is bent and placed behind the other, which is stretched.

Thus, it is clear that the Gupta figurines were made both by hand and mould according to the requirements. Among the secular objects of this age are mostly male and female figurines. All of them exhibit characteristically refined taste and charm of this period. Some of the female and human heads are so charming that everyone wonders at the skill of the artist. The most outstanding features of the Gupta figures are the expressions on their faces.

In this study, such indeterminate specimens as well as unidentified fragments of the plaques have been mentioned under this topic. Some of them are obtained from Lumbinī. Most of them are female figurines with heavy and bulging hips and prominent rounded breasts made of husk-mixed clay. The figurines of this type were entirely hand made. A bust of the female from Lumbinī is bedecked with a necklace in the form of a row of impressed roundels. A damaged tiny terracotta plaque from the surface in Lumbinī has only hanging hands. A head from Lumbinī appears quite individualistic with its hair indicated by incised-lines.

Animal Figurines

The terracotta animal figurines are scattered on the surface of the mounds in different areas. They are also found in the occupational layers. From the study of these figurines, it is clear that animal figurines were produced in greater number than other figurines. A large number of terracotta animal and bird figurines were meant undoubtedly to be children's toys. Some of them might have been made by the family members of the artists. Toys were quite popular in this area during ancient period. As recorded in *Bhadda sāla Jātaka* prince Vidudhabha questions his mother as to why he does not get gifts like horses, elephants and toys which other princes were receiving from their maternal side. Among animal figurines, elephant, bull, horse, ram, dog, deer and birds are found in larger proportion at Banjarāhi, Nipānia and Lumbinī.

Crude animal figurines when decorated become more realistic and beautiful. The artists show a preference for elephant. Animals are made of baked clay.

Other specimens, viz. dog, deer, ram, birds, are also modelled or moulded in usual tradition and technique in the contemporary society. All the specimens are made of fine-grained clay. They are usually red in colour and fairly well-burnt, often with a grey core. Grey specimens and a few of smoky-red figurines are treated with black slip.

Terracotta objects

Clay being a cheap and simple media for artistic expression and also within the reach of common people, terracotta objects were generally made of it. Besides human and animal figurines, beads and bangles are also found in this region. Miscellaneous terracotta objects include toy carts and toy-wheels, discs, flesh-rubber, dabbers, balls, ear-ornaments, stoppers, musical instruments, lump of clay and lamps.

Dabber

Only eleven specimens of dabbers have been reported from this area. Two specimens with a solid handle and having a grey core, made in red fabric are reported from Lumbinī.

Seals and Sealing

Seals and sealings belong to kings, nobles, private individuals, government officials and public institutions. They were used for sealing letters and parcels and also to authenticate documents or to serve as signature. Documented-seals bear in their engravings the impress of an artistic impulse of the people. Some of them were also used as passports, which enabled the couriers to get entrance to a particular place. Another class of seals and sealing bear religious and secular formulae. They were most likely used for propaganda and given to the visiting devotees.

Lumbinī and Kapilvastu being the pilgrimage centre for the Buddhists from the ancient period, different group of people, viz. poor and rich, king and merchant, had issued seals and sealing to be given to the visitors as token after their visit of the sites. The seals and sealing from the sites help us to identify the antiquity of the culture of this region like any other Buddhists sites in India. Almost all the seals and sealings are made of terracotta during the third-second centuries BC.

Seals

The seals carry engraved legends in negative form in order to produce its positive form on any soft material like mud when impressed. One of them, a chalk stone seal is very remarkable. When impressed on wet clay it produced pictographs. The soft stone seal has a circular working edge and a long handle. There are three symbols on it. Two of them are taurine in two rows looking like four *Devanāgari* script and the remaining one is a four petalled flower with a dot in the centre of a circle. *Damaru*-shaped handle has a circular hole across the body to suspend it from a string (No. 30) (National Museum, 1998:27). Mishra has also reported nineteen terracotta seals with inscription in Gupta characters from a stūpa of the same period in course of his excavation of trench LMB-1 at Lumbinī, in 1984-85 primarily a religious site where monks lived. It is known *Dhamma* stūpa. However, no further information about these seals is available. Seals are available in Lumbinī because it was primarily a pilgrimage site during ancient period.

Sealing

Terracotta sealing of various size and shape are made out of fine alluvial clay. Seals, which are well-fired, are bright-red in colour though ill-fired ones are not so bright-red in colour. Almost all the sealings were issued by the organisations and individuals in this area.

Since the sites of Lumbinī and others on the periphery of Kapilvastu turned into pilgrimage centres and fell on the trade route from the Himālayas to the Gangetic plain. Various classes of people, including traders, monks, nuns, kings and nobles must have visited these sites and enriched them by issuing and offering seals and sealings as a token of their visit of the region. A lot of seals and sealing available on the surface from here are missing as they might have been dismantled due to lack of proper information about their significance among the local people. Only a limited number of these are available to help us to reconstruct the social, religious and cultural life ways of the contemporary people, as well as, to establish the identification this area with ancient Kapilvastu.

Beads

Beads from stratified layers and these collected from the surface are taken into consideration for comparative and typological analysis. Beads from here are of great interest. A large number of materials were employed to make different varieties of beads. It is interesting to note that the forms and manufacturing techniques of beads in the area are similar to the typical North-Indian beads from settlements dating as far back as the third century BC. These provide proofs of the trade connections, which existed between Hastināpur, Ahichchhatra, Kausambi and Nepāl in that period. Some of these beads are unbored or partly made. This indicates that, probably, bead manufacturing was a local industry of Kapilvastu. In many cases, they could hardly be even approximately dated.

A lot of beads in various mediums have been reported during excavations. However, some of them are not properly classified and studied. Some of them are kept at Lumbinī museum. The researcher has grouped these beads on the basis of the materials from which they are made. Semi-precious stone beads are also classified on the basis of the technique in certain cases. Special care was taken to select the material for a particular type of bead. This shows the skill and expertise available in the area in bead making technology.

Plasticity of clay for preparing easily any shape and design, its ubiquitous availability without any cost and being within the reach of common person were different factors responsible for the popularity of terracotta beads. All the three methods—moulded, hand-made and wheel-turned were adopted for manufacturing terracotta beads. Fine clay from rivers and tanks was used for its manufacture. Some of these beads are unbored, indicative of the fact that it was a local industry. It would not be far from truth if the ancient site of Tilaurākoṭ is called 'a mine of terracotta beads' on the basis a large number of beads found in the limited excavation of the site. Some of them are with red-coloured surface having a slip or wash on it. These were broadly used in Lumbinī area.

Bangles

Bangles being the most popular ornament of women and clay being a cheap material and easily available were generally used for making it. Fragments available in different diameters reveal that children, girls and woman of different ages used it as ornament. Both hand-made and mould-made terracotta bangles are available. The former are mostly circular in section, plain in design and irregular in thickness. Mica-mixed clay is used to provide it a glittering surface. This variety is rectangular in section with rounded corner. Some of them are incised with vertical strokes or lines over the sides across the length by sharp-tools to decorate it with design. Mould-made bangles are mostly triangular in section with rounded corners. This variety is decorated with geometrical designs and a series of incised lines over the sides across the length of the bangles. The inner part of the bangle, which touches the skin, has a smooth surface in both the varieties.

Coins

A coin is a piece of metal of prescribed weight, with designs or legends on them produced and issued under the direction of an authority (private or public) for its use as a medium of exchange. Various designs or legends are produced on the surface of the metal by punching, stamping on one or both faces and casting. Silver and copper coins made with these techniques are found from here in course of excavation and exploration. These coins play a very significant role in the reconstruction of the early history of this area.

Punch-marked Coins

Punch-marked coins are the earliest coins of India. The term 'punch marked' means that punches were applied irregularly at various points on the surface of the coins marking symbols or signs on them. Punch-marked coins are found both in silver and in copper. These coins were first introduced, probably, during the pre-Mauryan period because a reference to them is made by Kautilya. The earliest evidence of coins from the excavations at Tilaurākoṭ and Lumbinī happen to be of copper and silver punch marked coins. Coins in silver and copper are irregular in shape and are in different shapes, viz. oblong, rectangular, circular and square. These coins bear no inscriptions instead they carry different symbols, viz. different forms of hills, trees, birds, animals, reptiles, human figures, sun, six-armed symbols, caduceus, floral and geometrical designs, religious symbols, etc.

Punch-marked coins are generally dated from sixth to second centuries BC. These coins remained in continuous currency up to the first and second centuries AD. These are made of pieces cut from hammered sheets of metal. They are in irregular size and shape, roughly square or rectangular. There are edges on alternate sides, indicating cut marks on them. These sharp edges are seen on all the four sides. Rough sides and non-standard shape and size of the coins exhibit the negligence of the mint-master. Due to the lack of proper excavated reports and sufficient information it is not possible to assign a definite chronological sequence to the periods of their issue. The distinct relative variations in fabric as thin, medium and thick and symbol represented on them makes it possible to some extent to divide the punch marked coins into three groups mentioned below.

Kushāṇa coins

The successor of Kujula Kadaphises and Vima Kadaphises issued copper coins in continuation of the earlier tradition. Vima Kadaphises was succeeded by Kanishka who also issued copper coins. On the coins of Kanishka, the king is shown standing dressed in tunic *shalwar,* mantle held in double clasp at the chest and a low round cap, pouring incense at the alter and holding a spear. Huvishka introduced a few new symbols on the reverse of his coins. On his coins, the figures of the deity are depicted. The next ruler Vāsudeva issued some coins. The figures of the king, Śiva, etc. are depicted on the obverse and reverse of these coins. His coins remained in circulation even a few centuries after this period. From this region, Kushāṇa coins are found in good number. Some of these are exhibited at Lumbinī museum. This indicates that these coins were in regular circulation in this area.

Vima Kadaphise's Coins

One specimen of the coin of Vima Kadaphises was found in a trench at Lumbinī having the figures of Śiva and *nandi* on the obverse and reverse (Mishra, 1996:44). Japanese Buddhist Federation has not published its details even now.

Muslim Coins

Many Muslim coins have been obtained from Tilaurākoṭ, Lumbinī, Nipaniā and Lakshmipur in course of exploration. One of them from Nipaniā is an issue of Muhammad Shah. The copper coin is 1.6 cm in maximum diameter and 2.66 gm in weight. On the obverse the legend (a's), Sultan (U' l-A') Zam 'Alan' (d) Dunya wad-Dim is depicted. On the reverse, his name 'Muhammad Shah' with in a double circle is seen. The Nagari legend may have read 'Sri Sultana Alavadin' and a date seven hundred and odd (A.H.) in figure. Allah-Uedin Khalji was the ruler of the Khalji dynasty during 1296-1315 AD in India.

One thousand Muslim copper coins are found nearly one meter below the surface at Lakshmipur in course of digging of a canal. These coins were put in a clay pot. All of them carry on the obverse the legend Sultan (U'l-A') Zam, Alau '(d) Wa'd-Din and 710 and on the reverse is engraved issuer's name' Muhammad Shah (Fig. 25). These are 1.5 cm in diameter and 3.35 to 2.95 gm in weight. A difference in weight may be due to their worn out condition. The figure of date 710 A.H. corresponds to 1310 AD, when Alau'd-Din Khalji was ruling India.

The hoard appears to be a private collection of an individual buried in the habitation area at Lakshmipur. It indicates the prosperous condition of the people. These coins from Lakshmipur are very valuable in studying the relationship with other contemporary sites in India. Sen King of Palpa had also written Hijari Samvat in their documents as on the coins of in this area.

These coins are very valuable for understanding various cultural modes as well as economic condition of the contemporary times. Almost all the coins of the ancient Indian dynasties were in circulation in this area. Copper coins with four-spoked wheel might have been local issues of the Kapilvastu principality. Muslim coins found in hoards reveal that the area was under their control during thirteenth-fourteenth centuries AD.

Metal Images

Being light and easy to carry on ones back from one place to other places a large number of Buddha's images were moulded and imported, evidently in order to meet the increasing demands of cult objects. The metallurgical centres in Eastern India seem to have influenced the art of metal-casting in Nepāl. The most favoured technique was known as retardataire in Nepāl. The *cire-perdue* or lost wax method was also known to the Nepāli artist. A large number of Buddhist images were made in this area, of which only some specimens are available now. One of them, a bronze figure of Padampāṇi, and, another a Gaṇeśa image, are remarkable specimens of this area.

Padampani avalokitesvar

A bronze figure of Padampāni measuring 11 cm in height from Lumbinī is shown holding a stalk of a fully-blossed lotus in the right hand (Mitra, 1972:203). The deity wears *dhoti* without *kachchha*, a folded scarf around his waist elaborated double bangle, a plain hara, kundalas, a waist-band and a short *mukuta*, probably a part of a turban. The attribute in the left hand is seen like a *Vajra* with its both ends in the form of prongs. The figure belongs to the late Kushāṇa period type of stone sculptures.

Devotee

A bronze figure of a devotee of late Kushāṇa type from Lumbinī is shown wearing a *dhoti* held by a girdle and a folded scarf around the thigh and decorated like the preceding Avalokiteśvar images. It is 8 cm in height and is shown standing in *abhanga* pose with folded hands with its back portion being solid and concaves (Ibid.).

Ornaments

Beads, rings bangles, ear studs, armlets and anklets have been found in course of excavation and exploration in this region. Apart from beads and bangles, other specimens have been classified on the basis of their use. Copper was used for the maximum variety of ornaments, specially rings and bangles.

Pottery

Pottery from the excavated and explored-sites help us in understanding basic cultural components of the various periods of human occupation. The ceramic evidence from the western Terai region of Nepāl is very interesting. In course of excavation excavators discovered clear-cut sequences of cultures beginning from painted NBP ware phase to the period of Imperical Guptas. The ceramic tradition of this region is similar to the one at Hastināpur. Thus, the archaeologists rightly compared the chronology and ceramic tradition of the area with that of Hastināpur.

The most characteristic shape in grey ware is dish with convex sides and beaked edges. The pottery is thick in section having horizontal and vertical bands. The clay used was well-levigated. The fragments of grey ware when struck produce a metallic sound. Northern black polished ware is thin and perfect in treatment.

The red-slipped ware is abundant in quantity in the trenches as well as on the surface of the ancient mounds. Dishes, bowls and basins are representative types of this ceramic tradition as well. Red ware pottery and terracotta seals with Brāhmi scripts were found in the same layers. The quality of clay is very fine and is also well-fired.

Northern Black Polished Ware

North black polished ware was popular throughout the western Terai region of Nepāl succeeding the painted Grey ware. The treatment and finish of the ware looks perfect. The surface is usually coal-black and rarely steel-grey or silvery. In some cases, it has golden-brown patches. The core is either grey or reddish. The part immediately below the surface is generally dull-red. N.B.P.ware fragments are thin and well-baked and are made of good quality of clay. This region is completely dominated by the NBP ware, rather than the black polished ware, as is seen in the eastern parts of Uttar Pradesh in India. Fragaments of black-polished ware are thinner in section and are not as perfect in treatment as NBP ware. Fragments of this ware are similar to that of the pottery of period III at Hastināpur. It is datable in c.6th-5th centuries BC.

Dishes, bowls, saucers, small basins, lids with tapering sides, small vases with different types of rim and carinated *handis* are the representative types in this ceramic. There are deep or shallow bowls with convex, receding or progressively widening sides, small basins with receding sides, lids with tapering sides, some with a projection for flanged vessels and small vases with different types of rims. Fragments obtained from Lumbinī are displayed at Lumbinī museum, which have been reported from here.

Red ware

This type of ceramic is usually associated with the Mauryan Period. Some of the fragments in red ware are painted in circular line. In some cases, the black portion is so well merged with the red that it is difficult to find out the main feature. Mainly bowls, basins and vases are reported. However, these shapes are not peculiar to this type alone. It is usually of medium fabric with some red-slip on it.

CHAPTER **6**

Architecture

During the rule of the Śākyas a large number of residential buildings, chaityas and monasteries of the Buddhists were built in this area. Surface findings as well as exposed structures during excavations in the limited area; represent the existence of drains and tanks. Chinese accounts are also useful in knowing something about ancient architecture. During the twelfth-thirteenth centuries, after the rise of Mohammedan rule in India, kings, princes, priests, tradesmen, philosophers, musicians and artisans migrated from India to this region. They got freely mixed-up with the local people here and contributed much in the fields of religion, art and music of the inhabitants of this area. The structural remains are classified into religious architecture on the basis of their nature, use and variations in shapes, size, model, technique and traditions.

Religious Architecture

The cultural life of the people in Lumbinī is dominated by three great religions, viz. Buddhism, Muslim and Brāhmaṇism which have been co-existing here in a most intimate manner and from relatively early times, interacting with each other without being conscious of it even. It is difficult to point out the lines of demarcation on the behavioural level. However, certain motifs and symbols are peculiar to Buddhism and Brāhmaṇism, which help us to find out its real nature. The archaeological remains of the monuments of Lumbinī are associated with Buddhism.

Buddhist Architecture

Most of the ruined structures in Lumbinī are Buddhist architecture, viz. monolithic stone pillar, stūpa, vihārs and temples. Due to the mingling of new architectural elements, designs and ornaments in course of more than two and half millennia, it is not possible to visualise today the original form of these remains. However, the foundation walls and other structures provide indication to distinguish their features and the periods of their reconstruction and repair.

Monolithic Stone Pillars

Monolithic stone pillar is an ancient component of Buddhist architecture, art, religion and culture. During his last days, Gautam Buddha declared that, 'after I am no more, O Ananda! Men of belief will visit with faithful curiosity and devotion, the four places where I was born ... attained enlightenment ... gave the first sermons ... and where I passed into *Parinirvaṇa*'. Due to the declaration of Gautam his devotees started erecting various stūpas and monolithic stone pillars at these places in his memory. From the reign of Emperor Aśoka this tradition is authenticated. It became popular in the Buddhist world. Having been a great patron of Buddhism Aśoka had erected many monolithic stone pillars as well as stūpas all over India and in Nepāl, especially at Patan and the Western Terai region. Pillars were fashioned from the stone blocks quarried at chunar in UP. It seems that artisans trained in Greco-Persian tradition were invited and engaged in making these pillars with selected Indian artisans. These pillars, bearing inscriptions, belong to the Mauryan period are popularly known as *lats*. Tall tapering monolithic pilllars of polished sandstone are surmounted with sculptured capitals, rising to an average height of about 12.1916 m from the base to the summit. S.K. Saraswati has opined that these *lats* should be included within the scope of sculpture, rather than architecture, because of being unrelated to any large architectural composition and having richly decorated capitals. However, scholars have also given the details of the monolithic stone pillars as interrelated component of architecture, which seems to be justified and not biased in nature.

Main feathers of the Mauryan pillar are: (i) it is not placed over a base, (ii) its shaft is monolithic, but not in Persipolitan style,

(iii) wood carver or carpenter's technique is used to decorate it. The Mauryan pillar seems to have been copied from the original timber construction in which pillars were made of complete logs of wood. They are fashioned out of brown chunar sand stone and stand directly on the ground without any masonry platform or base. Plain and circular shaft is chiselled out of a single block of stone slightly tapering upwards. A separate capital is fixed at the top of the shaft. The capital consists of three parts, viz. bell-shaped reversed lotus (commonly known as the Persepolitan bell), surmounted by an abacus or drum on which animal figurines are made in the round. Most of these animal figures carry mythological meanings. The animals made on four sides symbolise the four quarters of the universe, viz. the elephant being the guardian of the east, the bull, as at Rampurva, of the west, the horse of the south and lion, as in Nandangarh, of the north (Brown, 1976:9). The elephant symbolises the birth of Buddha (Sharma, 1995:161), the horse of, *Mahāparinirvāṇa*, the lion of the Śākya dynasty and the bull of non-violence. The animal sculptures surmounting the Aśokan pillars became chief components of Buddhist architecture. Thus, the monolithic stone pillars of the Nepalese Terai, which were erected by the Indian emperor Aśoka in the third century BC, are executed as an important component of Buddhist architecture. Aśoka started his pilgrimage of Buddhist sites with venerable Upagupta from Patna and visited Vaisali, Rampurva, Arreraj, Lauria-Nandangarh, Triveṇī, Parāsi, Bhairahawā and Lumbinī. He got monolithic stone pillars erected at these important places.

Three monolithic stone pillars of brown chunar sandstone are available in Lumbinī, the birthplace of Lord Buddha, Niglihawā and Goṭihawā, within the territory of ancient Kapilvastu. Pradhan has claimed that besides the above three, there are probably two more Aśokan pillars in Nepāl. Having been installed by Aśoka in course of his pilgrimage after Kaliṅga war there is known as Aśoka pillar by the local people. Pillars at Lumbinī and Niglihawā bear Brāhmī inscription in Pāli language of the Mauryan period. The foundation of Lumbinī pillar was not allowed to be excavated by the authorities it is not clearly known as to how they were made to stand. The shaft, plain and circular in section, is a slightly tapering upwards and is chiselled out of a single block of stone. The capital surmounting it is made separately in another piece of stone and is fixed at the top of the shaft. Unfortunately, the abacus or drums of the pillars are not found in good condition. However, their buried fragments were available in the course of excavation. Crowning figures on the abacus was horse as is also mentioned by the Chinese pilgrims (Beal, 1994:18-25). Although the pillar is not available *in situ*, broken fragments of it were found in course of excavation.

The Lumbinī pillar

Lumbinī, the birthplace of Buddha, was discovered in December 1896 in course of exploration under the leadership of Rana and Fūhrer. A most interesting piece of antiquity, the sandstone pillar carrying characteristic Mauryan polish and having tiny blackish specks, was found here which provided a documentary evidence of Emperor Aśoka of third century BC (Fig. 28). The pillar is made of chunar sandstone, as are other Aśokan pillars in India and Nepāl. The height of the extant part, above the rough hammer-dressed surface meant to be buried below ground, is 7.391 m. The crowning elements of the pillar, which were unknown, are lying on the paved platform in front of the Māyādevī temple. At the height of 3 m 41 cm above the rough surface of the stone pillar is engraved an inscription in five lines of *Priyadarsi* (Aśoka) recording that after twenty years of his coronation he had come to the spot where Buddha was born. He had also erected a stone wall around the place as well as a commemorative pillar. Aśoka exempted the village of Lumbinī from paying taxes except only one/eight of the product (Führer, 1972:33). The pillar tapers slightly upwards. Its circumference at the base is 2 m 51 cm and near the inscribed portion, it is 2m 25 cm. At the top of the pillar, it is 1 m 97 cm. The pillar has vertical fissure down to the pillar and its top is broken off, probably, by lightening, as noted by Hiuen-Tsiang. The capital of the pillar was bell- shaped. Its base, broken into two halves, still exists. The capital shows the usual festoon in the face of the big cyma under which there was one 30.47 cm deep hole of 12.5 cm diameter in which was fitted the copper mortice that was fixed above the shaft. Its slender tapering towards the top, mirror like Mauryan shining polish and sophisticated chiselling indicate that it was made by the skillful Mauryan masons. The horse surmounting the top was broken into pieces due to lightening flash which penetrated into it from above, the effect of which can be seen at the top even at present. Mukherji has also noticed the bell-shaped capital of Aśokan pillar, broken into two halves and stored in the temple compound (Mukherji, 1969:34). In course of excavation of the site many pieces of chunar sandstone, with and without Aśokan polish, and some of the pieces of the Aśokan pillar-capital were also recovered. It proves that after the erection of the pillar by Aśoka it was destroyed, possibly by thunderbolt and lightening. In course of excavation at the Māyādevī temple foundation two pieces of the pillar were found in the central chamber and one piece in the side chamber (Uesaka, 1997:8). Rijal has claimed that 15 chambers were filled in third-fourth centuries AD. Three pieces of the Aśokan pillar were found in the filling of the first temple complex. They carry evidences which indicate lightening stroke that fell the Aśokan pillar in about third or fourth centuries AD. Hiuen-Tsiang, therefore, had seen it in the seventh century AD. However, Fa-Hien did not mention any information about the Aśokan pillar and Māyādevī temple.

Führer and Rana did not excavate the basement of the monolithic stone pillar at the site. They measured Aśokan pillar and found 91.3 cm of it below the surface of the soil and 2 m 95 cm above the base of the pillar. Mukherji also could not go down to the foundation. Mitra wanted to reach at the bottom of the pillar to know the height of the hammer-dressed portion and its contrivance. She could not go beyond 51 cm below the polished portion because of the intervention of the commissioner (on tour).

Railing

Railing attached to a building is the basic component of the Buddhist architecture from the ancient period. Its popularity soared to the climax in the post-Mauryan epoch by about the second century BC, when important stūpas like Bharhut, Sanchi, Mathura, Saranatha, Bodha Gaya and Amaravati was built or enlarged. This architectural feature might have begun during the period of Aśoka as we find a mention of *'Silā-vigada-bhicha'* in the Rummindei (Lumbinī) pillar inscription which indicates, most probably, the presence of some kind of railing around the Aśokan pillar installed at the birthplace of Lord Buddha. An inscribed *harmika*-railing with typical Mauryan polish was brought to light from Saranatha. During the Suńga period, every portion of the stone railing was richly carved in bas-relief portraying incidents of the Jātakas, or scenes connected with the life of Buddha (Brown, 1976:14). The openings in the stūpa railing form the entrance where imposing gateway were erected.

However, the nature of railing construction in the region is not very clear. All around the Aśokan pillar at Lumbinī, a square brick-railing, 1 m 76 cm wide and 86 cm in height, was constructed. According to Mukherji an ancient brick-railing around the Aśokan pillar in Lumbinī was exposed during the excavation of the site. The walls of enclosure show three phases of construction. The earliest courses, 1.675 m in height, were built by using usually very large bricks with a sort of dentils, which are the ancient in style. The middle wall, 81.24 cm in height, is dated in the subsequent period. The upper portion of the wall was the latest construction. It exhibited about 20.31 cm width dentils, each made of two bricks. On the west, the height of the fallen wall was about 91.43 cm. Mitra had excavated a narrow trench on the north side of the Aśokan pillar to check the nature of the enclosure-wall mentioned by the former excavator in his report. According to her, the brick-railing no longer existed on the west of the pillar. Probably, it got disturbed in the excavation in 1933-34 conducted under the leadership of Rana.

A number of stūpas as well as vihārs built in this complex must have had systematic and scientific railings around them as an excellent component of the architecture. However, due to lack of proper excavation and exploration of the sites, many of the evidences may not be available to us at present.

Stūpa

The word stūpa refers to a Buddhist monument, generally of a pyramidal or dome like form, erected over the sacred relics of the great Buddha. Edgerton defines stūpa as a relic mound tope. It denotes *thopa*, to cover, heap, collect, or, *thupam* up in Hindi meaning to cause to prop or be propped. In Pāli *thuipikata* means heaped up or heaped of an alms bowl. Stūpa thus became a symbol of supremacy and stability of an order. Stūpas commemorate essential moments of the life and famous miracles of Lord Buddha. It is an ancient architectural element in the Buddhist world. Originally, it contained the relics of Buddha and represented *Pariniravana*. It became religious component to those who wanted some concrete form to worship before the image of Buddha. The practice of erecting stūpas over corporal relics is of pre-Buddhist tradition. Earlier stūpas or chaitays, either in the shape of a tumulus or made of perishable materials, must have been in existence before Aśoka. It is clear from the declaration and instructions given to Ānanda by his master, Lord Buddha that his bones and other remains were to be kept under a dome after cremation. It is thus clear that stūpas were popular in the Buddhist religion and society right at the time of the death of Lord Buddha.

In the *Mahaparinirvāṇa Sutta* of *Dighanikaya,* it is mentioned that after the death of Gautam Buddha in Kuśinagar, the relics were divided into eight portions and allotted to Ajātasatru, king of Magadha, Lichchhavis of Vaisali, Śākyas of Kapilvastu, Bulis of Allakapa, Kolias of Rāmagrāma, Brāhmaṇ of Veṭhādipa, Mallas of Pāvā, and Mallas of Kuśinagar. At last Droṇa, the Brāhmaṇ who divided the relic, received the vessel of cremated body and the Moriyas of Pipphalivana, who arrived after the division had been made and claimed a share of the relics, received the ashes of the funeral pyre. The Buddhists regarded this particular form of structure as an object of supreme veneration. It was changed from simple mound of earth into ostentatious structure of architectural importance later on and became the chief emblem of the Buddhist faith. The Buddhist stūpas are categorised into five groups, viz. (a) *Sāririka*, those erected over the corporal relics of Buddha, his disciples, Buddhist teachers and saints (b) *Paribhogikā*, erected over the objects used by Buddha, like robe, begging-bowl, cloths, etc. (c) *Uddesika*, commemorative of the Buddha's life, (d) Votive, those which were small in size and mostly erected by the pilgrims when they visited the sacred places and, (e) *Dhamma* stupa, those built over religious books written on paper, metal, stone or wood. Banerjee has categorised them into three groups and excluded votive stūpas. He did not refer small excavated stūpas in the western Terai region of Nepāl. Bidari has mentioned five group of the stūpas.

Main components of the stūpas have been changing according to the interest of the builders and situation from the ancient to modern period. In the beginning, the stūpa used to be a low hemispherical dome (*aṇda*), rose on a basal cylinder (*medhi*). Circumambulatory path was provided around the *aṇda* and on the top of the *aṇda,* a *harmika* was made enclosing the *chhatra* or a series of *chhatras*. Later on lower circumambulating path of the stūpa was constructed and the railing was made of wood, stone or brick adjoining the elaborate entrances. The exterior component of the solidly-constructed stūpa was smoothened with lime, clay or concrete plaster. Later the *medhi* was filled-up with appropriate packing materials to provide additional strength to the stūpa to bear the weight of its huge hemispherical top. Due to the influences of Hindu temple architecture, various components of the stūpas were decorated and other additional parts were also added to it.

Unfortunately, the main (original) shape, size and features of the ancient stūpas are not available because of later reconstructions from time to time. In the begging earthen funeral mounds were made of layers of mud, which used to be separated from one another by thinner layers of *kankar* and ashy clay. The earliest definitely dated stūpas were made by Mauryan Emperor Aśoka. They are provided with hemispherical dome of brick-work with *medhi* as its base. It is surmounted by a dome or umbrellas with square railing. The top of the drum was also utilised as an elevated processional path during this period. Brick stūpas of Aśoka with veneer of hammer-dressed stone, was converted in the second century BC into an almost hemispherical dome flattened near the top, crowned by three superimposed umbrellas, *yasthi*, *harmikā* and *vedikā. Medhi, sopanā* and circumambulation path were also added as the elements of the stūpas. The earliest stūpas were built solid. But in later times, when ostentatious stūpas of great height came to be erected by filling the core used to be filled with earth or rubble in order to economise the building materials, i.e. brick or stone as the case may be. During this period box-chambers built by network of walls were also filled with earth.

From the Kushāṇa period onwards the drum (*medhi*) grew in height as compared to its diameter and turned into a tall cylinder dominating the dome. Projected niches were made, as in temples, to install the images of Buddha or other divinities of the Buddhist pantheon. During the Gupta period, four images of Buddha were kept at four cardinal points of the stūpas. In the Gandhara period, the drum was built in diminishing terraces and the facade was elaborately embellished. The low hemisphere of the earliest stūpas was changed into a tall figure with ornamental tower on the platform, drum and *chhatravali*. The shape and size of the stūpas were so radically changed that it became difficult to recognise the original form and its importance without the knowledge of the intermediate stages. The changing modes as well as the stages in its development could not be studied without the support of the stone and metal miniatures, rock-cut specimens due to the absence of the preserved complete superstructure. Not all the structures can be clearly classified into various periods in chronological order due to reconstruction and repair from time to time. Each stūpa shows the impact of many periods (Fig. 32).

Buddha had forbidden his disciples to make his images. As such stūpas were built after his death at the spots related with him during his lifetime to commemorate him. His followers in Lumbinī might have built many stūpas in the fifth century BC (Pandey, 1985:54). Pre-Mauryan stūpas were enlarged by Aśoka during his visit of the place in the third century BC. This stūpa was buried under the plinth of the brick temple, which was excavated under the aegis of the LDT and JBF during 1992-97. The earliest structure of the site had been exposed to the north-west corner of Māyādevī temple. The texture of the brick used to build a rectangular room was very rough as it contained much husk and straw. These rough bricks could probably be dated tentatively in the pre-Mauryan period. Thus, it is clear that building activities had already been started in Lumbinī area during the lifetime of Lord Buddha himself.

Pre-Mauryan stūpas were repaired and rebuilt during the Mauryan period features and tradition of which are clearly seen in the structures available in course of excavation. Thirty-one stūpas have exposed in Lumbinī complex. The stūpas during this period were plain with two steppings at the basement. These monuments seem to have been built with kiln-burnt bricks and their interior chambers being filled-up with lumps of clay. Above it was built low hemispheres on squarish drums, including *harmikas* on the top. However, not all these parts of the stūpa are in existence today. The remaining portions of the excavated-stūpas throw light on the cultural style of the Buddhist followers of the region, especially of Lumbinī (Fig. 29).

About 1.52 m north of the Māyādevī temple a square based stūpa of Mauryan period was discovered. The top portion of the stūpa was cut to the depth of 91.4 × 80.9 cm probably during the excavations in 1933-39. On the foundation of the stūpa there was a cylindrical gold casket with some charred human bones and other ritual offerings. The lid of the vessel was broken into pieces, most probably in the course of excavations conducted between 1933-39 and the remains in it were found scattered over the ground (Rijal, 1975-77:32). It is known as S.6 and unique *saririka* stupa of Lumbinī (Bidari, 2003:202). Relics did not identify due to missing inscriptions.

Lumbinī, being the birthplace of Gautam Buddha, may have contained many stūpas in past in the pre-Mauyan period. However, almost all the stūpas found here seem to have been constructed during the Mauryan period. Their original shape and size were changing from time to time due to the repair work and their enlargement. Various phases of the monuments have been described when discovered in archaeological excavations (Mishra, 1996:42). Mauryan stūpas of the region are plain with their basements having two steppings. These seem to have been built with kiln-burnt bricks. The interior portion of these stūpas was filled up with clay-lumps. They carry low hemispheres on their squarish drums including *harmikas* on the top. In course of excavation, Mukherji had postulated that the foundation of the original temple of Māyādevī is embedded in the mound . This could be proved only after a scientific excavation of this site. During the archaeological excavations of the Joint Team of DOA, LDT and JBF, foundation of the present temple was exposed. The foundation of Māyādevi temple is based upon fifteen square chambers in the grid of five rows from east to west and three columns from south to north. Two kinds of NBP (Black and Brown), typical red ware, punch-marked coins and copper coins were recovered in the chambers belonging to Mauryan period. A piece of natural rock (a hard conglomerate) having dimensions of 70 cm × 40 cm × 10 cm with its axis running in south to north direction was found in the central chamber. It has been interpreted that Aśoka had built a square *Bodhi mandal chaitya* consisting of nine box chambers with the stone marking the 'birth spot' in the first central chamber. In the second phase six more chambers were added to make a total of it 15 within the centre of a concentric square huge Bodhi stūpa at the spot.

In third century BC, the Mauryan emperor Aśoka had opened the seven original stūpas and redistributed relics of Lord Buddha into 84,000 parts on which equal number of stūpas were built all over the Jambudipa. During this period he might have built the brick stūpa and erected the monolithic stone pillar at Lumbinī. During the excavation of the site Mukherji had exposed many stūpas in the periphery of the Aśokan monolithic stone pillar in Lumbinī. 15.24 m south-west of the pillar a mound of rubbles of brick-walls was discovered on its southern and western slopes. It was thought to be the cross-walls of a stūpa. 4.87 m north of the Māyādevī temple one another stūpa was discovered. It was already exposed by a saint. To the west of the hermitage a third stūpa of kiln-burnt bricks, square in plan, was also exposed by him. To the south-west of the temple he exposed the remains of the next stūpa, which was defaced on the north-west side. It was square in plan with rectangular projections on all its sides, rising in regular gradations of courses in rather plain mouldings. The lower portion of the round form stūpa represented some moulding remains.

To the east of the former stūpa many other stūpas were

discovered in dilapidated and defaced condition. It is impossible to know their shape and size clearly. Near the bank of the tank, four diminutive stūpas were discovered in a line, and a fifth one to the north-east of the fourth. The southern wall of the basement is better than other portions.

To the west of the pillar two votive stūpas were exposed during the archaeological excavations of Rijal. To the north of Māyādevī temple remains of a group of sixteen stūpas were found (Fig. 32) .The original structure of these stūpas was lost due to their reconstruction from time to time. Besides these stūpas, there are five other stūpas in a row. One of them, the first stūpa from the east, is ruined down to the core. Its original structure was reconstructed. The second stūpa, belonging to the Mauryan period, was disintegrated by the tropical climate of the Terai region. Its top was made watertight in course of its repair. The third was ascribable to the phase of the second stūpa. It was erected in round shape by adding clay and brick-bats all around. Remaining other two stūpas are also ruined up to the core. They were repaired in their original form. The top course of the fifth stūpa was completely lost, but it was reconstructed with the brick-bats of the Mauryan period.

In course of excavation, Mishra had discovered some very important stūpas among the ninteen big and small stūpas in the complex of Māyādevī temple in Lumbinī. They belong to different periods. They were of various size and shapes. One of it is 10.66 m to the north of Māyādevī temple, and the other, is inside a big square stūpa. Two rectangular stūpas of the Mauryan period were also discovered. They were plain and with two steppings in the basement. To the south-east of Māyādevī temple a big square stūpa, belonging probably to the Aśokan period (3rd century BC), was exposed during excavations in 1984 and 1985. It represented various periods of repair from time to time, and had contained casket and other relics in it. At a gap of 60.9 cm from the original structure a line of 63.47 cm thick wall was added encasing the earlier stūpa providing a new outer elevation to the stūpa. At a gap of 1 m 52.3 cm from the interior face of the stūpas during second century BC, a processional path had been made by filling the gap between the structure with earth and a 63.4 cm. thick wall around it. It was reconstructed on the top and 1.21 m wall was added all around the square basement during the Kushāṇa and Gupta periods respectively. Ninteen seals with inscriptions in Gupta character were found in another square stupa. It is only one *Dhamma* stupa of Lumbinī complex. Bidari has reported that findings of Mishra may be stupa nos. 12-31. On the top of the stūpa, nine votive stūpas survived in the medieval period. Thus, it is clear that the shape and size of the original stūpa was changed from time to time (Mishra, 1996:42). Lack of proper details and drawings their technique, tradition and informations are not so clear.

All the above-mentioned evidences reveal that the tradition of stūpa was developed from Pre-Mauryan period to the medieval period in Lumbinī complex. However, their main features are not clear due to the repair and reconstruction of these monuments from time to time. Pre-Mauryan and Mauryan stūpas also reflect the impact of the Suṅga and Kushāṇa periods. The shape of the stūpa is in the form of a hemispherical dome of solid brick work, which is filled with earth-packing. Procession-path is also constructed round the exterior of the drum with railings. Small votive stūpas were also built in Lumbinī by the pilgrims. Earlier stūpas were built on a low hemispherical dome rose on a cylindrical base and were provided with *harmikā* and *chhatrāvali*. The exterior components of the solid brick work were smoothened with lime, clay or concrete plaster. The *medhi* was filled-up with mud or other appropriate packing materials to provide additional strength to bear the weight of hemisphere. However, all the ancient stūpas were disturbed. Stūpas of later period are well-decorated and it's various components i.e. *chhatrāvali, āmalaka, kalāśa* and *vāyupuraka* were added to the superstructure. A comprehensive knowledge of these can be obtained only after an extensive archaeological excavation in future.

One of the new stupas of the Lumbinī complex is Great Lotus Stupa. It was completed with the financial support of Tara Foundation of Germany in 27 February 2004. It was inspired by Tibetan tradition, based on the writing of the Drigung Kagyud scholar Rigdzin Choskyi Dragpa (1595-1659). It is built like a Mandala, with the shrine in the middle and four directions, corresponding to the different Buddha families. Daily ritual performances and meditation is carrying out in the Meditation hall. Painting and wood carving work is done in Nepalese and Newari style under the supervision of Drubpon Rinpoche and Ferdinand Stange. The stupa cum meditation hall is in the centre of the complex. Many accommodation blocks and rooms have been built around the main monument. Spiritual heads of Drigung Kagyud tradition, monks and guests live here. Ten monks and helpers can stay to perform religious practice in accordance with the tradition of this complex. To create peace and harmony trees, bushes and flowers have been planted around the stupa. Fresco paintings as well as stone images are remarkable at the complex. Huge prayer wheels have been kept at the four corners of the shrine. It's main gate is also well elaborated with floral and vegetal designs and model. The world peace Stūpa named Nipponzan Myohoji of 41.5 m in height and 59 m in diameter is completed in November 2001. Images of Buddha are kept in the four directions, which are belonging to the four events in His life, viz. *Mahaviniskramana*, Enlighten, *Dharmacakra* and *Mahaparinirvana* (Figs. 1-6). Components of the superstructure are based on their model and design. Dharmodaya Sabha has built a huge stupa at plot no. WB-3, on the east of Korean Monastery. Its design and model is similar to the stupas of Kathmandu valley.

Vihār

In the beginning, followers of Buddha used to stay in a forest, under a tree, on a hill side, in a glen, in a cemetery, in a mountain cave, in the open air, in a forest glade and on a heap of straw. During three months of the rainy season, they took shelter in the caves or under trees or in sanctuaries, begging around the periphery of their abode. Thus, a monastery or vihār was a hostel of the Buddhist monks during the lifetime of Gautam Buddha. In the beginning, vihārs were made of thatched bamboo and wooden huts for taking rest. They are known as vihārs, *aramas* and *Saṅghārāmas*. Dwelling places were provided to the monks and nuns by the local merchants. Monasteries were built to fulfil the basic needs of the *saṅgha* as places to walk, to retire during the night and to stay during the day. During Buddha's lifetime, the monastic complex consisted of vihāras (dwelling rooms), *parivenas* (cells or private chambers) koṭṭhakas (gate-chambers or porches), *upattana–sālās* (service halls), *aggini–sālās* (hall with fire places), *kappiya–kutis* (store-house outside the vihāras), *vachcha–kutis* (privies), *chankamas* (promenade), *chankama–sālās* (rooms with promenade), *udapanas* (wells), *udapana–sālās* (sheds attached to wells), *janta-ghara* (bath-rooms), *janta-ghara–sālās* (halls attached to bath rooms) *pokkharani* (tanks) and *mandapas* (halls) (Horner, 1952:223). The vihār is the site where the monks and nuns inhabited with facilities for begging in neigbourhood and ensuring a proper atmosphere for meditation. The complex developed as an organised educational institution and academic centre of Buddhist learning due to the activities of the *Sangha*. Mahavihar was known as university in ancient period.

The earliest monasteries were made of perishable materials like wood and bamboo. These were mostly flimsy structures with no set plan. Rock cut caves were also used as the dwelling places. The later monasteries were not so different from the former. Progressive attempts to elaborate and ornament the shrines were made. The basement of the vihār is built on a quadrangular plan consisting of a series of cells enclosed from three sides and the remaining one side was used as the entrance gateway. The cells are built around the courtyard providing communication to the monks. To the rear-back row of the cells, the image of Buddha was housed for worship the monks during their rest. Stone pavement was built all around the courtyard to be used as a circumambulatory path of the shrine. Verandah, bathroom, drain, shrine, courtyard, kitchen, refectory, privy, storeroom, assembly-hall and scullery are provided in the structure of the vihār. To both sides of the entrance gate cells are built. One of them is used as a guardroom and the other for Goddess Hariti. In the courtyard of the complex, a well is built to supply drinking water to the monks and nuns residing in the vihārs. Verandah is used as the waiting place for the guests, monks and nuns visiting to the complex.

Places of residence in the east were generally with the rooms opening on to an interior quadrangle making plain outside walls to secure both privacy and protection. However, the construction of the vihār may differ according to the interest, needs of the sects and changing modes of the architectural styles of different ages.

Lumbinī is quite fertile from the point of view of Buddhist architectural remains. Lumbinī, being the birthplace of Lord Buddha, monks and nuns lived there forming their *Saṅghas*. During his visit Aśoka built a huge stūpa and installed a monolithic stone pillar to commemorate the spot of nativity of Lord Buddha. On this occasion monks and nuns required vihāras to retire in the night and to stay during the day at Lumbinī. Some of the ruins of the monasteries have been exposed in course of excavation (Mishra, 1996:40-42). In 1898 Mukherji had exposed the square structure of a low mound to the south-east corner of the Māyādevī temple. The mound yielded a mass of solid brick-work. Its original structure was not exposed due to incomplete excavation of the site. About 33 m 52 cm south-east of the temple there was another mound (monastery) of which some walls were running north-east and south-east. The complete structure was, however, not exposed on this occasion. Although he could not expose all the monuments, he expressed hope that the site is enriched with the ancient mounds. During excavations in 1984 and 1985, Mishra discovered four vihārs to the south of Māyādevī temple. These monuments are built in a row from east to west. Exposed monuments reveal that the might have been encircled by stūpas as well as the Aśokan stone pillar, which are partially exposed even now. 1 m. 21.9 cm west of the vihār no. 1 is situated vihār no. 2 dated in the Mauryan period. This original structure is 16.20 m (east-west) long and 14.75 m in breadth (north-south). There are living rooms in four directions and a meeting hall in the centre. It measures 4.21 m × 4.185 m in size. Rebuilt Kushan structure has yielded fourteen rooms in three directions, except to the east where there existed a courtyard (Ibid.). In the western portion of the complex there is a verandah facing to the east.

To the east of the former vihār no. 2, exists vihār no. 3, which was built in three phases from the 2nd century BC to the 4th century AD. The earliest two structures of 2nd century BC-2nd century AD highly very damaged, excepting the outer walls, probably, due to reconstruction in later period. The size of the structure (during the Gupta period) is 13.56 m in length (east-west), 13.10 m in breadth (north-south) with eleven rooms in three sides, excepting the west (*trisālā*). In the centre of the complex there is an *aposthagarasālā* measuring 3.96 × 3.04 m in size. 13 m 41 cm long drain started from the eastern room and diverted to the south through a 'L' shape hall. The structure of the drain was built on the pattern of closed drains of bricks in the Kushāṇa and Gupta periods. There were two water storage-tanks measuring 91.4 cm × 81 cm and 73.63 cm × 38 cm in the south-east row of rooms of the vihārs. Both are 1 m 21 cm in depth. The excavator has proposed that these rooms might be the kitchen of the monks and nuns. The size of the rooms are 2 m 18 cm × 1 m 77 cm, 2 m 48 cm × 2 m 3 cm and 3 m 12 cm × 2 m 61 cm. The size of the entrance passages to the east and south-east direction of the complex measure 81.2 cm, 86.3 cm and 88.8 cm.There are three buttress walls in the internal part which measures 3 m 83 cm in size. One of the walls measures 2.31 m × 71 cm in length and thickness respectively.

Vihār no. 1 consists of living room for the monks and a meeting hall in its three sides except the west. Two stūpas, one square and the other circular in size, are built in the courtyard of the vihār. They were rebuilt in *trisālā* pattern in the Gupta period.

Only three rooms of vihār no. 4 have been recovered to the east of vihār no. 3 which is extending to the east, out side the bar. The size and shape of the rooms are very small as such they might have been used as single mediation site of the monk and nuns. The drainage system and water storage tanks indicate that the architectural-engineering was quite advance in the region during the Mauryan and Kushāṇa periods. Residential rooms were larger than meditational rooms in this complex. Altogether thirty one small meditational rooms have exposed with out lecture and meeting hall in this block.

In course of times, all the surface findings have been removed by unknown persons. Not so many hidden structures are exposed due to limited excavation and exploration. Thus, not all the features of the vihār complex could be found into chronological order. Exposed walls also overlapped due to the repair and reconstruction from time to time at the same place. The earliest position of the perishable materials, i.e. wood, bamboo and dry-grass, are not clearly known. However, generally vihārs where built on a quadrangular plan consisting of a series of cells being enclosed on three sides and the remaining open side was used as a gateway. Cells of different size and shapes were built around the courtyard providing communication to the monks and nuns in the complex. Verandah, bathroom, drain, kitchen, meditation-room, store-room, assembly-hall and other apartments were provided in the structure of the vihārs. In this structure the image of Buddha was housed to be worshiped by the devotees during their leisure period. After the collapse of the structure of the vihār, remaining fragments of Buddha images are found in courses of excavation from the site, especially from the Lumbinī complex. Modern structures of Lumbinī vihārs represent its significance and throw light on the nature of ancient vihārs of the region. According to Master Plan of Lumbinī new monasteries, stupas, sacred ponds, bridge, guesthouses and hotels have been built by the proper institutes and donor agencies. One of them Royal vihar, in front of archaeological garden, was built with the patron of Lumbinī Dharmodaya Samitee in 2009 vs. Image of Buddha is enshrined in the eastern portion of the hall. Its wall paintings are entirely belongs to the events of Lord Buddha, viz. birth, Mahabhiniskramana, Mahabodhi, Dharmackra, Mahaparinirvana, etc. as described in Buddhist literatures. Window, door, door-jam, doorframe, strut and tympanums are carved with floral, vegetal, sthamba sakha, naga sakha, Tara and gandharbha as the Chhusyabhal, Musyabahal and Itumbahal of Kathmandu valley (Fig...). Wooden art of this vihar is very fine and unique in this sacred complex.

Dharmaswami Maharaja Buddha vihar, in front of the Māyādevī temple and immediate north of Royal vihar, was inaugurated on the auspicious occasion of coronation of king Birendra on 2 March, 1975. King Mahendra had provided ten *kattha* land Mustange Dharmaraj to build this sacred vihar in 1968. Buddha images of the fifteenth century and Astasasrika prajnaparamita, written in golden colour, were also received by Namagyala gumbha. It was built by the support of the people of Mustang. Shining image of Buddha is enshrined in the sanctum. Fresco painting is remarkable of this monastery. According to Buddhist tradition and literature figures of white elephant, birth scene of Buddha, Bodhisattva, athletic competition of Buddha, *Mahaviniskramana, dharmcakra*, curd offered to Buddha by Sujata, meeting of Buddha and his father, honey offered to Buddha by monkeys, *Mahaparinirvana*, etc. scenes have been painted by the Tibetan painters, named. Unique figure of 26th Chonyz Thichena Rinpochhe is also painted in this sacred complex. Door, window, strut, tympanum and other architectural elements represent the Pagoda style and model.

Gautami Nun's vihar, east of peace lamp and south east of Hinayani complex, was built during the period in 1995-2002. Gautami temple, Buddha hall, kitchen, guesthouse and sacred pond are main architectural elements of this complex. U-Chela of Verma had donated a Buddha image and 165 chaityas. Huge stone image of Buddha is kept in the centre point of artificial tank by Jyapu Mahaguthi of Kathmandu. This complex was constructed by the nuns collecting donation in various sites. *Pariyati* education is also teaching in the public schools and in this monastery under the aegis of the nuns. It is also educational centre. Monastery of Myanmar is also build in Vermese style. Many buildings have been built by the Thai Royal monastery, north-east side of the central canal, with the subsidies and donations from Thai and foreign Buddhists. At present, it has four Thai-styled cells with the donations of faithful Buddhist for monks, one two-storied refectory, one kitchen, one two-storied multi-purpose building for pilgrims, one three-storied multi-purpose building for pilgrims and a meditation centre. Uposatha hall designed by Architect Phinyo Suwannakiri, a national artist, is also completed. It contains hall in four directions, shrine hall, grand pagoda, lodgings for senior monks and buildings for special guests as projected.

Zhong Hua Buddhist Monastery, in the western Mahayani

complex, was built by Buddhist Association of China in October, 1998. It was designed by the Ancient Architecture Designing Institute of Zhe Jiang Province of China. It covers an area 25,600 square meters. Main entrance hall, Mahavira hall, the east side hall, the west side hall, the meditation, dinning hall, and the abbot hall are built in this sacred complex. A link wall is made around the architectural complex. Winding corridor is built to connect all halls together. Its style and model is based on Qing dynasty's official buildings and Tang dynasty's temples. In 1999, a group of monks was sent to enter here by the Buddhist Association of China.

Buddhist Temple

The Buddhist temple architecture is not very different in technique, style and form to that of Jaina and Brāhmaṇical temples made in a particular zone in various phases. However, isolated temples were erected on the pattern of stūpa-shaped sanctuaries. In most cases, the temples have survived up to a height above the ground and were constructed with *adhisṭhāna, jańgha* and other superstructures providing different additional components to the body. The structure of the temple consists of square flat-roof, pillars and pilasters, a bell-shaped lotus, decorated door-jambs, single opening with its cubical cella. These are the basic parts of the type of temples in sikhara style. Buddhist texts have also mention temples in the context of the diferent types of abodes. The *Chullavaga* and the *Mahavagga* describe about five kinds of abodes (*panch-Lenami*). The *Buddhacharita* of Aśogohsa has stated *Śākyeśvaralaya* and chanting of sacred *mantras* within a temple. Buddhist temples are known as *Gandhakuti, Bodhighara, Gṣiha-chaitya, Chetiya-ghara, Pāṭimaghara* and *Bodhi-rukh Pasada*. One of them, the *Gandhakuti* (chamber of perfume) is very popular form in the Buddhist architecture. The *Vinayapiṭaka* mentions four types of houses, viz. *Karerikuti, Kosambakuti, Gandhakuti* and *Salalghara* (Upadhyaya, 2018:200). The above-mentioned description reveals that in the beginning *Ghandhakuti* was the name of a simple cottage which was known later on as Buddhist temple. Such a Buddhist temple of Aśokan period is found at Bodha Gaya.

Lumbinī has been associated with Buddhism and is known as 'Buddhist land'. Many structural remains as well as unexcavated mounds are scattered all over the area in Lumbinī. However, because of limited archeological activities, the evidence of separate existence of temples is quite limited, except the Māyādevī temple of Lumbinī. The sikhar style temple of Māyādevī was not found in its original shape and size because it was never reconstructed for a long time, i.e. from the Mauryan period to the eighth century AD. The original basement of the temple was 26 m east-west and 21 m in north-south direction from out side of the walls. It's inside walls measure 20 m east to west and 16 m north-south. There are 15 chambers arranged in five rows in east-west and three rows in north-south direction. All the chambers are rectangular in size except chamber 2, 5 and 8, which are square in size. A conglomerate stone (a pebble sand stone of the Siwalik hill) was found at the centre of second row in chamber 2 on the west side of central row on the east west axis. Various antiquities including punched silver coins and numerous NBP ware pieces were found here. From the *kundas* polished pieces of Aśokan pillar of chunar sandstone were also found (Rijal, 1996:3). The temple is in *saptaratha* pattern and made of moulded bricks. Five phases of the temple construction, viz. the Mauryan, the Suṅga, the kushāṇa, the Gupta and the Late Gupta have been noticed in course of excavation. The box chamber of the structure is called *maṇdala.*

The *maṇdala* structure was built as high platform to erect the earliest Gupta temple to install the nativity image of Māyādevī. In the third phase, the stone marker was covered by a square votive platform in front of the nativity sculpture. During the fourth stage, a s*aptaratha* temple was erected over the Gupta temple in 8-9th century AD. From 1200 AD the site was gradually forgotten by the pilgrims due to the decline of Buddhism and Muslim invasion in the region. During his exploration and excavation Mukherji mentioned the structure of the ruined temple of Māyādevī in Lumbinī. It was in curvilinear style and a s*aptaratha* type in plan, measuring 3.65 × 3.04 m. A sanctum was provided at the rear back with six flight of steps from the east. The size of the temple was 14.62 × 9.14 m in length and breadth respectively. Mukherji had noticed four successive phases of construction. The lowest position of the wall was plain with two courses of bricks being ornamented and carved in circular design. A floriated cyma was seen standing above it. Lotus-petals, *gala* (neck), *dasa*, cyma and *kumbha* were executed on the walls. He is of the opinion that there should be remains of the old temple structure below the present temple. Rijal exposed the eastern plinth of the temple, but he did not mention any detail of it in his report. The temple was linked up with the Śākyan tank by a cause-way for taking a bath by the devotees before worshipping in the shrine (Fig. 31). The foundation of Māyādevī temple has deteriorated due to the unusual growth of roots of a Linden tree. JBF and LDT have signed on an agreement in September 1990 to restore Māyādevī temple. In June 1991 another memoranda for the same purpose was signed. The tribunal team of LDT, DOA and JBF has conducted archaeological work in the Māyādevi temple complex during 1992 to 1996. During this work six phases of the various periods of the structure were exposed. In the first phase, Aśokan bricks were found on the north-west corner of the temple. On this spot, Rijal had found an oblong brick structure with rammed floor measuring 4.72 × 3.78 m during 1976–78. An oblong structure below the Mauryan square stūpa was found there. The bricks measure 38 × 25.3 × 7.6 cm in size. The pre-Aśokan structure was, perhaps, destroyed during constructions in the Mauryan period.

During the period of Aśoka the construction with burnt bricks and perhaps, with stone members, was done around the Nativity site. Antiquities related to the Mauryan period-coins, punched silver coins and numerous Northern Black Polished (NBP) sherds and earthen ware were also found.

In the second stage, a rectangular shaped chamber on east-west axis, measuring 1.87 m, 1.22 m in north-south direction, was located directly above chamber 2 of stage I. In the centre four pieces of sand stone were found of which two were rectangular in size. The whole temple was again encircled by a compound wall with brick-paved floor for circumambulatory path. The third phase of the temple was encircled with five irregular pits in which stone pieces of the same proportion might have been erected in the style of an *Apsidal* square cell. The important architectural element is the corbelled niche with a few stone pieces in it. The conglomerate stone (70 × 40× 10 cm) was found in this part, having a corbelled niche. The size of the brick was 32.89 × 24 × 6.32 cm in this phase (Figs. 26 &27).

The fourth phase of the temple yielded the Nativity Mathura sand stone panel and the brick platform measuring 1.5 × 1.3 × 0.45 m. It is clear that the temple was built during the Gupta period. Phase five of the temple was built in the last phase of the Gupta period. The temple was built in s*aptaratha* (seven bayed) and sikhar style with square sanctum, which was similar to the temples of Kudān, Paisiā, Tilaurākoṭ, Bikuli and Chetradei of the region. The sixth phase of the shrine was erected four years before the discovery of Lumbinī by Führer. The small temple was rebuilt two more times between 1892 and 1939.

The structure has been under the patronage of LDT and JBF in course of its restoration. Being very important monument of the sacred site of Lumbinī, the old temple should be protected and preserved in its original shape and size as recommended by Tange in the master plan. In course of excavation during 1984-85, Mishra had exposed two basements of Buddhist brick temples and a 12.1916 m long wall. Most probably, a compound wall running east to west had also been found in the southern side of Māyādevī temple, which was repaired. After the excavation of Māyādevī Temple fifteen chambers, conglomerate stone and Nativity sculpture of Buddha are preserved. Stūpa components have been added at the superstructure of the New Temple.

Monolithic pillar is belonged to the Buddhist architecture. Plain and circular shaft is executed slightly tapering upwards and is chiseled of a single block of stone. A separate capital was fixed on it, which is missing at present. The capital consists of three parts, viz. inverted bell-shaped base, abacus and a horse figure surmounting the superstructure. Unfortunately, the animal figure on the superstructure is not available. Pillar of Lumbinī bears Brāhmi inscription of Aśoka, has provided important information about the Mauryan period. Ruined stūpas are represented by their hemispherical dome built in solid brick-work and filled-up with earth packing. The early stūpas are plain. They are disturbed due to repair and reconstruction work from the pre-Mauryan period up to the Gupta period. Votive stūpas dedicated by the pirgrims are also in the Lumbinī complex. General structure of the vihār is based on quadrangular plan consisting of a series of cells enclosing it three sides and the remaining open side being used as a gateway. Verandah, bathroom, drain, kitchen, meditation-room, store-room, assembly-hall and other apartments are provided in the vihār structure. Residential and meditation blocks were constructed in Lumbinī complex. Buddhist temple of Lumbinī is built in Nāgar style. After the excavation of the temple area, its original shape is changed at present.

Wells

Ring wells were built in many residential complexes, vihārs and the Royal complex to provide drinking water in ancient period. Its method, model, technique and materials were used according to the geographical location and interest of the builders. In Lumbinī ring well is made of kiln-burnt bricks. The ring well is significant from the utilitarian as well as religious points of view even now.

The Śākya tank of Lumbninī was originally oval-shaped (Fig. 31). In the Buddhist literature it is called *Puskariṇi* or *Siddharth kupa*. Māyādevī was provided with hot and cold water before and after the birth of Siddhartha (Beal, 1994:25). The Chinese pilgrim Fa-Hien had also mentioned that in Lumbinī garden, queen (Māyādevī) entered the pond and bathed there. It denotes the significance of the sacred pond. On the south of this tank is standing a sacred old Pipal tree (Fig. 33). It is the symbol of peace and harmony. In the seventh century AD, Hiuen-Tsiang had also pointed out the bathing tank of the Śākyas, which had bright and clear water like mirror, and its surface was covered with mixed flowers. This tank undoubtedly represents the bathing tank of the Śākyas as mentioned by Huien-Tsiang (Mitra, 1972:198). As the legend goes, on the occasion of the birth of Lord Buddha, dragons had poured down first cold water and thereafter warm water from their mouth to wash the prince. These details prove that the tank was in existence until seventh century AD. The tank must have been buried or filled up with rubbish in course of times. In 1939

Rana got it cleaned and made it *pakka* by using kiln-burnt bricks. 15.2395 m square tank shows six terraces and a flight of steps far descending up to the water level. After the birth of Lord Buddha in Lumbinī garden, the tank was changed into a sacred pond, which was being used by public before this event. In 1993 in course of draining out the dirty water of the pond, two artesian wells were exposed to the north-east and south-west corner of the pond measuring 170 × 160 and 130 × 114 cm in size respectively. Bidari is of the opinion that Lumbinī being the ancient trade route these wells might have been constructed here (Bidari, 2003:215). It is the case of inquiry. With in the structural remains of vihars of Lumbinī a terracotta ring-well as well as some antiquities belonging to sixth century BC were found from the lowest level. A large number of Kushāṇa figurines are also reported from the habitation-mounds, as well as, two brick-wells from the upper level. During 1970-71, three more such type of the new wells were exposed in the area. A brick-well, datable to the Kushāṇa period, was discovered from the nursery field of Lumbinī in 1983. It was exposed upto the bottom with 29 courses of solid concave bricks which were well elaborated with the symbols of horse, elephant, boar, palm tree, conch, etc. At the bottom of the well a few Kushāṇa spouted pots as well as faceted pots used for *Nāga* worship were found.

Reiyukai Japan built the building of LIRI. It has built with specific purpose in studying philosophy, religion, culture, art and architecture. It contains library, lecture rooms, study rooms, a dormitory and office rooms. In the centre of the complex, a large space is provided to research scholars and informal contact. There are two-stories of brick masonry arches and reinforced concrete at the core. In this complex reception hall, reference hall, dormitory, living quarters, lecture rooms, administration rooms and meeting hall are provided. Museum building is made of a central exhibition hall, surrounded by the four mezzanine spaces and the ground floor space. The two mezzanine spaces on the west side and ground floor are used for administration, workshop and laboratory for archaeological research. Art remains of Lumbinī and pictures of Buddhist monuments from Kathmandu as well as India are kept in the main hall.

CHAPTER **7**

Pilgrims and Pilgrimage

Concept and Motives

The institution of pilgrimage plays an important role in generating 'a circulation mechanism' in which all the social strata of Buddhism participate. The institution of pilgrimage in the Buddhist world is as old as the lifetime of Buddha. When Buddha was lying down on the death bed at the age of eighty in Kushinagar his disciples, monks and nuns had surrounded him. Buddha advised with feeling of holy reverence and awe, viz. the place where the *Tathagata* was born (Lumbinī grove), the place where he had reached perfect enlightenment (Bodh Gaya), the place where the first time he had proclaimed the law (Deerpark near Varāṇasi) and the place of his final extinction (Kushinagar). These facts reveal that Lumbinī was declared as the sacred spot to the pilgrims and was regularly visited by the monks, nuns and devotees at this sacred-place.

In the present situation of conflict and violence, there is much emphasis on the linguistic, geographical, regional and social diversities created by the political activities and dogmatic religious body. They are playing a vital role in integrating the societies of this part of the world into one cognate order. The motives of the earning of the religious merit consist of holy places and *dracaena* of the deities. The religious merits support and lead one to attain *Nirvana* at the end.

Tirtha phala and Tirtha practices

According to the orthodox view, a pilgrimage is not a pleasure tour, and if undertaken with such motives it fails to become a *tirtha-yatra.* One of such opportunities is furnished by the discipline of pilgrimage which is not an end in its but only one of the means to the high tested end. The merits of pilgrimage range from immediate relief from *tirtha-yatra* troubles to the expiation of sins and gaining the ultimate Reality. There is no automatic spiritual reaction to the mechanical act or rite; the mental *tirthas* are more effective than the physical ones. Sacred complex as well as the activities done by the nuns, monks and devotees also supports to secure a co-ordination between pious life and highest knowledge.

Fasting, sexual abstinence, abstinence from unguents, soft bed and luxuries rejection of the aid of the vehicles or animals for making journey, and walking without shoes in *tirtha* have been enjoined on the pilgrims with a view to producing righteous mind by disciplining the body.The pilgrims worship the deities of the site while chanting the Buddhist *mantras* offering the prayers and different kinds of gifts and finally doing *darshan.* The throwing of fruits, flowers, money and shaved-hair is also considered to be meritorious. Living at a *tirtha* or *barsavass* of at least four month is considered to be an important means of obtaining salvation or *nirvana. Parikarma* of the *tirtha* is also an important act. The liberal feeding accompanied by *dakshina* to monks, nuns and hungry is also a commendable practice during pilgrimage.

Pilgrimage of Lumbinī

The Buddhist texts *Lalitavistār, Jātak Nidan kathā, Divya vadana* and *Mahāvamsa* have stated Lumbinī as the birthplace of Lord Buddha. When Buddha was lying down on the death bed at the age of eighty in Kusinagar his disciples, monks and nuns surrounded him. On this occasion, he advised to visit Lumbinī, the place where the *Tathāgata* was born. Thus, Lumbinī was declared as the sacred spot to the pilgrims and was visited by the scholars, nobles, Royalities and devotees. According to *Kundala Vadana* of *Divyavadana* having led King Aśoka into the Lumbinī jungle, venerable Upagupta indicated with his right hand and said '*Asmin Maharājā pradase bhagavan jatah*', meaning 'Oh Great king! Here the Blessed one was born!'. King Aśoka made an offer of one hundred thousand gold coins and established the first *cetiya* or pagoda. In the next chapter *A śoka vadana of Divyavadan,* we find the description of the site. In the Aśokan pillar of Lumbinī it is inscribed that 'Here *Bhagwan Śākyamuni* was at the Lumbinī village'. It is translated by Führer as to mean King *Piyadasi* beloved of the Gods (or dear to the Gods), having been anointed 20 years came himself and worshipped saying: 'Here Buddha Śākya muni was born', and he got a stone (capital) representing a horse, and the stone pillar erected. Because here the worshipped one was born, the village of Lumbinī has been made free of taxes and a recipient of wealth. According to Hultzsch it means, 'when king, beloved of gods, had been anointed twenty years he came himself and worshipped (this spot).' Here Buddha Śākyamuni was born. He got a stone bearing horse made at this place. Hiuen-Tsiang's remark that the capital of the pillar contained a horse figure confirms to this interpretation. 'As quoted by Rhys Davids, Būhler also says that 'a stone horse was made and put on a stone pillar'. King Aśoka installed the stone column with a clear legend inscribed on it that it is the spot of Lumbinī where the blessed one was born. In Lumbinī a brick railing was erected at a distance of 48.76 cm from the base of the pillar and it had dentils also. After the visit of Emperor, many monks and nuns had started visiting the place. A large number of monasteries and vihārs must have been built for their stay in this sacred complex. A large number of artifacts of the Mauryan, Suṅga, Kushāṇa and Gupta periods were recovered in course of various excavations. It is thus clear that it continued to be a place of pilgrimage since the third century BC till to date.

Chinese pilgrims have given a more accurate and authentic description of Lumbinī. Shui-Ching-Chu describes that at Lumbinī the Aśokan tree, which was gripped by Māyādevī at the time of Siddartha's birth, was still in a living condition and an image of Māyādevī was placed there where devotees used to offer *puja* articles. The spot where Siddartha's feet touched the earth first, Aśoka got the Siddartha's footprints shielded with stones. His description has been ratified by the noticable findings discovered during the joint excavation of the DOA, LDT and JBF from 1993 to 1997. It is clearly seen that Aśoka had shielded the Siddhartha's footprints with stones in order to secure it. This significant news of the findings of the excavation was publicly declared by then Honourable Prime Minister Sher Bahadur Deuba on February 4, 1996. According to Fa-Hien in Lumbinī the queen (Māyādevī) having entered the pool to bathe, came out on the north side, and after walking twenty paces, raised her hands and grasped the branch of a tree. She brought forth the Heir Apparent facing to the east. On reaching the ground, the Heir Apparent walked seven steps, and two dragon-kings washed his body. At the time of washing, the tank was used. In this context, Hiuen-Tsiang had stated that there was the bathing tank of the Śākyas, the water of which was clear as a mirror and the surface of which was covered with a mixture of flowers (Fig. 31). 24 or 25 paces to the north of this there was fallen Aśokan flower tree on the birthplace of Bodhisattva. To the east from this place there was a stūpa built by Aśoka-*rājā* on the spot where the two dragons bathed the body of the prince. Bodhisattva walked without assistance in the direction of the four quarters, seven spaces in each direction, and said, 'I am the only Lord in heaven and earth; from this time forth my births are finished'. To the east of this stūpa were two fountains of pure water, by the side of which two stūpas were built. To the south of this was a stūpa, where Sakra, the Lord of Devas, received Bodhisattva in his arms. Close to the site there were four stūpas to denote the place where the four heavenly kings received Bodhisattva in their arms. When Bodhisattva was born, they wrapped him in a golden coloured cotton vestment, and brought him to his mother, and placed him on a golden slab (*bench*). They said, 'The queen may rejoice indeed at having given birth to such a fortunate child! If the Devas rejoiced at the event how much more could the men. By the side of these stūpas there is a great stone pillar, on the top of which was the figure of a horse built by Aśoka. It was broken off in the middle and fell to the ground due to the contrivance (thunder stroke) of a wicked dragon. By the side of it is a little oil river flowing to the south-east, where Māyādev? had brought forth her child to wash and to purify herself. After Hiuen-Tsiang many other pilgrims had visited this place from time to time. One of them was Wu-Kung who came in 764 AD. Due to the absence of records very little is known about the condition of the area. The monumental and habitational structures, stone sculptures, terracotta human and animal figurines, fragments of pottery belonging to the Mauryan, Suńga, Kushāṇa, Gupta, Vardhan and Sena-Pāla periods, found here prove that Lumbinī was well-populated till the early-medieval period and was frequently visited by the monks, nuns and other devotees from time to time. The names of Jitari Malla (1287-89 AD) and Ripu Malla (1312 AD) were engraved on the stone columns (pillars) at Nigalihawa and Lumbinī garden. It consists of the words, '*Om mani padme hum, shree Ripumallaschiran jayatu, 1234'*. The former portion is a Mahayani Buddhist prayer and the later portion means 'prince Ripu Malla, be victorious for long 1234'. The year 1234 in the Saka era, corresponding to 1312 AD. Bhuwan Lal Pradhan has claimed that Sikandar Lodi (1489-1517 AD) and Aurangzeb (1668-1707AD) were mainly responsible for the destruction of cultural heritage and property of the Lumbinī-Kapilvastu region. During the reign of Mukunda Sena I (1540-1575 AD), Mukunda Sena II (1750-82 AD) and Mahadatta Sena (1782-93 AD) in Pālpā the previous religious condition in the region could not be retained. The site was lost in the dense forest until the discovery of General Khadga Shamsher JB Rāṇā, Governor of Pālpā.

In 1967, U-Thant the then General Secretary of the UNO had visited Lumbinī and after that, he offered the help of the United Nations for the development of Lumbinī. Due to the keen interest of UNO, Prof. Kenzo Tange of Japan prepared the architectural Master Plan of the Lumbinī garden and Lumbinī Development Committee organised various plans of development in this region. Late King Mahendra had shown keen interest in developing Lumbinī as a sacred complex for all the human beings. In 1985, Lumbinī Development Trust was created as an autonomous and non-governmental organisation for the creative work instead of Lumbinī Development Committee. Then His Royal Highness Prince and present King Gyanendra Bir Bikram Shah Dev, then Chairman of LDT, paid a visit to the United Nations and had addressed the International Committee for the Development of

Lumbinī in 1986. At that time King Gyanendra had also visited Japan and Korea to promote awareness and to develop friendly relationship with each other. In 1986, King Gyanendra lit a torch of Eternal Peace in Lumbinī in commemoration of the International Year of Peace. In each year, many national and international VIP and VVIP come here for their pilgrimage in Lumbinī. King, Queen and Prime Minister of Nepal, Ambassadors of Japan, United Kingdom, India, Pakistan, China, South Korea and Myanmar for Nepal had visited Lumbini on 16 May 2003. On 27 May 2003 Queen, Prince and Princess of Bhutan had also visited here. President of Japanese Reiyukai, Ambassadors of Śri Lanka and Thailnd, Cultural Advisor of UNESCO and Culture Vice-Minister of China had come for their visit during July 2003 to April 2004 in Lumbinī (LDT, 2004, 1:7). Minister for International Development of United Kingdom and the Head of DFID Nepal had also visited Lumbinī on 29 July 2004 (LDT, 2004, 2 : 4).

Composition of Pilgrims

To analyse the pilgrimage of Lumbinī in modern times a sample of 100 pilgrims representing the various cross-sections of Buddhist society was drawn up from hotels, monasteries, dharmasala and lodges. The flow of pilgrims visiting the peace city is almost uniformly large round the year. By the pilgrimage of the Lumbinī, they shall receive all kinds of worldly pleasures, peace, progencies and exemption from different kinds of ailments and obstacles in the life. A large number of people since the ancient period have continued to come here from China, India and other western countries. The pilgrims from more than seventy countries, viz. Japan, South-Korea, Thāiland, Taiwan, China, India, etc., come here on the occasion of festivals and proper season to offer their prayer and respect to the deities (Table 12.5 & Fig. 34). Buddha Jayanti, Barsavass, Chaitra *sukla purnima,* etc. are the main occasions of festivities and much rejoicing in Lumbinī. During the period of their visiting, they offer prayers and oblations and represent their devotion to the monasteries, temples and Stūpas in traditional manner (Fig. 35).

The pilgrims and local people of Lumbinī often hesitated from filling up the questionnaires. Table No. 7.1 presents the profession of the pilgrims as follows:

TABLE 7.1 : Showing professions of the pilgrims

Sl.No.	*Professions*	*No. of pilgrims*	*Percentage*	*Remarks*
1.	Peasant	26	26%	
2.	Business	12	12%	
3.	Higher professions (Doctor, Lawyers, Engineers etc.	13	13%	
4.	Students	22	22%	
5.	Monks & Nuns	7	7%	
6.	Menial Services	10	10%	
7.	Other professions	10	10%	

Above table 7.1 represents that 26% peasant, 22% student and 13% of higher profession visited Lumbinī in course of this field study. Businesspersons as well as monks and nuns from various countries also visited the place.

TABLE 7.2 : Showing percentage of literacy among the pilgrims

Sl.No.	*Educational qualification*	*No. of pilgrims*	*Percentage*	*Remarks*
1.	Illiterate	18	18%	
2.	Literate	31	31%	
3.	Matriculate	5	5%	
4.	Intermediate	13	13%	
5.	Graduate	7	7%	
6.	Postgraduate	12	12%	
7.	Buddhalogists	5	5%	
8.	Professional qualification (Technicians)	9	9%	
	Total	100	100%	

Table 7.2 shows 18% of the pilgrims of Lumbinī were the illiterate persons and 31% of them were only literate. 5% pilgrims among them were matriculate and 13% were intermediate passed. 7% graduate, 12% postgraduate and 5% Buddhalogists had come for pilgrimage during this study period. Monks and nuns from various

countries were expert in Buddhist literature, art and architecture. The educated pilgrims have known the significance of Lumbinī and they come here to visit Māyādevī temple, Aśokan pillar and monasteries. Some of them are interested to see ancient Telār river, described in Chinese accounts. They feel that Buddha's peace has motivated them to come to the sacred complex and offering donations to the poors, Lumbinī Development Trust and proper local NGOs to build building and create peace . At present Lumbinī has become a particular site of attraction for its great natural and scenic beauty, the school, campus and university students of Buddhist countries visit this place for educational tour and pilgrimage.

TABLE 7.3 : Age-group of Pilgrims

S.No.	*Age range*	*No. of pilgrims*	*Percentage*	*Remarks*
1.	Below 20 years	12	12%	
2.	21-40 years	34	34%	
3.	41-60 years	28	28%	
4.	Over 60 years	24	24%	
5.	Answer not obtained	2	2%	
	Total	100	100%	

Table 7.3 represents 40%, the highest number of pilgrims of Lumbinī are of the age between 21 and 40. 28% of the pilgrims are of age 41 to 60 years. In the last phase of the life over 60 years, 24% among them has visited during here. Below 20 years group has come usually with their family members and teachers.

TABLE 7.4 : Team of pilgrims

Sl.No.	*Visiting team member with*	*No. of pilgrims*	*Percentage*	*Remarks*
1.	Alone	10	10	
2.	Family members	22	22	
3.	Friend and relatives	12	12	
4.	In groups (Mass)	48	48	
5.	Couple	8	8	
	Total	100	100%	

Table 7.4 shows the pilgrims composed of various sizes such as single, couple, family and group visitors and the largest number of visitors belonged to group visitors, which include 48%. Pilgrims from Thāiland, Taiwan, South-Korea, Japan, Myanmar and India usually come in groups for three days. 22% of pilgrims come with their family members, viz. parents, brother, sister, grand-father and grand-mother at Lumbunī. 10% age of 18-35 come alone. 8% couple come to pilgrimage and perform some rituals at the Māyādevī temple complex or at proper monasteris to fulfil their wishes. This study reveals that mass tourism (pilgrims) should be emphasised providing miminum visa-charge and other proper facilities to them.

TABLE 7.5 : Modes of stay of pilgrims

Sl.No.	*Accommodation*	*No. of pilgrims*	*Percentage*	*Remarks*
1.	Monasteries-Lumbinī	24	24%	
2.	Hotel & Lodges-Lumbinī	35	35%	
3.	Indian hotels	11	11%	
4.	Bhairahawā Hotels	26	26%	
5.	Relatives' and friends' houses	44%		

Table 7.5 presents that 35% of the pilgrims stay in the hotels and lodges of Lumbinī and 24% of pilgrims accommodate in the monasteries. Several monasteries have been built here for the pilgrims by the national and international donor agencies. Monasteries have not fixed the accommodation charge to the pilgrims, but they can donate own their well. This study reveals that monasteries have not captured pilgrims from business point of view. 26% of the pilgrims stay at Bhairahawā bazar, 22 km east from Lumbinī. Similarly, 11% of them go India across the border after their visit. 4% of the pilgrims stay in the houses of their relatives and friends at the time of their visit of Lumbinī. They generally visit archaeological garden, monastic zone, meditation-centres, bird-watching including Saras and Nilgai watching, dance, sing and enjoy themselves by undertaking various kinds of entertainments. Lumbinī is the prime location of accommodation for majority of the visitors. Majority of the visitor use air route

for their visit. Travel and Tour companies or agencies directly come from India taking pilgrims and return within a short span of time after bird's eye view at the sacred complex of Lumbinī.

TABLE 7.6 : Number of pilgrims

Area	*Number of pilgrims*				*Total*	
	Male		*Female*		*No.*	*%*
	No.	%	No.	%		
National	26	26%	14	14%	40	40%
International	45	45%	15	15%	60	60%
Total	71	71%	29	29%	100	100%

Table 7.6 shows that among the foreign pilgrims, the number of the male pilgrims is 45% and that of female pilgrims only 15%. The male pilgrims of Nepāl constitute 26%, whereas the female pilgrims are 14%. National pilgrims are 40% in comparison to the 60% pilgrims coming from international. The number of male pilgrims is always higher than that of the female pilgrims. Almost the foreign tourists usually come from more than seventy countries, especially from Japan, South Korea, Thāiland, Taiwan, Myanmar, China and India.

In an attempt to assess the attitude of pilgrims towards the sacred complex in general, we inquired about their pilgrims cycle, their motivators and their knowledge of the sacred complex in Lumbinī. Pilgrims were motivated by their kinsmen, family members and friends.

CHAPTER **8**

Sacred Performances

Siddhartha Gautam Buddha was against the tradition of icon-worship in his life. He had advised to build stūpas all over the world in course of popularity to his disciples. Various *ārāmas* were built to reside monks, nuns and other followers in India and Nepāl in ancient period. Their residing sites were not only the shelters, but also the sacred complex to pay homage and respect to Buddha's teachings and his personality. In the beginning there were no any special rites and rituals to conduct hard and rigidly. Buddha was known as super human being. In course of development of Buddhism, the icons of Buddha came to be executed and installed in the holy shrines for their regular worship. Vihar and monasteries became main residing places to the monk and nuns. Compartments of the vihar have been constructed from the utilitarian-view point of residing and worshipping. Sacred performances have been conducting by Theravadi, Mahāyani and Vajrayāni according to their tradition in Buddhism.

Lumbinī is one of the sacred complex where the Buddhist Vihar and Stūpas had been constructed in ancient period. Foundation of the monuments has been exposed in Lumbinī complex. According to Master Plan of Lumbinī to the immediate north of circular levee, Monastic zone is separated to build various Stūpa, vihar and monasteries by national and international organisation and Governments. The eastern complex from central canal has allocated for Theravadi or Hinayāni and western complex is for Mahāyan sect. Buddha's icons have been installed in the sanctorum of the shrines. Daily treatment of the shrines took the form of sacred performance. Various performances have been conducted with full preparation, devotion of mind and sense of obligation. Lumbinī frequently occurs in various Buddhist literature and Chines account. Mauryan, Sunga, Kushan and Gupta periods were popular for sacred performances and even made generous donations to see sacred performances continue uniterruptedly. The sacred performances of Lumbinī can be divided in two broad catagorises, viz. (i) daily performances and (ii) special performances. Daily performances have been conducted by the concerned vihar and monastery authorities and special performances have been conducted by the devotees and jointly by the monasteries on the occasion of fourteen night full moonday at the site of Aśokan pillar.

The management of the initial performances is done by the authority of the concerned monasteries of Lumbinī. According to the contract letter between Lumbinī Development Trust and concerned institute only five *Bhikshus* and five helpers can stay in a monastery. Particularly the *Bhiskshus* conduct regular morning performances at their monasteries. Nepālese monks and nuns are also associated with Theravad and Mahāyan sects. For the daily worship of the shrine and protection of the monasteries, monks, nuns and care-takers have been appointed and their functionaries honestly carry out their duties. The main performances in the premises of the shrines in Lumbinī can divide into two shifts as follows:

Morning worship

The morning worship in the complex of Lumbinī is done at 7 to 8 a.m. after opening the gate of the shrine. Visitors are also permitted to worship and offer their oblation materials to the deities. First, they clean sanctum and wash icons in water. Courtyard and premises of the shrines have also cleaned by the sweepers. Icons of Buddha have been decked with garments and ornaments, which are already prepared for worshipping. Rites and rituals of Theravadi, Mahāyani and Vajrayāni are different on the basis of their national tradition and rules. At the time of worship *sutras* are chanted by the devotees. Homage to triple gems has been chanted in every morning in course of paying devotin to Buddha and Buddhism.

Homage to Triple Gems

Namo Tassa Bhagavato Arahato Samma Sambvddhassa.

(Adoration to him, the Blessed one, the worthy one, the Fully Enlightened one.) (Three Times)*Okasa! Aham Bhante Tisaranena sadhin panchasilam dhamman yacami, anuggahan katwa silam detha me bhante.* (permit me! I, ask, venerable sir, for the five precepts together with the three refuges.Venerable Sir! Please have compassion on me and grant me the precepts.)

Dutiyampi okasa..............me bhante
Tatiyampi okasa..............me bhante
For the second time...........
For the third time...........

THE THREE REFUGES

Buddham saranam gacchami
Dhammam saranam gacchami
Dutiyampi Buddham saranam gacchami
Dutiyampi Dhammam saranam gacchami
Dutiyampi Sangham saranam gacchami
Tatiyampi Buddham saranam gacchami
Tatiyampi Dhammam saranam gacchami
Tatiyampi Sangham saranam gacchami
(I go to the Buddha as my Refuge
I go to the Dhamma as my Refuge
I go to the Sangha as my Refuge
For the second time I go to the Buddha as my Refuge
For the second time I go to the Dhamma as my Refuge
For the second time I go to the Sangha as my Refuge
For the third time I go to the Buddha as my Refuge
For the third time I go to the Dhamma as my Refuge
For the third time I go to the Sangha as my Refuge)

THE FIVE PRECEPTS

1. *Panatipata veramani sikkhapadam samadiyami*
2. *Adinnadana veramani sikkhapadam samadiyami*
3. *Kamesumicchacara veramani sikkhapadam samadiyami*

4. *Musawada veramani sikkhapadam samadiyami*

5. *Surameraya majja pamadatthana veramani sikkhapadam samadiyami*

1. I take the precept to abstain from killing.
2. I take the precept to abstain from stealing.
3. I take the precept to abstain from adultery.
4. I take the precept to abstain from lying.
5. I take the precept to abstain from liquor that causes intoxication and heedlessness.)

THE EIGHT PRECEPTS

1. *Panatipata veramani sikkha padam samadiyami.*
2. *Adinnadana veramani sikkha padam samadiyami.*
3. *Abramhacariya veramani sikkha padam samadiyami.*
4. *Musavada veramani sikkha padam samadiyami.*
5. *Surameraya majjapamadathana veramani sikkha padam samadiyami.*
6. *Vikala bhojana vermani sikkha padam samadiyami.*
7. N*acca, gita, vadita, visuka, dassana, mala, gandha, vilepana dharana mandana, vibhusanattan veramani sikkha padam samadiyami.*
8. *Uccasayana mahasyana Veramani sikkha padam samadiyami.*

1. I take the precept to abstain from killing.
2. I take the precept to abstain from stealing.
3. I take the precept to abstain from incelibacy.
4. I take the precept to abstain from lying.
5. I take the precept to abstain from liquor that causes intoxication and heedlessness.
6. I take the precept to abstain from taking food at an unreasonable time.
7. I take the precept to abstain from dancing, singing, music and unseemly shows from the use of garlands perfumes and ornaments; and from things that tends to beautfy, and by adorn (the person).

8. I take the precept to abstain from (using) high and, luxurious seats (and beds).

(This eight precepts observed mostly on the uposath day.)

THE TEN PRECEPTS

1. *Panatipata veramani sikkha padam samadiyami.*

2. *Adinnadana veramani sikkha padam samadiyami.*

3. *Abrahamacariya verammani sikkha padam samadiyami.*

4. *Musavada veramani sikkha padam samadiyami.*

5. *Surameraya majja pamadatthana veramani sikkhapadam samadiyami.*

6. *Vikala bhojana vermani sikkha padam samdadiyami.*

7. *Nacca, gita, vadita, visuka dassana veramani sikkhapadam samadiyami.*

8. *Mala, gandha, vilepana, dharana, mandana, vibhusanatthana veramani sikkha padam samadiyami*

9. *Uccasayana maha sayana veramani sikkhapadam samadiyami.*

10. Jata, Rupā, rajata patiggahana veramani sikkha padam samadiyami.

1. I take the precept to abstain from killing.

2. I take the precept to abstain from stealing.

3. I take the precept to abstain from incelibacy.

4. I take the precept to abstain from lying.

5. I take the precept to abstain from liquor that causes intoxication and heedlessness.

6. I take the precept to abstain from taking food at an unreasonable time.

7. I take the precept to abstain from dancing, music, singing and unseemly shows.

8. I take the precept to abstain from the use of garlands, perfumes, ornaments and from thing that tend to beautify and adorn (the person).

9. I take the precept to abstain from use high and luxurious seats and beds.

10. I take the precept to abstain from accepting gold and silver. (The ten precepts also observed on the upsosatha day).

(Vimalananda, 2043:1-7)

These *sutras* denote Buddha, Sangha and Dharma three refugees; for bidden killing, stealing, adultery, lying and liquor that courses intoxication and heedlessness. The eight and ten perceptions are directly concerned to the practical teachings of Lord Buddha. All these activities support to create mental peace, harmony and compassion in human beings. These are useful to all the creatures. These utterances mainly belong to Theravada. Royal Monastery of Dharmodaya committee, Thāi monastery, Calcutta monastery and International Nun's association use these *sutras* in course of their worship. They have also slight difference in their countrywise traditions. Thāi Bhikshus are more hard and rigid in their *sutras.*

At the time of the worship of the deity, the musicians of Mahāyani play on their musical instruments and sing Buddhist songs praising the glory of the deity. The main substance of their *sutras* or *mantras* is the summary of Buddha's teachings. The people who have joined the morning worship of the deity participate with the monks and nuns. They offer prayer in honour of the deity and utter the holy teachings and practical elements of Gautam Buddha. Chinese, Korean, Vietnam, Germany, Nepalese, etc. Mahāyani of western complex in Lumbinī conduct regular prayer of Buddha and his teachings. Japanese and Manang monasteries of Lumbinī use *tantrika sutras* in course of their worship.

Nipponzan Myohoji, Lumbinī Dojo has been chanting *'NA-MU-MYO-HO-REN-GE-KYO'* with drum beating from 4.30 to 6.30 a.m. in the morning (Peace Pagoda, 2001:2). First, they chant *mantra* and walk around the shrine (Fig. 1). After sometime they visit Lumbinī area chanting *mantras* with drum-beating (Fig. 36). About one and half-hour they walk at the villages in the periphery of Lumbinī, especially Mahajidiya, Parsa, Paderiya, Mayalawar and Lavani to inform Buddha's teachings and aware the local people. They think, revise and recite the following *mantras:*

Even when all the living sees, at the kalpa's end,
The conflagration when it is burning,
Tranquil is the realm of mine
Even filled with celestial beings
Parks and many palaces with every kind of gem adorned
Precious trees full of blossoms and fruits
Where all creatures take their pleasure;
All the gods strike the heavenly drums
And ever more make music,
Showering mandarava flowers
On the Buddha and his great assembly.
My Pure Land will never be destroyed,
Yet all view it as being burned up,
And grief and horror and distress
Fill them all like this.:

(Shanti Stūpa, 2001:7)

This passage is their main base of worship and Buddhism. Their activities have been originated from this utterance.

Evening worship

Theravada, Mahāyan and Vajrayān have also conducted evening worship and chanting *mantras*. *Mantras* and process of chanting is similar to morning activities.

Special performances

Apart from regular meditation and worship of the shrines, the concerned monasteries and devotees have also conducted special performances. Pandey priest had performed three years before regular and occasional worship at Māyādevī temple. Priest Gangaram Pandey used to worship at the shrine and devotees had also lit butter-lamps to pay respect to Buddha. This tradition of worshipping at Māyādevī temple has been forbade by the authority at present. All the monasteries and institutes of Lumbinī conduct full moon day worship and prayer at the site of Aśokan pillar in each month (Fig. 37). Upon arrival at Lumbinī Sacred Garden where prince Siddhartha was born, they would find out a peaceful and appropriate area for concentration of mind and paying respect to the Triple Gem. Such area may be under the *Bodhi* Tree near *Puskarini* pond or Aśoka Pillar in the west as seen proper. When all get ready, they start with lighting three incensed sticks and two candles and then, with all offering placed before them, recite the following Sacred Pail verses to pay their worship to the Triple Gem together.

Araham Sammasambuddho Bhagava
(The Buddha is an aharta who had perfectly extinguished all fires of cravings and defilements and was self enlightened.)
Buddham Bhagavantam Abhivademi.
(I pay homage to the Buddha, who is Blessed, Self-Awakened and fully enlightened.) (Prostrating)
Svakkhato Bhagavata Dhammo
(The Dharma was well taught and delivered by the Buddha).
Dhammam Namassami
(I pay worship to the Dhamma.) (Prostrating)
Supatipanno Bhagavato Savakasango
The Sangha is the Buddha's disciples who well behaved and practiced Dhamma).
Sangham Namami
(I pay respect to the angha.) (Prostrating)
Paying Respect to the Buddha
Namo Tassa Bhagavato Arahato sammasambbhassa. (3 times)
(I pay homage to the Blessed One, Perfect One, fully-enlightened One.)

Devotees then gently handle all offerings, including flowers, colourful clothes, pack of candles, etc. prior to chanting the following sacred Pali verses to pay respect to the Buddha's birthplace.

For Paying Respect to the Buddha's Birthplace

Imasmim Lumbinī vane Jatakale, Asabhivaca, Yena Bhagavat Bhasita, 'Aggohamasmi Lokassa, Jetthoha masmi Lokassa, Setthohamasmi Lokassa, Ayamantima Me Jati, Natthidani Punabbhavoti'.

Idam Kho Pana Thanam, Samvejaniyam, Saddhassa Kulaputtassa, Dassaniyam, Imehi Sakkarehi, Imam Samvejaniyam, Abhipujayami, Imam Samve janiyam Sirasa Namami, Sotthi Me Hotu Sabbada.

(On the date of His birth in the Lumbinī Sacred Garden, the Buddha proclaimed his speech, 'I am the most excellent person of the world. I am the most progressive person of the world. I am the noblest person of the world and this is my last birth. From now on, I will never be reborn again and again.'

The Lumbinī Sacred Garden is the place of urgency where all faithful persons should come to admire. I pay homage to this Lumbinī Sacred Garden with these offerings; I pay respect to this place of urgency with unwavering belief and faith. May I always have a happy and prosperous life forever?

After that, we should place our offerings in a suitable place before prostrating for 3 times and reciting the following sacred Pali verses to pay respect to the Triple Gem.)

For Paying Respect to the Triple Gem

Itipi So Bhagava, Araham Sammasambuddho, Vijjacaranasampanno, Sugato, Lokavidu, Anuttaro, Purisadammasarathi, Sattha Devamanussanam Buddho Bhagavati. (56)

Svakkhato Bhagavata Dhammo, Sanditthiko, Akaliko, Ehipassiko, Opanayiko, Paccattam Veditabbo Vinnuhiti. (38)

Supatipanno Bhagavato Savakasangho, Ujupati panno Bhagavato Savakasangho, Nayapatipanno Bhagavato Savakasangho, Samicipatipanno Bhagavato Savakasangho,Yadidam Cattari, Purisayugani, Attha Purisapuggala, Esa Bhagavato Savakasangho, Ahuneyyo, Pahuneyyo, Dakkhi neyyo, Anjalikaraniyo, Anuttaram Punnakkhettam Lokassati. (14)

(Should we have sufficient times, we may recite additional sacred Pali verses to pay respect to 28 Buddhas, Jinapanjara Pali verses, Ten fold Parami, or any Pali verses that we always recite. After that, we should sit meditation to concentrate our mind prior to recalling the Buddha's sublime and endless kindness and making our wishes.)

Pilgrims coming from the distance places and such pilgrims often conduct special worship to the deities with elaborate rituals and different kinds of offerings. The time of the solar and lunar eclipses is some particular days of the years. They feel attainment of peace and happiness in this world and ultimately for the attainment of salvation in the next world. The above-mentioned days in the months of *Vaisakha, Sravana, ṃswin, Kartika* and Chaitra are the particular days of worship and festivites in Lumbinī. Devotees offer butter-lamps, money, flowers, fruits, sweets, clothes and other kinds of articles according to their economic condition. The devotees worship the deities and there after they come back to their homes with optimum inner satisfaction. Those pilgrims, who come from far off places, generally come for the special worship of Buddha and his disciples. Some people make a vow to perform the pilgrimage of Lumbinī to worship Buddha. Local people who make a request to the god for a male progency and get a son, immediately come to Lumbinī with their family members. Some people of Lumbinī region come for the first shaving of the head (*mundana*).

Lumbinī is a significant Buddhist *tirtha sthala* where the people come for pilgrimage from Buddhist as well as non-Buddhist countries. Many pilgrims as well as visitors come for their pilgrimage. To pay devotion to Lord Buddha is a kind of ancestor worship, which is deeply rooted in the families living in the neighbourhood of Lumbinī. The people of all castes and creeds worship Buddha with no discrimination of sex and age.

CHAPTER **9**

Fair and Festivals

The fairs and festivals are an integral part of the Buddhist as well as Hindu civilisation. These are the main attraction of the lifestyle of the people and preserve the social customs, the religious beliefs, art-tradition and economic condition of the cotemporary society. Festivals have been celebrated not only for socio-economic and religious concept, but also as a source of entertainment. So ever in religious work, people feel the entertainment by praying, singing, dancing and meeting with the people and feasting was the source of religious activities. Due to the mixed settlement of Hindu, Buddhist and Muslim people in the periphery of Lumbinī, they celebrate Buddha Jayanti, Varṣāvāss, Dashain, Deepāvali, Chhaṭa, Māghi, Śivarātri, Basanta panchami, Holi purṇmā, Rāmanavami, Parikaramā and Chaitra sukla purnima fair and festivals on proper occasions (Figs. 38 & 39). They are of national, regional and local significance. Vihar, Stūpa, monasteries and temples of Lumbinī have been associated with the Hinayān, Mahāyan and Vajrayān sects according to Master Plan (Fig. 40). Thus, a systematic table of the festivals of proper sects is given below to understand their significance.

TABLE 9.1 : Annual Fair and Festivals

Sl. No.	*Name of the Festivals*	*Day of Observation*	*Month of theYear*
1.	Buddha Jayanti	Purnima	Vaiśākha
2.	Varṣāvāss	Purnima	Asār-Aświn
3.	Durgāpujā	Pratipadā-Dasami	Aświn
4.	Deepāvali	Trayodasi -Diutiyā	Kārtika
5.	Chhaṭa	Khaṣṭhi	Kārtika

6.	Māghi	1st day	Māgha
7.	Basanta Panchami	Māghasukla Paṇchami	Māgha
8.	Śivarātri	Krishṇa trayodasi	Phāguna
9.	Holi	Purnima	Phāguna
10.	Rāmanawami	Śukla navami	Chaitra
11.	Chaitra purnima	Śukla purnima	Chaitra

These festivals have great religious significance, but it is not possible to trace their origin and whole traditions to observe. However, they may be briefly described here in order to get a clear idea of their sacred complexities.

Buddha Jayanti

Buddha Jayanti is celebrated on Vaiśākha Sukla purnima or full-moon April-May, associated the four major events in Buddha's life, viz. his birth, *Mahaviniskramana,* his enlightenment and *Mahaparinirvana.* When Māyādevī, queen of Suddhodhan of Kapilvastu, was going to her maternal house at Devadaha Siddhartha Gautam was born in Lumbinī garden in 563 BC. According to Buddhist literature, he immediately took seven steps and each steps left a lotus flower where his foot touched the ground. After the forecast of the sage Asita and Kaudinya, king isolated Siddhartha in the royal palace, providing him all the pleasures and facilities for his entertainment. One day he went outside the castle walls and saw a sick man, old man and third a dead body. At last, he met to a saint, a holy man and he felt that it was the source of free from preceding three pains of the world.

At the age of twenty-nine, he left palace, wife Yasodhara and son Rahula. It was the day of Vaiśākha *sukla purnima* in course of his *Mahaviniskramana.* His enlightenment was also held on the day of *Vaiśākha sukla purnima* in Bodha Gaya. Then, he became the Lord Buddha. At the age of eighty, he left his body at Kusinagar. This is known '*Mahaparinirvana*' in Buddhist literature and society. Buddha passed his life sharing his teaching to human being, which is known Buddhism. Under the auspicious of the Buddhist followers, Buddha Jayanti festival is celebrated with various activities in Buddhist countries. Lumbinī, being the birthplace of Siddhartha Gautam Buddha, is the main Sacred Complex to the Buddhist (Fig. 41). On the occasion of *Vaiśākha sukla purnima* LDT and Institutions of Lumbinī have been celebrating Buddha Jayanti in each year. LDT, the authority, organise a three-day programme on the occasion of the Buddha Jayanti and Lumbinī Day. The main Organising Committee is constituted, especially under the chairmanship of Honourable Culture, Sport and Civil Aviation Minister to conduct various activities. The preparatory organising Committee is formed under the chairmanship of Vice Chairman of Lumbinī Development Trust. Other sub-committees are also organising for proper works. In 7 May 2004, sub-committees were formed to celebrate 2548th Buddha Jayanti and Lumbinī Day 2061 at the holy birthplace of Lord Buddha. On 23 May 2005 and 13 May 2006, 2549 and 2550 Buddha Jayanti and Lumbinī Day were also celebrated forming various Committees under the leadership of LDT (Fig. 42).

On this occasion, the main functions are cleaning of sacred site and a large number of monk, nun and devotees come to the sacred complex along with flower, water, *dipa, prasada,* etc. to worship the idol of Buddha at Māyādevī temple. Organising Committee has managed discourse on Nepāl Television and Radio stations under the topic 'Role of Lumbinī in peace and Development'. In 2005 the topic was 'Lumbinī: Glory of Nepāl' for essay competition, speech on Radio Stations and oratory competition among inter college and inter schools of this area. Inter-School oratory competition and intercampus essay writing competition on the topic 'Role of Lumbinī in peace and Development' was also organised on this occasion. Panditarama and Goyanka Meditation centres also organise special camps in the evening.

The second day or the main celebration day is also performed with several functions. Monks and nuns of Lumbinī come at the site of Asokan pillar to conduct their regular worship on *Purnima*. The statue of the Buddha is kept in a chariot (*khata*) and taken in a procession in Lumbinī area amidst music of the musician, songs of the women, prayers of the males and sacred slogans of Buddhism, such as *Om Namo Shanta Rupya, Om Namo Buddhaya and Om mani padame hu*. Finally, after reaching the proposed site some monk, nun and Buddhist scholars deliver speech highlighting the deeper significance of the Buddha's sermon and Buddhism to the mass who gather there. On this procession, Honourable Ministers, Monks, Nuns, His Excellency Ambassadors, associated with Buddhism, Buddhist scholars, Members of LDT and local people also take part in the programme. The third day, last day of the celebration, the chief guests also provide prizes and certificates to the winners in eassy writing and oratory competitions and distribute scholarship to the students of the local disadvantage groups and society. Lumbinī International Buddhist Society, Cross Flow, Monasteries of Lumbinī and other non-governmental organisations have also organized free medical camps in Lumbinī Area.

Peace March

Fuji Guruji began construction of peace pagodas in Nepāl and later worldwide. He also organised peace Marches to pray for worldpeace and to awaken consciousness among men. Guruji was awarded with Jawaharlal Nehru Award for International understanding in 1978. The citation mentioned, 'As pacifist and an advocate of universal and complete disarmament the relevance of his life and his message cannot be over emphaused". 74 peace pagodas have been completed in Japan, India, Śri Laṅkā, England, USA, Austria and Nepāl. After the death of Guruji his disciples and devotees have been succeeding to build peace pagodas and walking peace marches in the different parts of the World. The first peace march in Nepāl was organised by Nepālese Buddhists and Nipponzan Myohoji from Kathmandu to Lumbinī covering 440 km in October, 2001. This peace march has been organised by the peace loving people of the World. From 2002 to 2005, many monks and young generation have been involving in peace march. On the occasion of 2549 Buddha Jayanti and Lumbinī Day a motorcycle team was involved in peace march from Kathmandu to Lumbinī on 23 May 2005 (2062 Jestha 9). It is the sounding process for peace all over the World.

Barsavassa

In ancient period Buddha advised to his disciples to take shelter during the rainy season from Asara *Sukla purnima* to Aswin *Sukla purnima* (June to September) due to heavy rain. In order to safe their lives, they stay at any place about three months without passing night-rest at other site. They follow up the rules and regulations based on Vinaya pitaka. They perform one month religious activities known as '*Kathinadana*'. Devotees of Buddhism provide food, drinks, medicine and dresses to them during this period. Dress donation process is known as '*Kathina chivar*'. Devotees offer basis requirement of the *Bhikshus*, who live in Barsavassa.

A *Bhikshu* cannot leave his shelter without permission of head monk for some times. If he needs to go outside for sometime, he must return at night at the shelter. They can go outside with the permission of their head in case of illness or urgent work. In special cases, they are permitted to stay out of their *vasa*. Sometime, if the rainy reason is longer than three months they should stay in Barsavassa. It is their regular duty.

Durga Puja

The people of Lumbinī celebrate the festival of Durga puja for fifteen days. It is known as Dashain, *Tika* or *Dasahara*. It is associated with the worship of the *Sakti* cult in which she is worshipped in her different manifestations. On the first day of *Ghatasthapana* the local people of Lumbinī install ceremonially the *ghata* to be worshipped till the day of *Vijayadashami*. The head of the family offers flowers, sweets, fruits and clarified butter and distributes *prasada* each day. From the installment of *ghata* to the sixth day of *Durga Puja* only simple worship is conducted at *pujakotha* of the households. The seventh day, on *phulapati* special worship is offered to the deities. Flowers, *pati*, unbroken-rice and other *puja* articles are managed in the *puja kotha*. The eighth day is known as *Kalaratri*. On that day, goat, buffalo, cock, duck and pigeon are also sacrificed to the goddess. Activities of *Mahastami* and *Mahanavami* are similar.

On this occasion, the devotees undertake a *parikrama* (circumambulation) of the goddess shrines, which is known *Nava Durga Parikrama*. Many secular activities are performed in order to achieve proposed goals. *Vrata, upavasa* and *puja* are main activities during this period. On the tenth day, the members of the family worship Vijayadasami Navadurga bhawani early in the morning. At the proper time of *Tika* the ceremony of *Tika* starts. The younger people of the families go to receive *Tika* and *jamara* from their elders. The young people go to respect the elders at the village. They finish the *puja* and other activities of *Navadurga bhawani* from this day. *Kojagrata purnima* is also a special day of Dashain festival.

Basanta Panchami

The festival of Basanta Panchami falls on the fifth day of the light fortnight in the month of *Magha* (January-February). This festival is associated with the worship of nature on the setting of *Basanta Ritu,* which is known as the king of season (*ritu raj*). It is also considered as the occasion of worshipping of *Kamadev*. The most popular function on the day is the worship of Saraswati, the goddess of learning. The goddess of *Manjushree*, the Buddhist deity, is also worshipped on this occasion. In Buddhist religion, *Manjushree* is considered as the goddess of education, arts and crafts.

Lumbinī has been the important prominent site of Buddhist learning. The *Saraswati Puja* is performed here with great devotion. On the occasion, in all the educational centres, viz. primary, lower secondary and secondary schools and institutions install the images of goddess Saraswati and worship her by the students and teachers. Various cultural programmes are also conducted, especially *bhajan, kirtan*, drama and dancing. Artists, musicians, students and teachers offer flowers, unbroken rice, sweet, banana and other *puja* articles to pleasure her. Due to the absence of permanent temples of Saraswati in Lumbinī and its outskirts, the devotees make the icon of Saraswati and worship her. Goddess Sarsawati is worshipped in most of the families.This is also an occasion to initiate a young child in learning or it is known as *vidhyarambha* or *aksharamabha*.

The local people to pay attention on this auspicious day visit these sacred centres. The priests perform *shodashopchar puja* and offer the deties mango-flowers *(amra manjen)* and flowers. They address her with other names as *Sarada, Jagatamata* or *Jagatajanani.*

Śivaratri

The Śivaratri festival takes place on the day of *Falgun Krishna trayodasi* and on this day there is a big gathering of the people at Śivalayas of Lumbinī area. According to Hindu tradition, Śiva was originated at that night. As the tradition has it, Śiva was married on this auspicious day. The devotees do not celebrate his first marriage with Sati, the daughter of Raja Daksha. The devotees all over India celebrate his second marriage with Pārvati, the daughter of king Hemant of the Himalayas, as Śivarātri (Vidyarthi, 1979:65). The festival of Mahaśivarātri is celebrated as the birthday of Śiva. Devotees spend this day and night by singing the *Bhajans*, the song of Śiva and reciting Śiva *Purana*. *Bhajan, Kirtan* and proper stories of Śiva are told by the sage and mendicants.

Parikramas

The tradition of parikrama (circumambulation) in Hindu and Buddhist scriptures has been considered as the best method of replacing out all sins and unlawful activities during one's life period. There are a number of sacred centres like Bodh Gaya, Kushinagar, Saranatha, Kapilvastu and Lumbinī, where the devotees go for *parikrama* and attach great religious significance to these sacred centres. At the last stage of his life, Gautam Buddha had advised to his disciples that they should visit at these sites, associated with him. Master Plan is also prepared on the basis of Buddhist philosophy. Plan is divided into three parts on the basis of worldly-life (*grihastha*), cultural complex, study area, religious sector and ruins of human civilisation from north to south respectively.

Three segments of Lumbinī represent the life-circle of human beings on the basis of Buddha's life and style. Monks and nuns circumambulate Hinayāni and Mahāyani monasteries according to their belief and customs. Apart from their sect, they usually do *parikrama* from north to south. Annual peace *parikrama* of peace Stūpa (Nipponzan Myohoji) is also performing from northern to southern sector of Lumbinī. Buddhist monks and nuns, who come from Buddhist countries, usually visit around the Māyādevī temple to fulfil their wishes.

CHAPTER **10**

Sacred Specialists

The monks and nuns of the Buddhist shrines have been defined as sacred specialists like in the Hindu complex. Most of the sacred functionaries have specialised themselves in the knowledge of the Buddhist texts as well as chanting *sutras*. Pilgrims believe that the rites of the ritual conducted by the authorised specialist will lead them to have peace, harmony and compassion. There is hard and fast rule in Hinayān sect than Mahāyan. Monks and nuns come from all the ethnic groups and castes. To train the persons to work proficiently as a functionary, *sravane* have trained and taught at Buddhist schools and councils of Lumbinī. Nuns of Gautami vihar have been teaching *Pariyati* (Buddhist) education at the vihar complex, schools of Lumbinī and Parasi area. This plan has supported to produce skillful manpower in this sector. Some of the functionaries of Lumbinī have obtained higer education in Buddhist studies from renowned universities of the world. The Government of Nepāl and non-governmental organisation have been teaching Buddhist homage to Triple Gems and Buddhist teachings at schools of Lumbinī. There are professional guides of Lumbinī Development Trust and in private sectors. Religious and conscious local people help to the pilgrims who come for the pilgrimage of Lumbinī. Monks and nuns of Lumbinī are the main functionaries of the Buddhist shrines.

Apart from them *sravane*, priest, musician, pale, gardeners and barbars are also involved in the premises of the shrine. Ancient Māyādevī temple was known as Rummendei (goddess), where the traditional priest was appointed to conduct daily performances. After the excavation of Lumbinī complex, the temple, Aśoka pillar and structural remains of vihars were exposed. First of all Jayasri Mishra was appointed in the post of priest of Māyādevī temple. After his death Gomati Mishra, Bhagavati Prasad Mishra and his son-in-law Ganga Prasad Pandey became priest of this temple. According to Ven. Bimalananda, they had conducted daily performances under the supervision of Lumbinī Dharmodaya Committee. Before dismantling the Māyādevī temple one priest and one guard quota was provided to take care and conduct daily rituals by the H.M.G. of Nepal through the channel of *Malapota* (*land revenue*) office. Chandra Bhusana Pandey, son of Ganga Prasad Pandey, became Buddhist named Vivekananda at present. The tradition of worshipping in the sanctom-sanctorium of Māyādevī temple has been forbidded by the LDT.

According to the Rule and Regulation of LDT, 2058 only five Bhikshus and five their helper have been permitted to stay in each Buddhist shrine in Lumnibī. During the period of building construction, proper skilled and semi-skilled workers of the concerned party are also permitted to stay here. Due to the fixation of the numbers of monks and nuns to live in Lumbinī each monastery has limited number of functionaries. They are awarded by the titles of *Sthavir* and *Mahasthavir* based on their knowledge in Buddhist literature and seniority of their position. The juniors respect the senior monks and nuns. Almost all the functionaries of the monasteries are monks and nuns (Figs. 43-46). According to their professions, they can be grouped into the following catagories:

Monk and Nun

Duties and responsibilities are slightly different among the Hinayān, Mahāyan and Vajrayān sects in Lumbinī complex because of their countrywise cultural traditions and rules. Among them Hinayān (*Theravadi*) sect is hard and rigid to follow up original tradition. However, other sects are liberal and flexible on the basis of changable movement and motive of the contemporary society. They are liberal for cultural changes and transmission in the synchronous times. Head of the monastery receive the highest regard by the pilgrims and the local people. *Vinaya* rules have been strictly followed up by the Theravadi. Walking on *pindapatra,* wearing *panisukula* robes (discarded cloth taken from the rubbish heap or from the charnel ground), dwelling at the foot of a tree and taking medicine picked in stale orize are the four *Nissaya* or resources.

The four-akaranaya *kicca* (things that should not be done) are indulging in sexual intercourse, stealing others property, killing living being and speaking boastfully with regard to special state that one has not attained. *Sila, Samadhi* and *Panna* are the three trainings (*sikkha*). *Sila* means control of body and speech so that they should be correct and orderly. The action of guarding one's heart unwaveringly is *samadhi* and throughly knowing the mass of *sankhara* (all conditioned things including the body and the mind) is *panna.* Monk and nuns should have obeyed these rule and regulations in proper way. If they do not follow these rules, they are punished because of their offences. There are seven kinds of *Apatti* (offences) among them. Committed on offence of this class is served from the status of a *Bhikshus* is known *parajika. Sanghadisesa* means a *Bhikshus* having committed on offence of this class must dwell under discipline in order to clear himself of the offence. Remaining five classes of *apatti* include confess fault of the monk or nun to the *sangha* or to a *gana*. There should be minimum 2 or 3 *Bhikshus* in a *gana*. There are six reasons why a *Bhikshu* should comment *apatti.* These are, viz. lack of shame, he does not know that it is an *apatti*, he is doubtful, but still goes and does it. He thinks that he ought to do something when in fact he ought not; he thinks that he ought not to do something when in fact he ought to do it. He does something without thinking (does not mindly). The four *parajika* are the Bhikshus who indulge in sexual intercourses commits a *parajika*, kills a human being or causes him, takes something without permission and who boasts of *uttarimanussadhamma* (i.e. states of *Dhamma* superior to the human state) which he has not in fact attained commits a *parajika.*

Bhikshus, who does behave or action against their rule and regulations, is punished by the *gana.* There are thirteen *sanghadisesa* (formal meeting) in course of their unlawful activities and behaviours. Being sexually excited who touches the body of a woman commits a *sanghadisesa*. Being sexually excited speaks that a woman should enjoy herself by indulging in sex commits a *sanghadisesa*. A Bhikshus who acts as a meditator leading a man and woman to become husband and wife as well as hut (12 *sugata* spans length × 7 spans wide) to built great than this and without first permission of *sangha.* Being angry and misbehave with other Bhikshus by means of a stratagem or pretext and *sangha* destruction commits a *sanghadisesa*. Theravadi strictly follows up these traditional rules and regulations, especially Thāi, Myanmar, Śri Laṅkā and Calcutta Mahābodhi society monasteries in Lumbinī.

According to Ven. Phra Nirandarn Sihanam (Fig. 43), secretary and member International Buddhist Monk in Lumbinī (Theravada), the three fold trainings (studies) are *sila*-morality-training in higher morality, *Samadhi*-concentration, meditation in higher mentality and *panna*-wisdom and in higher wisdom (Appendix-7). Bhikhu Maitri (Fig. 45), chairman of International Buddhist Society Lumbinī, belief on self and do good, be good as a monk in the Buddhist world (Appendix-6). Mahāyan and Tibetan Lamaism are not so hard and rigid in course of following rules and regulations. Ven. Dr. Lam suggests that every one should be hard worker to keep peace and harmony (Fig. 44 & Appendix-8). Monk and nuns of China, South Korea, Vietnam, Japan, Germany, Mananga of Nepāl and Tibetan Lama are liberal and easily accept social changes in the contemporary society. International Buddhist Federation is also constituted to conduct various religious activities in Lumbinī complex. Buddha *puja* has been conducting at full-moon day in each month as a common platform of all these sects of Lumbinī (Fig. 37).

Singer and Musicians

The devotional singer and musicians are in a large number, particularly at the shrines of Mahāyan. On the occasion of daily worship and on the days of important festivals in Lumbinī devotional singers and musicians usually sing devotional Buddhist songs to please the deities and the people who gather there. Buddha's teachings, philosophy, rules and regulations have been converted into devotional songs in the interest of the devotees. Dr. Lam, the president of International Buddhist Federation and Founder of Vietnam phat Que in Lumbinī, opines that the young people have less interest in the devotional songs of the shrines, especially local people at present. *Bhikshu* and *Sravane* bit the drums and play other musical instruments during the period of *puja*. At Nipponzan Myhoji, Santi Stūpa complex, *Bhikshu* always use musical drums and other instructions at the time of worship in the morning and at evening. These instruments are also used on special worships. Germany Lotus-Stūpa, Chinese temple, Korean temple, Manang-Sewa Samaja and Tibetan Lama monastery have also been using musical instruments in course of their daily worship at the shrines.

Traditional singers and dancers are employed and paid by the pilgrims and local people on the occasion of special festivals of Lumbinī garden. At *chaitra sukla purnima,* a lot of traditional singers and dancers have been involved in their activities. They sing Hindu as well as Buddhist stories as their favourite songs with musical instruments. They are engaged to dance and collect entertainment charge among the visitors. They are frequently employed by the pilgrims on contact for dancing at the time of the performances of the sacred rituals of various kinds in honour of Māyādevī temple. Professional singers and dancers have been associated with modern clubs, i.e. *Biraha*. Under the leadership of TRPAP, local people have organised their modern clubs where they make regular programmes of singing and dancing to entertain tourists and pilgrims in sacred complex of Lumbinī by these devotional activities, they earn money by which they have promoted their lifestyles and skills. Tourist guides of LDT and private sectors have played a vital role in the promotion of cultural activities in the sacred complex of Lumbinī. First, the pilgrims come at the premises of Māyādevī temple to pay devotional feeling. National as well as foreign pilgrims are not completely familiar with Master Plan of Lumbinī. If the guides of LDT or private sector properly lead them to the monastic zone, the pilgrims will show keen interest to visit Lumbinī in future. Otherwise, they will be unknown about this sacred garden and cannot convey its religious merits and values to their friend as well as relatives after returning from here. Now-a-days LDT has appointed especially tourist guides and TRPAP has also trained local tourist guides to promote pilgrimage activities in Lumbinī. Hotel and Travel Agencies of Lumbinī, Bhairahawā and other concerned area have also managed guidance of proper sites of this area.

Two meditation centers of Lumbinī have also played a vital role in the promotion of Buddhist culture, philosophy and pilgrimage tour. Meditation is a practice of training the mind in continuous movement-to-movement mindfulness throughout one's entire day. *Vipassana* or insight mediation is a form of Buddhist mediation from the *Theravada* tradition. As it is taught in the tradition of late Ven. Mahasi Sayadaw of Myanmar, Vipassana mediation consists of continuous mindfulness in sitting mediation, in walking mediation and in all general activities. All meditators are required to observe the 'Eight training precepts' and to maintain 'Noble Silence' throughout the course of a retreat. The ultimate aim and primary benefit of this meditation practice is the attainment of the four noble path knowledge, which take '*Nibbana*', the state of peace, as an object. Panditaram Lumbinī International Vipassana Meditation Centre has provided services to S. Korean, US American, Germany, British, Hungarian, Canadian, French, Swiss and Italian. Goeinka Meditation Centre is also providing mental training to the followers in each month. Experts of meditation centre are also propagating four noble truths and servicing of Buddhism. They are also known as sacred servicing of Buddhism as well as sacred specialists.

Temples of Lumbinī have appointed *pale* or guard for the protection of vihar, stūpa and gumba. Almost all the guards of these shrines are local people. They are also participated in course of daily performances at the shrines. Garland-sellers, bead-sellers, flower and other *puja* article-sellers are also directly associated with the activities of the specialists of this complex. Gardening is an interesting job due to the memory of Indira's paradise as mentioned in Buddhist literature. All the monastery, vihar and stūpa area have done hedge plantation of religious trees. Each shrine has appointed Gardener to protect garden complex and LDT has appointed five dozen gardeners for flowering and beautification of this area. In the premise of Māyādevī temple, some people sell *puja* articles, such as fruits, flowers, beads, bangles, images of Buddha, etc. for purpose of un-interrupted supply of the *puja*-materials to the pilgrims and the visitor of this complex.

The tradition of offering shaved-hair, at the time of the head-shaving ceremony of the small child, at Aśokan pillar is interesting for their optimum satisfaction. Professional as well as non-professional persons are involved in hair cutting in Lumbinī complex. Barbers are walking on to search their clients around sacred complex. They are also functionary of Lumbinī. They do not only shave the head of the people at the time of upanayan, marriage of the youths and antyesthi-kriya of the local people, but also bless the pilgrims to have peace and harmony. The local people generally engage to shave hair and beard at the time of special festivals in Lumbinī. At *chaitra sukla purnima* more than one hundred thousand people are gathered to celebrate their traditional festival in Lumbinī garden. On this occasion, barbers are also engaged in their professional duties. This tradition is mainly originated from the shaved-head of Siddhartha in course of his *Mahaviniskramana*.

Above-mentioned sacred specialists have played a vital role in the promotion of sacred complex of Lumbinī. There are some other types of specialists, which are employed by LDT. Management Committee, administrative and technical staffs of LDT have also mobilised the sacred performances based on LDT Act, 2042.

Lifestyle of the Specialist

The lifestyle of the sacred specialists of Lumbinī depends on their sects. Hinayāni are rigid and hard to follow their rules and regulations in traditional ways. Mahāyani are modernising their lifestyles and models on the basis of changing concept of the synchronous times. Bhikshus get up early in the morning about 4.00 a.m. and then perform the morning worship of the deities. Hinayān chant triple gems, *panchasila, astasila* and proper

Buddhist songs. Mahāyan also chant own *mantras* on their national tradition and rules. Bhikshus of Nipponzan Myohoji get up at 4 a.m. and start *puja.* After sometime they walk around the Lumbinī area about one and half hour. Sometimes, they reach to the villagers to inform Buddha's teachings and *sutras*. In the morning they take breakfast and engage themselves in their specified services. In the afternoon they take lunch before 12.00 a.m., Mahāyani and Lama are not strictly prohibited for their lunchtime. After their lunch, they take rest for about an hour.

They do not eat solid foods after 12 a.m. They drink liquid, viz. water, milk and fruit juice at dinner-time. Bhikshus are generally vegetarians and they take rice, pulse, sweets, milk, breads, fruits, edible roots of different kinds and various kinds of vegetables. Mahāyani monks and nuns are permitted to take non-vegetarian food also. They do not kill any creature, but are permitted to eat meat killed by others. Because of different followers of different sects of Buddhism, dress, colour and designs are also different. Theravadi *Bhikshus* wear yellow *sanghati* and various colours except blue and white colour in Lumbinī complex. Mahāyani are wearing shirt, *kurta, ganji*, socks, shoes and sandals in their position of living. Some of them in Vajrayān sect wear *saundaha, gemti, panden, chhuwa, tutunga, angi* and *banjura* due to the influence of Sherpa or Bhote culture in the northern side of Nepāl. General functionaries except Bhikshus usually wear shirt, paint, *dhoti, kachchhada, kurta*, coat, shoes, sandals and garments in proper seasons. Nuns wear *sadi, cholo, kambarbandha* and sandals. The colour is also similar to monks. Sacred functionaries pass their leisure time in the social activities to promote the lifestyles of the neighbourhood of Lumbinī complex. In course of field study of the researcher, monk and nuns were engaged in social activities around the villages of Lumbinī complex.

According to Bhikshu Maitri, International Buddhist Society was formed for social services to the disadvantage groups at the villages around Lumbinī. IBS has provided facilities of drinking water, drainage, literacy, non-formal vocational education, free-health service, etc. to the local people of Lumbinī (Appendix-6). Foreign donor agencies have also participated in these programmes. Five years ago on the way of counting Sarus Cranes nearly Lumbinī village, Thay Huyen Dieu saw the scene that people of this area were struggling to across the river. He felt very sad and constructed a bridge to faciliate them there. Since then, every day thousands of people go to the market; children go to school and patients can reach to the hospital very easily crossing the bridge. Due to the direct influence to the local people, every year the Vietnam Bridge Committee and the Local Villagers organize a festival day in order to encourage the people, particularly the younger generation to do good things in life. It is only an example of social work. Many social activities have been conducting by the monks and nuns at the remote villages, where disadvantage groups of people live, in the periphery of Lumbinī complex. They are also directly involved in the supervision and construction of their proper shrines. All the monasteries and institutions have been organised in a Federation of Lumbinī to develop Lumbinī complex. They are very interested to promote Lumbinī as a World Peace City (IBS, 2004: 35-38). These are only the examples of social work. Sacred specialists have been contributing to promote the life-styles of the people of Lumbinī and its outskirts.

Various worships are conducted by the head-monk of the vihar and monasteries (Fig.46). During the period of regular worship, all the monks and nuns of the concerned shrines are participated in a group. In the absence of head-monk, all the *puja* and performances have been conducted under the leadership of assistant Bhikkshu. The national or organizational authorities have appointed all the Bhikkhus of the concerned Vihar and Stūpa. Local monks and nuns have been involved freely in their duties and responsibilities.

CHAPTER 11

Conservation and Preservation

Art remains and monuments reflect the socio-economic condition and human civilisation of the contemporary society. The care and maintenance of cultural property transmits accurate history of the past life ways. Preservation of objects for the future is known collectively as conservation. Professionals who perform these activities are known as conservators. Conservators periodically examine objects, document, and their condition and, if necessary, treat and repair them. They distinguish between two treatment approaches: stabilisation and restoration. An object may be stabilised to maintain its integrity and minimise deterioration, or it may be restored to a previous state. During restoration, conservators may add materials that are not original to the object. Recommended practices call for restoration techniques and materials that preserve the characteristics of the object. Conservation requires specialised skills, facilities, and equipment that vary according to the type of object–paintings, buildings, sculpture, terracotta, bronze, wood, ivory and so forth. A painting conservator understands how to clean the surface of an oil painting whose surface has darkened or yellowed with age.

Conservators also establish preventive care measures, which provide optimum conditions to protect collections over time. All objects change over time because of physical or chemical deterioration and damage. Temperature, relative humidity, light, pollutants and handling are the primary threats to art objects of all kinds. Temperature and humidity levels must remain constant and moderate, avoiding excessively warm or moist conditions and fluctuations that can accelerate deterioration and encourage mold growth and insect activity. Exposure to ultraviolet light from daylight and sources such as fluorescent lamps must be controlled.

Rare antiquities and monuments are also slowly disappearing from the world and the unmovable objects are each day receiving same kind of damage due to human negligence, lack of proper knowledge and natural decay. These materials need to be conserved and preserved to transfer the cultural heritage from generation to generation. In order to preserve the artifacts and monuments, the sixteenth convention of UNESCO in Paris has passed a resolution on November 14, 1970 AD. The UNESCO convention in Paris passed a resolution after two year to conserve and preserve of the Historical, Cultural and Natural Heritage properties to the World Nations. Nepāl has signatured to this resolution in 1978. Among the eight important cultural heritage sites, listed on 'World Heritage Sites' of Nepāl, Lumbinī was also an important listed site in 1997 as 'World Heritage Site'.

Archaeological exploration and excavation have been carried out since 1895-96 in Lumbinī Garden Zone. Lumbinī museum has been operating to collect, categorise, display and study the findings of Lumbinī. Movable objects are grouped under the category of historical, cultural, science-technology and natural assets. Monuments are chemically treated and preserved. They can servive for long time against the natural deterioration and human activities. Due to the consciousness and foreign interest, the monumental structures of Lumbinī had *tar*-bared since 1972 (Figs. 26 & 27). These are the concrete infrastructures in the promotion of tourism in Lumbinī. They support to generate income and changing the lifestyle of the people. According to Master Plan, the sacred garden is an archaeological complex. Māyādevī temple, Aśokan pillar, *Puskarini* pond, stūpas and structural remains of ancient vihars have been preserved within a short space (Figs. 26-30). According to the Master Plan of Lumbinī laboratory is proposed in the area of 1,200 square meter in Cultural Centre (Tange, 1977:17). It is not started even now. Conservation and preservation work is needed to protect the valuable and significant structural remains of the site.

Māyādevī temple has been restored from 1993 to 2002. JBF,

DOA and LDT had launched the project of restoration in 1993. However, the temple was not completed until 2003 due to their mutual misunderstanding for restoration. At last, Nepāl Government has completed its restoration in 2002. Its superstructure is made of concrete stūpa model consisting thirteen-*bhuwans, kalasa, amalaka* and *vyaupuraka,* pinnacle components. But, its upper structure has added additional part than former structure. Due to this portion, UNESCO has raised question to list in World Heritage Site. According to UNESCO, all the glass windows of the temple should be opened for proper ventilation. According to the UNESCO rules, brick-pavement in the complex of Māyādevī temple is also not permitted. The authority does not accept white wall painting of the temple. Basic requirements of UNESCO should be fulfilled in proper time in course of preservation and conservation. Remains of the fifteen chambers in the sanctum of the shrine are not scientifically preserved. The findings should be kept in proper sites like a conglomerate stone in bulletproof glass. Remaining portion of the excavated-temple is hanging as a cliff. It is need to replace the broken-bricks and rubbish from here. Otherwise, it will fall down on the site of Marker-stone. Wooden railing and iron framework need to be painted to protect from water and insects. Sometimes the wood can be slowly dried and moisture replaced by glycerin, which is retained by a skin of 10% poly vinyl acetate or shellac in alcohol.

Nativity sculpture of Buddha is kept on the wall, immediately above of the Marker stone. The remarkable unique piece of sculpture should be kept in glass-box in order to protect from hot weather of this region. When the devotees enter into the sanctum of the *Gandhakuti*, they search the presence of Gautam Buddha. Due to the absence of Buddha's idol in the sanctum of the shrine, devotees cannot feel as the birthplace of Buddha. LDT is not interested to keep the image of Buddha. However, the devotees' interest is to be kept an idol of Buddha in proper site at this temple for the memory of Buddha. Air-condition should be made for favourable atmosphere to preserve stone and wooden objects in the sanctum of the shrine. Aśokan pillar is standing at the back of Māyādevī temple. Temporary shed should be built to protect

Aśokan pillar. Due to the open station water saturated with Calcium Sulphate and Plaster of Paris need to be used to clean and protect its original features. Galvanised double iron-rings should be used to tie the broken parts of the pillar. According to local custom of the people, the hair of *mundan* is kept around the pillar. A proper point or box should be fixed for this purpose, which will support to create positive concept towards Lumbini of the local people. A donation box needs to be kept at any site of the pillar area, which will be used by the devotees on visiting here. Small pedestal should be built for the waiting to devotees in course of their worship. A horse figure should be surmounted on the pillar as described by Chinese visitors in ancient time. Chunar-sand stone should be used for this purpose within the limitation of archaeological norms and values.

Accurate size and shape of Siddhartha *Kupa* must be exposed in course of excavation. During the period 1933-39, Kaisher Shumsher Rana had excavated this pond, but there are the ruins of ancient wall-structures immediately on the south of the pond. Its present area 50 × 50 feet is not so reliable because of attached running walls of monuments (Fig. 31). At the bottom of the sacred pond, finding structural remains of two wells should be precisely identified to know their original shape and size. The pond is needed to be clean. An idol of Buddha should be kept in the middle of the pond to remember the birth and bath of Buddha. The old tree of *pipal*, on the south of the tank, should be cut down and either *Aśoka* or *pipal* tree need to be planted. The structural remains of ancient vihar has been exposed without any hesitation. Shrubs and rubbish are scattered all around the temple area. Visitors are walking on the ruins. Information booklets, leaflets, brouchurers and other proper information should be available to aware the visitors in course of visiting the complex of Sacred Garden. This programme will support to preserve archaeological remains of Lumbinī. Historical, archaeological, cultural as well as religious significance of the structural remains need to be mentioned on the hoarding-boards for the visitors. Chronological order, architectural techniques and traditions need to be labelled on each ancient excavated-stūpas and vihar structures at the site.

According to the Master Plan, circular levee around the archaeological garden must be completed to prevent flood from the high land on south-west corner of the project area. Otherwise, it is very difficult to prevent from decreasing the structural remains of this complex. Drains are also essential to control perennial water due to plain land. Now-a-days tar-bar should be strong and high in order to secure this complex. Entry-fee must be utilised for the promotion of this complex without hesitation. Structural remains of the stūpa, vihar, ring-well, etc. need immediate chemical treatment and good preservative chemical coating in proper time and objects.

Networking of internal transportation is not yet completed. New sectors should be constructed after preserving completed works. In monastic zone, various organisations and authorities of sixteen nations have been constructing vihar, stūpa, monasteries and *gumbas*. Some of them have been operating since a decade and some plots are not allotted even now. All the plots have been provided for 99 years. In this critical situation, building of first phase will be constructed due to the long-time of completion of the Master plan. On the east of central link Myanmar, International Nun's Association and Mahabodhi Society of India have been operating their regular activities in their plots (Figs. 11 & 14). Monasteries as well as other components of the concerned authorities are not neat and clean as sacred shrines. Their original colour and brightness is decreasing and discoloured due to lack of proper preservation. Lokamuni, Golden stūpa of Myanmar is going to be discoloured due to heavy rain, hot-weather and hot-air. At the four corner of the courtyard of this complex the animal figures, as surmounted on the top of Aśokan pillars in India, Pakistan and Nepāl during the reign of Aśoka, are not clear in facial expression. The temples built by Myanmar government are also changing their original colour and facing (Figs. 12 & 13). Shrines are not opened in proper time to the people, who visit here. Royal Thāi Monastery has allotted two plots in order to build Uposatha hall, Grand pagoda, refectory and chanting hall, lodging for monks, kitchen, office and residence for pilgrims (Figs. 16 & 17). Thai has completed construction work including internal connection road and bridge on north east.

Monastery of Śri Laṅkā seems to be rack and ruins lack of completation and protection of the site at present (Fig. 15). The authority is not active to complete this construction in time. LDT must be active to reinforce the donor agencies in proper time as mentioned in contract letter. On the west of central link Myanmar, Mananga Sewa Samaja (Fig. 18), Dharmodhaya Sabha (Fig. 19), South Korea, China (Fig. 20), Japan, Vietnam, Germany, Bhutan etc. have been constructing their monasteries, stūpa and *gumbas* in their national style, tradition and beliefs. China, Tara Foundation of Germany, Guesthouse of Korea, Dharmodaya Gumba and Manana Sewa stūpa have been operating. Almost of them are under construction. In this situation, the responsibility of conservation and preservation is depended on them for 99 years as mentioned in contract paper. Security is the main problem to the Institutions of Lumbinī. Boundary wall on the east and west is completed only 2.50 km. Apart from this part other sites are open from where one can freely enter to the Master Plan complex. First of all, all the infrastructures as well as physical developments of Lumbinī proposed on Master plan should be completed as soon as possible. Responsibility of conservation and preservation should be provided to the concerned authorities. LDT should be active to monitor and follow up them in free, fair and unbiasly in times.

Lumbinī museum has been hand overed to Nepāl by Indian Government. Artifacts of Lumbinī, photographs of Kapilvastu area, viz. Niglihawa, Gotihawa, Tilaurakot, Kudan etc.; replics and pictures of Indian art remains and monuments are displayed here. In reality visitors of this museum feel that they are visiting at any Indian site, but not in Nepal. Archaeological, anthropological, architectural and historical replics, photographs, VCDs as well as drawings, concerned to Buddha and Buddhism should be kept in this museum. All objects become change over time because of physical or chemical deterioration and damage. Temperature, relative humidity, light, pollutants, and handling are the primary threats to museum objects. Temperature and humidity levels must remain constant and moderate, avoiding excessively warm or moist conditions and fluctuations that can accelerate deterioration and encourage mold growth and insect activity. Exposure to ultraviolet light from daylight and sources such as fluorescent lamps must be controlled. Exhibition and storage areas must be pest-proof and free of indoor pollutants.

It should be provided adequate security, including protection against fire, theft, vandalism and accident. Collected objects must be insured in course of transmission and in permanent collections as well. When an object is moved, museum staff must observe accepted standards for the care and handling of objects with historic, aesthetic, or scientific value. Due to space constraints, museums usually can display only a small portion of their collections at a time. The rest must be stored using suitable equipment and materials under proper environmental conditions. Museum objects often require specially designed containers, drawers, shelves, or racks. Large objects such as aircraft or automobiles require specially designed facilities. Glass-windows as well as ventilations of this building are not sufficient to secure it. Iron-griddle should be kept inside the glass. Lumbinī International Research Institute building is under the supervision and operation of Japanese Reyukai. Its ground floor and dormitories should be well equipped. Architecture of these two buildings is unique as mentioned in Master Plan. These building must be cleaned from the moss. Air cooler system should be provided here.

Śri Laŋkan pilgrimage house has not been operated nowadays. It looks like a ruin of ancient civilisation. According to the authority of LDT, it is operatling by the Śri Laŋnkan hotelers. Mikasa hotel, middle class visitor accommodation, is also under construction. These accommodations must be operated in proper time by the pressure of the concerned authorities. Otherwise, these buildings will be collapsed due to their disputes. Hokke is operating for high class pilgrims.

CHAPTER **12**

Development of Tourism at Lumbinī

Tourism is a very important source for foreign exchange earning. It is an unrisky procedure for transfer of real resources from industrially capital surplus developed countries to developing countries. Tourism is a labours intensive industry offering employment to skilled, semi-skilled and unskilled manpower. The problems of unemployment and underemployment are more acute in the developing countries. It employs large number of people and provides a wide range of jobs. Apart from these area, a large number of specialist personnel required to work as accountants, housekeepers, cooks, waiters, and entertainers; semi-skilled workers, viz. porters, kitchen-staff, gardeners, chambermaids, etc. Furnishing and equipment industries, farming and food supply as well as souvenir industries provide indirect employment to the local people.

The basic infrastructure of tourism, i.e. roads, public awareness, sanitation, communication, transportation, water supply, airport, public utilities and accommodation units provide jobs for thousands of workers. The promotion of tourism can be a great encouragement to economic development. Cultural motivation has always stood as a unique vehicle for the cultural propagation through the process of tourism. It has always been an essential medium for broadening the limits of human knowledge. Mass of people travels to foreign countries to entertainment through usages, custom, fair, festivals, art, architecture, food and drinks of the host country. Tourism is an important medium of social and cultural development and is also of promoting lasting goodwill and friendship among the nations of the world.

Lumbinī being the birthplace of Lord Buddha thousands of Buddhist as well as other religious people come to visit in every year. It provides direct and indirect benefit to the people of this region. Pilgrimage, cultural, nature, mass, sustainable, endemic and domestic tourism can promote the lifestyle of the people in Lumbinī and its outskirt. Lumbinī Development Trust, the authority, has coordinated many physical, cultural, natural and architectural perspectives to promote foreign participant and to increase the rate of the tourists. According to Master Plan the projection of the tourists was 373500 in 1985. In the plan 15 % growth rate was proposed. 20% and 80% tourists by land and by air respectively were estimated (Tange, 1977:11). Important aspects of tourism in Lumbinī are as follows:

Mass Tourism

In the nineteenth century, the people had started to move in large numbers to places away from their usual places of residence. Railways, steamships, motorcars and aeroplane linked inter relation among the people of developed, developing and under developing countries. Rapid development in the means of transport and communication has changed the whole world one neighbourhood and has made travel an easy affair. Leisure, pleasure pilgrimage and recreation are the motivating factors of mass movement of people. Thomas Cook, the pioneer of mass tourism in England, had said that the earth in all its fullness and beauty is for the people (Bhatia, 1990). Nowadays a large number of people move from one country to another due to the cultural and natural attractions. Cultural tourism is the focus point of mass tourism at present.

Mass tourism can contribute unique benefits to the exploiting of the cultural heritage of a nation and can serve indirectly to improve the individual cultural level of both nationals and foreigners. 51.9% of the total visitors of Lumbinī came in group during 2003-4, which has particular implications for visit management such as the availability of sufficient toilets, orientation to the hoteliers, etc. (DEVA, 2004: VI). Tourist of Śri Lanka, South Korea, Japan, Taiwan, Thāiland and Myanmar usually come in mass. Lumbinī, the birthplace of Lord Buddha is the main motivating factor to them. From the Buddhist countries many visitors come in group. Tables 12.1 to 12.5 shows the number of the visitors; all of them at top ten countries come in mass.

Cultural Tourism

Lumbinī has the potentials of being a most important centre of cultural tourism. Māyādevī temple, Aśoka pillar, Puskarini tank, various ancient stūpas, vihar structures and finding relics have attracted many pilgrims and other visitors at this sacred complex. In ancient period king, nobles and other renowned persons had visited Lumbinī in course of their pilgrimage. The tradition has been continuing in an unbroken chain. On special occasion a large number of devotees visit from the various parts of Nepāl and foreign countries. Lumbinī represents not only monuments, but also the requisites, viz. unique lifestyle of the Hindu, Buddhist and Muslim people, local art, craft and indigenous religious activities.

Lumbinī, the birthplace of Lord Buddha, is a sacred complex not only Buddhist, but also for Hindu as well as other religious people due to the peace land. Siddharthanagar, the headquarter of Rupāndehi district, is the main entrance gateway of Lumbinī. Immigration office of Belahiya, Bhairahawā has been recorded the number of foreign tourists except Indian. Due to the open boarder and cultural similarity between Nepāl and India, it is difficult to find out discrimination and actual data. According to the report of Nepal Rastra Bank the number of Nepalese and Indian tourist in Lumbinī was 68272, 67545 and 81650 in 2000, 2001 and 2002 respectively. In 2003 and 2004, the number of the tourist was 78553 and 93269 respectively (NRB, 2005:112). The ratio of Indian and Nepālese tourist was 71% in 2004. In 2004, 16.6% in the total foreign tourists of Nepāl entered from the route of Siddharthanagar Belahiya. Among them 13% visited in Lumbinī complex. 66.7% tourists come for pilgrimage tour in this region (Ibid: 3).

Table 12.1 presents seven years scenarios of monthly tourist arrival trend from Belahiya, Sunauli gateway of Siddharthanagar. In 2000, 46174 tourists entered Nepāl from Belahiya gateway. In 2001, the ratio of tourist was decreased in 22.17% and next year

TABLE 12.1 : Monthly Tourists arrival Trend of Siddharthanagar (Belahiya)

Month	*2000*	*2001*	*2002*	*2003*	*2004*	*2005*	*2006*
January	3446	3242	2122	3364	3379	3737	4530
February	6749	6041	3035	5568	6849	5065	8717
March	7933	6321	5001	5553	8412	7823	9342
April	3484	2377	1552	1990	2163	2095	1289
May	1554	1030	733	935	876	790	925
June	684	453	479	493	566	771	804
July	1054	989	654	1269	1405	1207	1464
August	4368	4073	2673	3768	4572	5789	7059
September	2785	2620	1585	2633	2615	3981	4504
October	4653	3621	2455	5092	4938	6530	8917
November	5851	3503	3723	5518	6585	8214	8988
December	3613	1666	2426	3686	5453	5653	6114
Total	46174	35936	26438	39869	47813	51655	62680
Per cent		–22.17	–26.43	50.80	19.93	8.03	21.34

Source: Tourist Information Centre, Belahiya.

was decreasing in 26.43% ratio. In 2003 and 2004 its' numbers increased in 50.80% and 19.93% respectively. In 2005, the ratio of the tourists was increased only 8.03% than the last year. In 2006 the number of tourists increased in 21.34% than 2005. Tourists by aeroplane are not recorded here. This table shows that six months from October to March are very suitable for tourist industry in Lumbinī. The arrival flow of tourists is high in March, November and October respectively. June, May and April are dry months for Lumbinī visitors. Visiting schedule and proper programmes should be managed on the basis of tourists' wants and interest by the authority.

Due to the cultural and natural significance of Lumbinī many visitors visit at this sacred site. The survey of Lumbinī visitors has pointed out the types of visitors, purpose of visit, source of visit information, planned period of the visit and route (DEVA, 2004). Maximum number of visitors was 16-30 age-group and 70% among them visited first time at Lumbinī. Lumbinī is the main attractive site for first time visitors than repeaters'. Among repeat-visitors 55% were from Thāiland. Single, couple, family and group visitors usually come here in proper season. Large number of visitors involved in-group, which indicates the increasing position of mass-tourism at the site. 56% tourists had visited Lumbinī for religious purpose and remaining 44% for other purpose (DEVA, 2004). Family and friends were main their information sources for their visit. Visitors to Lumbinī from as far away as Japan, Taiwan and South Korea decide to come with the planning period of less than one month. Almost the tourists decide to visit Lumbinī refered by the travel agents, hotels and other related authorities after entering Nepāl. It means that there is lack of proper profile networking of Lumbinī information in these markets.

Majority of the tourists use air route for their visit at Lumbinī and do not use the services of Tour Company and Travel Agencies. Lumbinī and Bhairahawā have provided 59 and 26 per cent accommodation to them respectively. Only 11 per cent has find accommodation in India. About 25 per cent tourists accommodated in the monasteries and 16 per cent in lodges. In 2007 hotel association has opposed against the accommodation in monasteries. Remaining visitors mostly used hotel accommodation of various categories. Length of stay of about 90 per cent visitors was up to 3 days their average length of stay of merely. South-Korean and Thāiland have the most willingness to extend their stay with 16 per cent of the tourists each from these countries preferring to stay for longer period (Ibid.). The tourists who enter from India in Lumbinī stay only 1.5 days in Nepal. Tour and travel agencies of India come directly Lumbinī and return after some hours at the same day without night rest here (NRB 2005:3).The most interesting thing at Lumbinī is recorded Māyādevī temple to the tourists. Beggars and fake monks' activities have created least interesting feeling to the tourists during their visit at this complex. In 2004, the over all impression of the international tourists about Lumbinī was found to be encouraging as the majority of the tourists expressed that their impression was very good and excellent.

TABLE 12.2 : Top Ten Countries Annual Visitors at Belahiya (Siddharthanagar)

Sl.No.	*Countries*	*2000*	*2001*	*2002*	*2003*	*2004*	*2005*	*2006*
1.	Śri Lanka	9035	9017	7938	10642	14357	17748	24818
2.	Thailand	3058	2350	2318	5058	7198	8439	9912
3.	South Korea	2395	2745	2715	4073	3939	3909	4395
4.	Myanmar	1920	1289	1002	1515	2291	-	3405
5.	Japan	4180	3348	2118	3138	3092	2535	2713
6.	Netherland	-	-	-	-	-	1524	1456
7.	UK	3509	2566	1436	1699	1703	1493	1430
8.	Israel	1828	1737	1383	1996	1995	1701	1366
9.	USA	1844	-	-	907	1068	1006	1129
10.	Germany	-	1273	831	939	1097	860	1058
11.	Other countries	18405	11611	6697	9902	11073	12440	10998
Total		46174	35936	26438	39869	47813	51655	62680

Source: Tourist Information Centre, Belahiya.

According to the number of visitors at Belahiya, main entrance gate of Siddharthanagar to Lumbinī, in 2006 Table 12.2 shows the ten top countrywise tourists. Main visitors are of Śri Lanka, Thailand, South Korea, Myanmar, Japan, UK, USA, Israel and Germany. In 2002, visitors were only 26438 due to Maoist movement in Nepal. After the seize fire of the Maoist, visiting ratio of the foreigners rapidly increased in 2005 and 2006. In the comparison of 2002, the number of visitors was increased 137% in 2006. From 2003 to 2006, the ratio of the tourists is increasing in positive way. Apart from the above-mentioned countries, tourists of Australia, Canada, Cambodia, Malaysia, China, Vietnam, France, Dutch, etc. are also visiting here in proper season. Their main target of visit is Lumbinī and it's periphery.

Table 12.3 presents twelve years tourist arrival trend of Lumbinī. The ratio of tourists was 26.85% increased in 1996 than last year. From 1997 to 99, its ratio was decreasing at least 51.56%. Next year ratio was increased in 31.92%. In 2001 and 2002 arrival ratio of tourists is not satisfied. In 2003 and 2004 were satisfied because of increasing rate 210.42% and 35.07% respectively. The entry ratio of the foreign tourists except India is increased 5.01%

TABLE 12.3 : Twelve Years Tourist Arrival Trend of Lumbinī

Sl.No.	*Years*	*Tourist Number of Arrival*	
		No.	*Percentage %*
1.	1995	20023	-
2.	1996	25400	26.85%
3.	1997	23280	–8.35%
4.	1998	22119	–4.99%
5.	1999	10715	–51.56%
6.	2000	14135	31.92%
7.	2001	10135	–28.30%
8.	2002	9037	–10.83%
9.	2003	28053	210.42%
10.	2004	37892	35.07%
11.	2005	39792	5.01%
12.	2006	49595	24.63%

#LDT

in 2005. In 2006 the ratio of the tourists increased in 24.63%. This scenario shows that peace, physical facilities, global communication and toleration among various group, religion, sex and communities should be provided to the guests.

Table 12.4 represents the major countries of tourist-flow in Lumbinī. Sri Lanka, Japan, South Korea, Thāiland, Taiwan and China are the main sources of foreign visitors. Twelve years scenario presents the attraction of Śri Lankan and Japanese tourists due to the Buddhist religion and philosophical influence. In 1996 and 1998, the number of Japanese was 9405 and 8247 respectively. In 2002, its number was decreased into 937. In 2003 and 2004, its ratio is increasing in 41.40% and 20.42% respectively in the comparison of last years. Its vast differentiation is the main cause of national and international violence and terrorism. The arrival ratio of the foreign tourists was decreased in –28.30 and –10.84 in 2002 and 2001 respectively. The ratio of Chinese tourists has been increasing in last two years than previous years due to the touristy-relation between Nepāl and China. Thāiland and Taiwan are also potential area in the promotion of cultural and pilgrimage tourism for Lumbinī.

TABLE 12.4 : Top Six countries Annual visitors of Lumbinī

		Years 1995-2006											
S.N.		*1995*	*1996*	*1997*	*1998*	*1999*	*2000*	*2001*	*2002*	*2003*	*2004*	*2005*	*2006*
1	Sri Lanka	1541	1798	19	1413	1375	2570	2657	2453	8673	12217	15520	21563
2	South Korea	2398	4030	2805	2481	1254	1390	891	1070	2903	3365	3053	3443
3	Japan	6454	9405	7906	8247	4192	2685	1354	937	2262	2724	2222	2165
4	China	366	463	604	160	260	266	277	486	621	912	1119	1659
5	Taiwan	2527	2875	2535	2863	701	981	242	245	1174	1650	1509	1471
6	Thailand	1948	1552	1425	3139	366	961	1147	1097	5164	7735	7828	9223
7	Myanmar	-	-	-	- - -	- - -	- - -	- - -	- - -	1099	2115	2106	2680
8	Others	4789	5277	6030	3816	2567	5282	3567	2748	6778	8086	7554	7391
	Total	20023	25400	23280	22119	10715	14135	10135	9036	28053	37892	39792	49595
	Percentage %		26.85	–8.35	–4.99	–51.56	31.92	–28.30	–10.84	210.46	35.07	5.01	24.63

Source: LDT, 2007.

TABLE 12.5 : Monthly Tourist Arrival Trend of Lumbinī

Sl.No.	*Month*	*2002*	*2003*	*2004*	*2005*	*2006*	*Remarks*
1	January	1498	3043	3160	4035	3751	
2	February	1903	3625	5690	4139	7508	
3	March	2352	3725	6298	5699	7655	
4	April	47	855	1321	991	546	
5	May	6	443	492	452	406	
6	June	18	239	350	450	454	
7	July	48	626	782	650	831	
8	August	321	2461	3590	4383	5948	
9	September	432	1653	1889	2770	3602	
10	October	247	3149	3220	4873	6962	
11	November	983	4316	5186	6584	6762	
12	December	1182	3918	5914	4766	5170	
Total		9037	28053	37892	39792	49595	

#LDT-2007

According to Table 12.5 March is the most favourable month for the visitors at Lumbinī. From August to March the flow of tourists is very high and local people also get chance to earn a lot of money by tourism industry. In 2003 the number of the tourists was increased in 210.42% than the last year. After 2003 the ratio of the visitors was increasing each year. In 2006 the rate of the visitors was increased in 24.63% than 2005. April, May, June and July are dry months for the international visitors due to hot weather and rainy season in the region. Due to the internal conflict, violence and unlawful activities the international visitors were not encouraged to visit Lumbinī and it's peripheral area at past. After the seize fire of the Maoist the flow of the visitors is increasing in per year. According to the wants and needs of the visitors GO, NGO and civil societies should manage and provide various facilities and services to them. The trend of the visitors supports to plan and manage the facilities to the authorities in proper time and situation. In March 2007, 12304 international visitors have come. The trend of 2007 is very satisfactory and ratio is also increasing than the last years.

TABLE 12.6 : Infrastructure of Tourism, 2000-06

Sl.No.	*Type of work*	*Quantity*	*Remarks*
1.	Community hall construction	12	
2.	Toilet construction	384	
3.	Hand pump installation	50	
4.	Drainage construction	2500 m	
5	Institutional development	900 persons	

#CFNT Lumbinī-2007.

Table 12.6 shows that Cross Flow Nepal Trust has launching various programmes at six VDCs, viz. Lumbinī Adarsa, Madhubani, Bhagawanpur, Ekala, Khudabagar and Tenuhawa. From 2002 to 2006 this project has provided facilities on free health and mobile clinic services, non-formal education, adult education, vocation training, school enrolment support and social mobilisation training. Drain construction, private toilet construction, social mobilisation and women empowerment programmes are also supporting for the attraction of tourists. 12 common halls are the meeting place of the local people. They gather and discuss about the plan and programmes of sustainable tourism at the villages. 384 toilets are also supporting to keep neat and clean the villages. Not only the adults but also the children are also conscious to use private and public toilets. 900 people are active for institutional development at the villages. 2.5 km drain in constructed to protect houses and roads in the rainy season. Due to public awareness and physical facilities the number of domestic and international tourists is increasing.

Indian tourists are also visiting in course of their Buddhist circuit tour. Their accurate data is not recorded at the Information Desk of Lumbinī. They usually come from air route and by land through Sunauli, Naugarh-Surjagarh, Chakar-Chaura-Pakadi and Bhagawanpur gateways in all season. They also expend some money and purchase local handicrafts.

Tourist guide who can speak native language of the visitors should be employed. Tourist materials, interpretator of the sites, cultural clubs and unique local handicrafts should be provided to the visitors to promote tourist activities at Lumbinī sacred garden area.

Role of TRPAP in Tourism

Tourism for Rural Poverty Alleviation Programme has launched to contribute to the poverty alleviation objectives of the government through review and formulation of policy and strategic planning for sustainable tourism development that are pro-poor, pro-environment, pro-rural communities and pro-women from 2002 to 2007. To demonstrate sustainable tourism development models for policy feedback, to develop institutional mechanisms for the sustenance of tourism development in Nepāl, to support the government to review and formulate sustainable tourism development policies and strategies and integrate them with wider conservation activities are its main objectives. This programme is running at 48 VDC's of Dolpa, Lumbinī, Chitwan, Langtang, Solukhumbu and Kanchanjungha. One of them Lumbinī area consists seven village development committees, viz. Aama, Bhagawanpur, Lumbinī Adarsa, Tenuhawa, Ekala, Khudabagar and Madhuwani. This programme has covered 37.9% population and 38.30% household of these seven VDC. TRPAP has been playing a vital role to develop Lumbinī as a model of tourism. It has focused on empowerment of Lumbinī Development Trust and the upliftment of local communities through various activities. Seven social mobilisers and one village tourism associate have contributed to enhance proper skills and self-help schemes to the local people to generate income for their living. Hotel-management, fish-farming, bee-keeping, rickshaw-pulling, unseasonable vegetable-farming, banana-farming, making-*Dhakkis,* moulding terracotta figurines, especially Buddha and Bodhisattva, group management, cultural programme, empowerment training etc. have conducted to special target groups (STG) at the proposed area (Fig. 47). To promote and enhance cultural tourism, a unique cultural organisation named 'Lumbinī Cultural Buddha *Biraha Geet Sadak Natak'* is formed to promote and conserve of local dance, singing, drama, painting, weaving, food, drinks, dress and ornaments of Lumbini area. After the proper search and inquiry social mobilizers have formed VDC level sustainable tourism development committees consisting members of various functional groups (Fig. 48). STDC supports to establish linkage among NTB, DDC, VDC, LDT and other proper institutes related to this area.

TABLE 12.7 : Tourism Infrastructure Development, 2004

Sl.No.	*Activities*	*Targets*	*Achievement*	*Distance*
1.	Road Maintenance	6	6	12.57 Km.
2.	Brick soling base of monkey tree (Khudabagar)	1	1	5 m. Radius
3.	Signpost & Flex Board	16	16	
4.	Visiting Information Centre furnishing (LDT)	1	1	
5.	Incinerator at major chok	5	5	
6.	Rubbish cart Madhuwani & Ama	2	2	
7.	Toilet construction	20	1	
8.	Eco-trait Maintenance LDT area	1	1	
9.	Rubbish Bins provided	20	18	

Source: TRPAP, 2007

Table 12.7 represents 12.57 km road maintenance, brick soling around the monkey tree of Khudabagar, 16 signpost and flex board and five incinerators have completed in course of infrastructure development of tourism. Two rubbish carts are provided to Madhuwani and Ama VDCs. Rubbish bins provide, toilet construction and eco-trail activities were carried out in 2004. The table shows that achievement was satisfactory.

TRPAP has developed the pre-requisites of tourism in the area of Lumbinī. This programme is supporting to alleviate poverty in the rural area of Lumbinī. Information boards, arrow boards, museum visiting information committees are managed in seven VDCs'. Table 12.8 presents 14 information boards and 30 arrow boards. A Tharu museum is operating at Sonabarsa of Khudabagar. Dress, weapons, utensils, agricultural instruments, terracotta pots, beads, bangles, ear studs, rings, necklaces, *bala, baju* and their cultural activities are exhibited. These artifacts and dummy represent the lifestyle and social customs of the Tharu, aboriginal tribe of the region. About fifteen thousand people are going to be benefited from this plan. This programme has provided opportunities to promote village tour, village-walk, pulling-cart-

TABLE 12.8 : Tourist Infrastructure Development, 2007

Sl.No.	*Name*	*Name of VDC*	*Quantity*	*No. of Beneficiaries*
1.	Information Board	Madhuwani	3	3120
2.	Arrow Board	Madhuwani	10	500
3.	Information Board	Bhagawanpur	1	500
4.	Arrow Board	Bhagawanpur	4	1000
5.	Information Board	Ama	1	500
6.	Information Board	Tenuhawa	5	3500
7.	Information Board	Lumbini Adarsha	1	700
8.	Information Board	Khudabagar	3	2100
9.	Arrow Board	Khudabagar	10	1000
10.	Museum	Khudabagar	1	230
11.	VIC	Khudabagar	1	230
12.	Information Board	Ekala	1	700
13.	Arrow Board	Ekala	6	600

#TRPAP

ride, weaving, rickshaw-riding, ceramic industries to the local people, which support to generate income. Tourism conservation programme, environment awareness programme and local resources mobilization programme are also launching in proper way. Lumbinī area is fertile for natural and cultural material productions. Natural heritages, viz. landscape-plain land, forest patches, river, ponds, wetlands and wildlife-animal-blue-bull, and bird like Sarus are available to attract domestic as well as foreign tourists. Archaeological remains, temples, monasteries, museum, Lumbinī International Research Institute, Bhojapuri, Pahadi, Muslim and Buddhist cultures, typical houses, dress and ornament, food and drinks language and lifestyle and hospitable management of the local people are known as cultural products. Due to the cultural and natural infrastructure of Lumbinī, TRPAP has chosen this area to promote lifestyle of the people.

In course of implementation of this program infrastructure development programmes, viz. signage standardisation (LDT and Belahiya), Tourist Hoarding Board, visitor information centre up-grading, nursery and water-pump (*Dhiki-pump*) plans were 100% completed. Institutional development activities, viz. community organisation formation 82%, functional group formation 94.74%,

Eco. club formation 100%, sustainable tourism development committee formation 50%, TEAP for groups 115.80% and SRT plans preparation 120% were succeeded. Institutional capacity building training and nursery operation training were 83.33% and 100% progress respectively. In the sector of institutional development, service standardisation training and exposure visit programmes were 85.33% and 50% successful respectively. Institutional human resource development, newsletter publication, news in media, local handicraft and success stories broadcasting by Radio Nepāl programmes had completed in 2007.

In the first quarter of 2004 staff capacity building training, stationeries support to CO, FGS, and STDC, workshop, insurance of ID card to group and VIC upgrading programmes were completed. Incinerator, TEAP, rubbish bin placement, STDC reformation, CMC operation, local level institutional capacity building training and environment awareness programmes had completed. The organisation provided furniture to Information Centre of Lumbinī and was conducted ten days local tour guide and hotel management training, 7 days basic hospitality and English language training was conducted for the rickshaw pullers of Lumbinī. Promotional documentary CD was also produced. TRPAP has done an appreciatable progress to product skilled-manpower for local sustainable tourism development in Lumbinī. This programme must be useful for regular employment in course of rural poverty alleviation in future. At present handicraft producers are actively preparing handicrafts using local raw materials, employment of hospitality-trained personnel at hostels, and local tourist guides are engage in their jobs. TRPAP is also promoting the surrounding areas of Lumbinī through the cannel of 'Lumbinī Buddhist Circuit Tour' networking at Ramagrama, Devadaha, Tilaurakot, Niglihawa, Gotihawa, etc. belonging sites to *Manushi* and Śākyamuni Buddha.

This programme has provided maximum outputs within a short span of six years period, especially positive feedback from stakeholder, well established institutional setting at VDC and district level. It developed the concept of model partnership between STDC and LDT-STDC, culture and biodiversity conservation. Lumbinī circuit and village tour promotion through documentary, wildlife and wetland conservation and trained human resources in tourism are main attractions for tourism development, which have been launched by TRPAP.

After the evaluation of this program during this period, some valuable suggestions are given to the authority. Action plan should be transparency or public audit and realistic in proper location, time and situation. Amicable relationship, low security staff mobilisation and high-sounding implementation should be limited in course of fieldwork in the synchronous times.

TABLE 12.9 : Institutional Development
VDC-wise status of Sustainable Tourism Development Committee (STDC), 2007

S.No.	*Name of STDC (VDC)*	*Contact address*	*Executive members*			*Chair-person*	*Manager*
			F	*M*	*Total*		
1	Bhagawanpur	Khungai-3/4	4	8	12	M	M (STG)
2	Ekala	Bhaisahiya-8	4	9	13	M	M
3	Lumbinī Adarsha	Padariya-4	4	9	13	M	M
4	Madhuwani	Mahilawar-8	2	9	11	M (STG)	M
5	Ama	Kakrahawa-9	4	7	11	M	M
6	Tenuhawa	Parsha-8	4	7	11	M	F
7	Khudabagar	Ramwapur-1	4	11	15	M	M
	Total		26	60	86		

Source: TRPAP, 2007

Table 12.9 shows that seven sustainable tourism development committees are formed involving 86 members for sustainable and endemic tourism development of the region in seven VDCs. Among them 26 members are women and 60 are men. Chairperson and manager of these groups are male except the manager of Tenuhawa. Female in curtain have been motivated to empower and involve in the social activities at present situation of the area. These groups will be capable to launch income generating programmes after ending the project in the area. Due to their awareness, leadership development, option of income generates and public interrelation, it will support to alleviate poverty in future.

TABLE 12.10 : Tourism and Environmental Awareness, 2007

	Name of VDC	*Quantity*	*No. of Beneficiaries*	*Supporrting*
1. Incinerator	Madhuwani	1	896	
2. Private Toilet	Madhuwani	29	232	
3. Dustbin	Madhuwani	6	960	
4. Push Cart	Madhuwani	1	960	
5. Incinerator	Bhagawanpur	1	920	
6. Privet Toilet	Bhagawanpur	42	336	
7. Dustbin	Bhagawanpur	2	300	
8. Push Cart	Bhagawanpur	1	920	
9. Drainage	Bhagawanpur	174 m.	550	
10. Incinerator	Ama	1	208	
11. Private Toilet	Ama	25	200	
12. Push Cart	Ama	1	208	
13. Drainage	Ama	196m.	9500	
14. Incinerator	Tenuhawa	1	200	
15. Private Toilet	Tenuhawa	29	290	
16. Push Cart	Tenuhawa	1	700	
17. Dustbin	Tenuhawa	2	400	
18. Incinerator	Lumbini Adarsha	1	700	
19. Public Toilet	Lumbini Adarsha	1	1000	
20. Private Toilet	Lumbini Adarsha	11	110	
21. Dustbin	Lumbini Adarsha	5	40	
22. Push Cart	Lumbini Adarsha	1	170	
23. Drainage	Lumbini Adarsha	150m.	550	
24. Incinerator	Khudabagar	2	1200	
25. Private Toilet	Khudabagar	34	238	
26. Dustbin	Khudabagar	4	50	
27. Push Cart	Khudabagar	1	650	
28. Incinerator	Ekala	1	1500	
29. Private Toilet	Ekala	33	264	
30. Dustbin	Ekala	6	100	

Source: TRPAP

In course of environmental awareness and tourism development six basic requirements have been developed in the area of Lumbinī. Table 12.10 shows seven incinerators in order to burn wastages and to keep neat and clean at seven VDCs. Motivating for toilet use 203 private and one public toilet are built with the patronage of TRPAP. The people of this area usually use open field for urinal. 25 dustbins are made for systematic collection of wastages of this area. For internal and traditional visit of Lumbinī area 6 push carts are provided to the local people. 520 m drain is also constructed for rainy season. All these physical facilities are developed for sustainable tourism of Lumbinī. It will support for generating income to the local people and environmental awareness.

TABLE 12.11 : Impact of Tourism, 2007

Sl.No	*Types of Facilities*	*Name of VDC*	*Quantity*	*Benificiaries*
1.	Improved cooking stove	Madhuwnai	5	40
2.	Bio-gas	Madhuwnai	2	20
3.	Improved cooking stove	Bhagawanpur	65	240
4.	Bio-gas	Bhagawanpur	3	30
5.	Bio-gas	Ama	4	29
6.	Bio-gas	Tenuhawa	1	9
7.	Improved cooking stove	Khudabagar	3	25
8.	Bio-gas	Khudabagar	3	30
9.	Bio-gas	Ekala	5	40

Due to the impact of tourist activities Table 12.11 reveals that people of Lumbinī are modifying their lifestyle and behaviour day to day. 73 improving cooking stoves are provided to the dwellers at Lumbinī. 18 bio-gas plants are also made here. They used cow dung for cooking food and other usage of fuels. After conducting this programme at the villages they became capable to use improved cooking stove and bio-gas. In one hand it has supported for health and hygiene and other hand is helping for tourist visiting programmes.

TRPAP, under the umbrella of Rupandehi DDC, has planned five years Endemic Tourism Development programme in 2005. Its main slogan is that Lumbinī, the birthplace of Buddha, is the pilgrimage of peace; endemic tourism develops Rupandehi (DDC, 2005: 27). Five and ten years schemes are stated in priority basis to develop tourism at Rupandehi district. Lumbinī is its focus point. Cultural and natural resources, manpower training, transportation and communication sectors are mentioned in this long-term plan (Ibid.).

Problems and Recommendations

Being the potential site of tourism Lumbinī is not developed lack of network of communication, transportation and other infrastructure needed for healthy-tourism. Therefore, some problems and recommendations have been pointed out for the promotion of healthy tourism in Lumbinī and its peripheral area.

1. Attraction Improvement : Tourists should be informed all of the sites, viz. monasteries, meditation-centres, LIRI, museum, New Lumbinī village etc., who visit properly at Māyādevī temple. Lumbinī Festival should be organised on the occasion of Buddha Jayanti in each year. Art reflects the accurate and authentic evidences of the past life ways of the people. Museum plays a vital role to collect, exhibition, conservation and preservation of the art remains. In this situation, concerned coins, architectural-fragments, sculptures, paintings, photography, replicas of Buddha, etc. should be collected and properly displayed in Lumbini Museum in the promotion of cultural tourism.

2. **Trained Tourist Guides :** Tourist-guides should be capable to interpret native languages of the guests, especially Thāiland, South Korea, Japanese, Chinese and Cambodian languages. Such training institutes should be conducted at local level and local people should be participated at these programmes.

3. **Preservation of Aboriginal Culture :** Local cultural activates like *Biraha,* music and dance should be organised. Tharu culture and their lifestyle should be preserved of Lumbinī area. Hotel and local community groups should be made aware for their cultural activities.

4. **Awareness Programme :** Awakening programmes should be carried out organising meeting, seminar workshop and symposium to make conscious of their sacred monuments, sacred rituals, sacred functionaries, religious processions and festivals. Local people should be motivated that these are the potential sources for the growth of tourism in the region.

5. **Training Programme :** Governmental and non-governmental organisations should also organise tourist awareness training programmes in the neighbour's villages of Lumbinī complex including and extending the programmes of TRPAP. The

youth of the locality should be trained to conduct tourist activities in future.

6. **Hospital-facility :** Thousands of local people as well as pilgrims come here for the purpose of tourism and daily activities. There is need a hospital with good doctors to provide health facilities to the local people and foreign delegates. The health service of International Buddhist society, Cross Flow and RK project is not sufficient at vast area.

7. **Drinking-Water :** Drinking water is directly provided from the boring-system. It is not purified with the use of proper chemicals and problem of *arsenic*. Purified water should be supplied using reservoir system after chemical treatment.

8. **Toilet** : Toilet facility should be provided near the temple, monastery and vihar to the visitors without charge. Otherwise open toilet-tradition will create great problem of pollution.

9. **Art and craft product** : The tradition of local art and crafts should be encouraged, i.e. basket and mat weaving, moulding the images of Buddha and local products should be supplied for sale in the market. It will encourage involving at the tourist activities to the local people.

10. **Tourism information centre :** A tourism information centre, especially for the motivation to Lumbinī, should be operated at Butwal, Bhairahawā Lumbinī-road (Buddha-choka), Kathmandu, Narayanagadha and other proper sites in Nepāl and foreign countries. TRPAP has promoted two Tourist information centers at Belahiya and LDT complex, which must be upgraded in proper way in proper situation.

11. **Tourist materials** : Having been so popular Buddhist pilgrimage site cheap and reliable informative tourist materials, viz. pamphlets, booklets, cassette, maps, VCD, tape recorder and photographs are not available in proper sites. These materials should be made available to the tourists having interest in knowing in details about Lumbinī.

12. **Transportation :** Qualitative rickshaws and bicycles should be provided as preferred means of visiting sites at reasonable rate at this complex. Gautam Buddha Airport of Siddharthanagar should be upgraded in International Airport to

increase the flow of tourists in Lumbinī.

13. **Environment Creation :** The authority should be careful for stopping the begging monks and beggars, controlling noise, cleaning the garbage and litters. Industries should not be established about 10 km east, north, south and west from the sacred complex of Lumbinī. About 3 km on right and left side of Siddharthanagar to Taulihawa road there should be strictly prohibited to establish polluted factories. It should be developed as a **Peace Land** of the world.

14. **Co-ordination :** LDT, CFNT, IBS, PPPP, DDC, VDCs and other such agencies have carried out integrated programmes for the development of Lumbinī and its out skirts for long times. Their action plan and programmes are duplication lack of proper co-ordination among them. As a whole co-ordination committee should be constituted among the governmental and non-governmental organisations not only for tourism but also social changes of Lumbinī area.

15. **Proper Advertisement and Management :** Various requirements should be available to increase the number of tourists as well as to increase their length of stay. National and international mass media, viz. TV, VCD, Radio, Internet and E-mail facilities should be used to advertise of this Sacred Complex. Local groups and communities should be aware to mobilise local resources to promote all the pre-requisites for attraction of the area in the international markets. LDT, local VDCs, DDC and STDC must be active to use natural and cultural heritages of Lumbinī complex.

CHAPTER 13

Changes and Modernisation

Introduction

Changing the social, economic, religious and cultural elements in human beings is natural process and eternal phenomenon. Core and skirt of any sacred complex always play a vital role to change and modernise the socio-economic factors. Since the stone age of human civilisation, concept of religion has continued promoting the social norms and values in synchronous times. The teachings of Buddha and Buddhism have been contributing to the development of socio-economic status, promotion of daily lifestyles, promotion of public awareness and humanity. The sacred places, associated with Lord Buddha, viz. Kapilvastu, Lumbinī, Bodh Gaya and Kushinagar have inspired to create peace, harmony and non-violence in twentieth century all over the world. Lumbinī, the birthplace of Buddha have been contributing in up holding the social values, economic condition and cultural phenomenon through the interaction with domestic and foreign tourists; agencies or organisations who are involved to build monasteries, meditation-centres and other development works, monks and nuns coming from various countries. UNO, foreign and national agencies have taken keen interest to promote and develop the lifestyles of the local people and sacred complex. INGOs and NGOs have conducted many plan and programmes in the periphery of Lumbinī, motivating by Buddhism and peace. Lumbinī is the main attraction of the devotees and donor parties to influence their plan and programmes in this area.

Ancient *Lumbinigrama* had buried in the earth before the exploration of Führer in the last decade of the nineteenth century.

Yadav, Lodha, Muslim, Kewat, Harijan, Brahaman, Kurmi, Mallha, Paswan, Teli, Tharu, Dhobi, Kumal, etc. castes reside around the sacred complex of Lumbinī (CBS, 2002:82-94). Some of them had emigrated from India and migrated from the middle hill region of Nepāl. Tharu is known as an aboriginal caste of this Terai region. Führer has purposed that Tharu were ancestor of the Śākyas of Kapilvastu, belonged to Buddha. This study is limited on the lifestyle and changes of the local people around the Master Plan of Lumbinī project, especially Āmā, Bhagawanpur, Ekalā, Khudabagar, Tenuhawa, Lumbinī ādarsa and Madhuwani VDCs. Priest, monk, nun and other people who reside in project area are also observed to know their changes and modernisation including physical development of the complex. Several kinds of changes have slowly crept into the traditional beliefs, customs, food and drinks, dress and ornaments, position of family members, literacy rate, vocational training, physical constructions, organisation of functional groups, increasing of income sources and cultural activities due to the verbal communication and project works of the guests, who come to visit Lumbinī. Elements of modernisation is clearly reflected in the management and maintenance of the lifestyle of the people, monks, nuns, hostellers, shop-keepers and worker who reside in Lumbinī area.

Before the formation of Lumbinī Development Committee, local people were not conscious to change and modernise their lifestyles lack of verbal communication of pilgrims and donated-property in the project area. After launching various programmes and project-works at Lumbinī, they got chance to employ in Master Plan as well as project-activities in their villages. The effect of modernisation has been felt not only in the nuclear part of Lumbinī, but also in the lifestyle of the people of the villages located on the outskirts of Lumbinī complex. Master plan, attractions of UNO donor agencies, schooling, networks of roads, metallic road from Siddharthanagar, plane-service, fast means of communications, i.e. telephone, television, e-mail, internet and various activities, conducted by NGOs are the main contributing factors to this change and modernisation. These modern facilities have played a vital role in the acceleration of complete lifestyle and socio-cultural activities of Lumbinī.

Due to the keen interest of donor agencies, NGO, INGO and governmental authorities have been launching various development activities through the channel of Rupāndehi DDC and separately in their interest. District Health strengthening programme (DFID), Nepāl Safe Motherhood programme (DFID), TRPAP, UNDP, SNV, Livelyhood Community Forest programme (DFID), Rural Urban Partnership Programme, PPPP, RK, IBS, PDDP, Cross flow, FINIDA, BP with poor and LDF programmes have been launching in this area. Their main target is to change and modernise the lifestyle of the people who reside in the core and outskirts of Lumbinī. The elements of changes and modernisation are reflecting on social, economic and cultural aspects of the people.

Social Aspect

Social activities have been running under the aegis of Rupāndehi DDC, which are inspired by the donor agencies.

TABLE 13.1 : Community Organisation

S. No	*VDC's Name*	*No. of Cos formed*				*No. of Members*			*Position of Female*	
		Male	*Female*	*Mixed*	*Total*	*Male*	*Female*	*Total*	*Chairman*	*Manager*
1.	Bhagawanpur	12	7	9	28	508	347	855	9	9
2.	Lumbinī Adarsa	17	4	1	22	554	112	676	4	4
3.	Madhuwani	10	8	5	23	272	266	538	9	9
4.	Tenuhawa	9	3	7	19	292	124	416	3	3
5.	Akala	15	2	5	22	427	99	526	2	2
	Total	63	24	27	114	2053	948	3011		

Source: Rupandehi DDC, 2005.

Table 13.1 presents community organisations in course of implementation of various programs and plans in this area. 114 groups formed consisting 24 female, 63 male and 27 mixed groups. Women of muslim family are also associated in female and mixed groups. 21% is single female group, which plays a significant role to abolish *parda pratha* in this community. 3011 members are organised in community groups. Among them 31% members of the groups are female and 27 are in leadership. At Bhagawanpur and Tenuhawa VDCs 855 and 416 members are organised in community works.This table shows that male as well as female are actively participated in social functional groups.

TABLE 13.2 : Social Mobilisation

S.No.	Name of VDC	Total FG	Total Members F	M	Total	STG Members F	M	Total
1.	Bhagawanpur	2	6	26	32	6	24	30
2.	Ekala	3	27	45	72	14	30	44
3.	Lumbinī Adarsha	3	12	53	65	7	22	29
4.	Madhuwani	7	9	110	119	4	63	67
5.	Ama	6	8	71	79	0	18	18
6.	Tenuhawa	3	19	21	40	9	6	15
7.	Khudabagar	3	3	38	41	3	24	27
	Total	27	84	364	448	43	187	230

Source: TRPAP, 2007.

Table 13.2 shows social activities to modernise the community of Lumbinī. Among 448 members of functional groups 84 are women in 27 groups. They are active to conduct social activities in their groups. Involvement of the women has played a vital role to change and modernise family and community life ways. In 27 groups there are 230 members of sustainable tourism. Among them 43 members are female. They are involved in social activities as well as income generating programmes at the villages. These programmes are directly and indirectly supporting to modernise the society of Lumbinī complex.

TABLE 13.3 : Social Activities by COs

S. No.	VDC's Name	Toilet Construction	Track & Trail	Community Hall	Community School	Well cleaning	Canal cleaning
1.	Lumbinī Adarsa	71	100 meter	1	–	–	–
2.	Madhuwani	10	1 km	–	1	–	–
3.	Tenuhawa	339	500 meter	1	–	1	–
4.	Akala	3	500 meter	–	–	–	500
	Total	423	2.100 km	2	1	1	500

Source: Rupandehi DDC, 2005.

Table No. 13.3 presents that 423 private toilet are constructed at four village development committees, viz. Lumbinī Adarsa, Madhubani, Tenuhawa and Akala. Use of toilet environmental as well as health and hygiene may be fresh and useful. Two community halls are providing opportunities to gather the villagers and discuss about the agendas of developing their life ways. One community school building is built for school going children. Number of school going children is increasing due to the facility at the village. Drinking water-cleaning programmes are also launching. 2.1 km basic track and trail is constructed at the remote area of preceeding VDCs. Road support for transportation not only for tourists but also villagers.

TABLE 13.4 : Health Service of IBS

Years	*Male*	*Female*	*Child*	*Total*
2050	6650	9750	6400	22800
2051	8600	9400	5800	23800
2052	9000	7500	7100	23600
2053	7950	8600	8650	25200
2054	10100	9700	6900	26700
2055	8900	8650	6200	23750
2056	7800	9600	8300	25700
2057	8100	8400	6200	22700
2058	6400	10400	6900	23700
2059	11400	12600	8300	32300
2060	14200	15700	12500	42400
2061	18700	16439	5965	41104
2062	17123	18268	7025	42416
2063	14820	9695	4831	29346
Total	149743	154702	101071	405516

Source: IBS, 2007

International Buddhist Society has been operating Amrit Free Health Centre with the support of Exchange Himalayan, French Organisation since 18 September 1993. It's main aim is to provide free service to the poor and uplift the living standards of the local people of Lumbinī area. IBS is providing ambulance service, minor irrigation project, door to door check-up program for pregnant ladies, *Bhikshu* training, scholarship, health camp, community awareness, non-formal education and health service programmes to the inhabitants of Lumbinī area. Among these health programme is very effective due to absence of government hospital in the area. This center has treated the patients of neuritis, leucorrhoea, gastritis, diarrhea's, paralysis, etc. Table No 13.4 presents that this centre has provided medical service to 405516 people within 14 years at Lumbinī area. Among them female and children are 38.14 % and 24.93 % respectively. The ratio of the patients is increasing per year. In 2050, 2054 and 2063 the number of the patients is 22800, 26700 and 29346 respectively. Among them female are high. Children are also properly cared by the specialists. The service of Amrit Free Health Centre is very popular and is also motivating to the local people towards Buddha and Buddhism. Death rate of the child and mother is also decreasing at this area. Their social and economic life ways are also changing.

TABLE 13.5: Trained Manpower

Sl.No.	*Types of Trainings*	*2002*	*2003*	*2004*	*2005*	*2006*
1.	First aid	23	30	37	42	48
2.	Mid-wife	23	30	37	42	48
3.	Clinical health education	459	700	850	1052	12500
4.	School health education	2095	2941	4225	5076	6078
5.	HE for NFE students	397	686	660	739	1050
6.	HE for leader of women groups	184	240	296	336	480

Source: CFNT, 2007

Cross Flow Nepal Trust has launched health, education, vocational training, school enrolment support, newspaper publication, celebration of international woman day, world child day, human right declaration day, world literacy day, condom day; institutional development training, social mobilisation, toilet, drain and public hall construction programmes at six village development committees, viz. Lumbinī Adarsa, Khudabagar, Ekala, Bhagawanpur, Madhubani and Tenuhawa. Within a short span of time these plan and programmes have played a dynamic role to modernise the life ways of the people at Lumbinī. Trainings in various sectors have launched for sustainable and modernise. Table No. 12.5 shows the skilled manpower in first aid, mid-wife, clinical health, school health, health education for non-formal students and women group leaders. Trained number of first aid and mid-wife is same from 2002 to 2006. Maximum number is 48 in 2006. 12500 members are trained in 2006. 5076 and 6078 members are involved in school health training programme in 2005 and 2006 respectively. Non-formal student and leader of women groups are participated in 1050 and 480 in 2006. These programmes have supported in public health and awareness at the remote villages.

TABLE 13.6 : Water-Supply Schemes

S.No.	*VDC's Name*	*Scheme-Name*	*Benifitted population*	*Cost per capita*	*Remarks*
1	Bhagawanpur	Suction Tube-well	1078	312	
2	Madhuwani	Suction Tube-well	588	403	
3	Akala I	Suction Tube-well	2848	175	
	Akala II	Suction Tube-well	2750	—	
	Akala III	Suction Tube-well	2534	—	
			9798		

Source: Finida, 2003: phase III.

Table 13.6 shows that this programme was carried out at Bhagawanpur, Madhuwani and Ekala VDCs. 9798 people were benefitted from this project work. Ekala VDC was the focus point in tube-well scheme. Finida has operated many programmes related with drinking water and sanitation of the region. Their lifestyle, food and drink, dress and ornament, social behaviours as well as traditions, viz. *bala vivaha, anamela vivaha*, dowary system and *parda pratha* have also undergone change and modernise due to these social activities. Here only a few people are using their traditional dress, ornaments and daily usage objects. The youths of Lumbinī area visit monastery zone for employment. They generally help the pilgrims and the people who come to enjoy the fair and festivals, especially Buddha Jayanti, by organising dramas, dances and music programmes and other kinds of recreational activities. In this process, TRPAP has formed a group of *Biraha Geeta*, traditional song of indigenous people, and sing on special request of the visitors in charge. Training of management capacity enhancement, group management, bee keeping, strategic plans, etc. are few examples of the training. Involvement of more women in the decision making level is the focus of TRPAP. At present household women are capable to come out from their houses and participate in the different training programme such as women empowerment as well as in social activities. Conducting programmes in Lumbinī and its outskirts have played a vital role to change and modernise the living standard of the local people day to day.

Economic Aspect

Centre of Rural Development and Self-help, Collective Development and Multi-purpose Co-operative, Pragatishil Women Development Co-operative, Indreni Rural Development Centre, TRPAP, FINIDA, CFNT, IBS and local agencies have been launching various programmes to promote the economic status of the people. These programmes have supported to fulfil the objectives of poverty alleviation underlined in the Ninth and Tenth Five year plans of Nepal Government. The self-reliant concept is needed in order to match with there source base of the poor communities, VDCs and DDCs, especially in the remote area. In order to focus further on the disadvantage and poor communities, the programmes have made a special provision of support fund for poor. TRPAP (Figs. 47 & 48), FINIDA, RK, IBS, CFNT and Bisweswar with poor programmes have played a significant role for sustainable development and income generation. Almost the plans and programmes have concentrate to the Sacred Complex of Lumbinī, associated with Buddha and Buddhism. FINIDA and BP with poor programmes had conducted rainwater using and household latrine schemes to the deprived and disadvantaged community together with the collaboration of DDC. Such collaboration among the same agencies has added a new dimension in addressing the needs of the poorer communities in rural area.

TABLE 13.7 : Physical Infrastructure Development

Sl. No.	*Facilities*	*Name of the VDC*	*Quantity*	*Benefited people*
	ACCESS			
1	Road Maintenance	Madhuwani	1600 m.	3013
2	Road Maintenance	Bhagawanpur	190 m.	960
3	Road Maintenance	Ama	2000 m.	8500
4	Road Maintenance	Tenuhawa	1000 m.	5000
5	Road Maintenance	Lumbini Adarsha		560
6	Road Maintenance	Khudabagar	3480 m.	1950
7	Pond rehabilitation	Khudabagar	200 m.	439
8	Road Maintenance	Ekala	3800 m.	3296
9	Pond rehabilitation	Ekala		1090
	ACCOMMODATION			
10	Resting Chair	Madhuwani	1	248
11	Resting Chair	Bhagawanpur	1	280
12	Resting Chair	Lumbini Adarsha	2	1100
13	Resting Chair	Khudabagar	2	439
14	Resting Chair	Ekala	1	1090

Source: TRPAP, 2007.

Table 13.7 represents road maintenance and pond repair-ing work was done at Lumbinī Adarsa, Tenuhawa, Khudabagar, Ekala, Ama and Madhubani VCDs. Due to transportation facilities it became easy to sell their products and marketing.

TABLE 13.8 : Irrigation and Tourism Factors

Sl.No	*Programmes*	*Name of VDC*	*Quantity*	*Beneficiaries*
1	Dhiki Pump	Madhuwani	32	256
2	Tourist Canteen	Madhuwani	1	10
3	Handicraft Prod. & Selling Center	Madhuwani	1	472
4	Drinking Water	Bhagawanpur	1	240
5	Sculpture Prod. & Selling Center	Bhagawanpur	1	240
6	Dhiki Pump	Ama	44	452
7	View Point	Tenuhwa	1	12000
8	Dhiki Pump	Lumbini Adarsha	27	450
9	Dhiki Pump	Khudabagar	39	214
10	Dhiki Pump	Ekala	57	464

Source: TRPAP, 2007.

TABLE 13.9 : Households having Agriculture Land, Livestock and Poultry

S.N.	*VDC's Name*	*Households Total*	*Having Agriculture land*	*Livestock only*	*Poultry only*	*Land & Livestock*	*Land & Poultary*	*Livestock & Poultary*	*Land, Livestock & Poultary*	*Non of all*
1.	Ama	1374	264	12	0	963	5	3	73	54
2.	Bhagawanpur	1372	247	16	1	759	15	5	255	74
3.	Akala	1230	109	21	4	596	10	10	415	65
4.	Khudabagar	605	102	8	0	242	16	5	192	40
5.	Lumbini Adarsa	1092	232	19	2	527	19	9	176	108
6.	Madhuwani	824	118	31	2	364	17	9	104	179
7.	Tenuhawa	1193	238	19	8	460	36	10	349	73
	Total:	7690	1310	126	17	3911	118	51	1564	593

Source: CBS, 2002

TABLE 13.10 : Households Operating Small Scale Non-agricultural Economic Activity by Type of Activity for VDC.

S.No.	*VDC's Name*	*Households Nos.*	*Having economic Activity*	*Not having economic Activity*	*Manufac-turing*	*Trade Business*	*Transport*	*Services*	*Others*
1.	Ama	1374	49	1325	2	28	0	2	17
2.	Bhagawanpur	1372	126	1246	10	83	1	10	22
3.	Akala	1230	202	1028	9	99	2	77	15
4.	Khudabagar	605	50	555	0	13	5	8	24
5.	Lumbini Adarsa	1092	139	953	2	69	20	14	34
6.	Madhuwani	824	114	710	9	83	2	2	18
7.	Tenuhawa	1193	238	955	3	80	6	53	97
	Total:	7690	918	6772	35	455	36	165	227
	Percentage%		11.938%	88.063%	0.455%	5.917%	0.468%	2.146%	2.952%

Source: CBS, 2002.

Table 13.8 represents the pre-requisites for agriculture and tourism development at Lumbinī area. Dhiki pumps are made at Madhubani, Ama, Lumbinī Adarsa, Khudabagar and Ekala VDCs. Tourist canton, handicrafts production and selling centers are at Madhubani and Bhagawanpur. Tourist view point is constructed at Tenuhawa. These activities are changing their lifestyle.

The economic condition of the people is very poor and opportunities of employment are limited. Table 13.9 shows that about 20% people depend on land, livestock and poultry farming in jointly. Among them 17% people are using only agriculture land. More than 50% among them depend on land and livestock. Livestock and poultry farming people are only 1.63% and 0.22% separately. They cannot save money from agriculture farming. Their income decides the lifestyle and status in the society.

Table 13.10 shows only 11.93% household people are engaged in economic activities and remaining are unemployed except quarterly involve in agriculture. 5.91% and 2.14% household people are engaged in business and services respectively. Industrial and transportation system is very poor.

The authority has also launched the programmes to promote the lifestyle and economic status of the local people.

TABLE 13. 11 : Number of Village experts by sectors

S. No.	*VDC's Name*	*Agriculture*		*Livestock*		*Community Health*		*Audit*		*Total*	
		Male	*Female*	*Male*	*Female*	*Male*	*Female*	*Male*	*Female*	*Male*	*Female*
1.	Bhagawanpur	3	-	1	-	-	-	-	4	4	4
2.	Lumbini Adarsa	2	-	1	1	-	-	1	-	4	1
3.	Madhuwani	2	-	2	-	-	-	-	1	4	1
4.	Tenuhawa	2	-	2	-	-	-	3	-	7	-
5.	Akala	-	-	1	-	-	-	-	5	-	-
	Total	9	-		1	-	-	4		19	6

Source: Rupandehi DDC, 2005.

Table 13.11 presents the experts by various sectors, viz. agriculture, livestock and auditing at the VDC level in this area. Programme under the aegis of DDC, total 25 experts have been trained within a short span of time in 2003-2004. Female are also trained in audit. They can do up-to-date their group-account as well as family budget.

TABLE 13.12 : Trained community members

S.No.	*VDC's Name*	*Vegetable Farming*	*Account & Record*	*Bee-keeping*	*Live-farming*	*Others*
1.	Bhagawanpur	-	20	-	-	-
2.	Lumbini Adarsa	25	22	-	-	-
3.	Madhuwani	35	15	-	25	1
4.	Tenuhawa	-	38	7	-	-
5.	Akala	46	47	-	-	-
	Total	106	142	7	25	1

Source: Rupandehi DDC, 2005.

In this context Table 13.12 represents 142 and 106 members of Bhagawanpur, Lumbinī Adarsa, Madhuwani, Tenuhawa and Akala VDCs were trained in vegetable farming and account respectively under the aegis of Rupendehi DDC. Seven persons of Tenuhawa were trained in bee-keeping sector. Bee-keeping is a suitable and cash-oriented industry in this area. 25 members were also skilled in modern concept for live-farming sector.

National resource center for non-formal education has launched community learning centres at Madhubani, Khudabagar, Tenuhawa, Ekla, Bhagawanpur and Lumbinī Adarsa village development committees during 2000 to 2006. This project was carried out with the joint venture of World Terakoya Movement France, National Federation of UNESCO Associations in Japan and International Buddhist Society Lumbinī. This project has focused the birthplace of Buddha, Lumbinī. Three community halls were built at Madhubani, Khudabagar and Tenuhawa villages. Literacy, environmental conservation, community development, women group, agriculture group, horticulture group, revolving fund management group, fish farming group, bee keeping group, goat rearing group and library management groups have formed for social and economical change in the rural area of Lumbinī. Table 13.13 presents it's real situation in action.

Table 13.13 : Functional Groups

S.No.	*Name of the groups*	*No. of group*	*Male*	*Female*	*Total Groups*
1	Women saving and credit group	11	0	259	259
2	Vegetable group	25	340	126	466
3	Poultry farming	3	20	27	47
4	Pigeon farming	1	7	0	7
5	Goat rearing	7	36	93	129
6	Fish farming	5	36	0	36
7	Bee keeping	3	22	9	31
8	Banana farming	2	23	2	25
9	Buffalo rearing	4	34	7	41
	Total	61	518	523	1041

Source: TRPAP, 2007.

Table 13.14 presents that from March 2002 to June 2007 TRPAP has conducted many trainings for poverty alleviation at seven VDCs of Lumbinī area. Its main focus area is sustainable and endemic tourism development of the area. To provide employment to the local people local tourist guide and advance guide, front office dealing, small hotel and lodge management, food beverage and service, rickshaw pullers and English language trainings are conducted. Service and production selling schemes are main target area of this project work. Handicraft production, terracotta images production, *katera* mat production, sculpture production, banana fiber design and packaging box trainings have carried during the project work. Female are involved in house keeping, moulding terracotta figurines, mat weaving, banana fibre production, improving cooking stove and food beverage and service training programmes. Training periods of these programmes are from 2 to 32 days. In sculptural production seven female are involved for 32 days. At last of the project work advance local guide and follow up trainings are carried out. 197 female and 403 male have involved in 28 programmes of trainings. These programmes are supporting to generate income, social change, interrelation among them, international understanding through the channel of the tourists, political awareness and cultural changes in their daily life ways. It is the consequence of Lumbinī,

TABLE 13.14 : Trainings

S. No.	*Name of the Training*	*Total Participants* F	M	Total	*Date of Training*	*Duration of Training*
1	Local Guide	0	19	19	24 March to 8 April 2002	15
2	Small Hotel & Lodge management	1	13	14	15 to 26 Sept. 2003	12
3	Food & Beverage Service	6	6	12	21 to 26 Sept. 2003	6
4	Front Office & English Language	5	8	13	21 to 26 Sept. 2003	6
5	Rickshaw puller's	0	50	50	31 May to 6 June 2003	7
6	Local Guide	0	18	18	13 to 24 June 2003	12
7	Housekeeping	19	2	21	19 to 24 June 2003	6
8	Handicraft Production	3	0	3		
9	Improve Cooking Stove	8	13	21	16 to 21 Sept. 2004	6
10	Small Hotel & Lodge management	3	22	25	2 to 11 Nov. 2004	10
11	Local Handicraft	20	0	20	23 April to 6 June 2004	45
12	Local Guide	3	22	25	13 to 24 June 2004	12
13	Mud Statue	12	11	23		
14	Mushroom Cultivation	8	15	23	23 to 28 Oct. 2004	6
15	Basic Hospitality & Rickshaw pullers	0	57	57	2004	
16	Sculpture Production	7	13	20	23 May to 24 June 2005	32
17	Muj Grass Handicraft design	19	0	19	29 May to 1 June 2005	3
18	Katera Mat weaving	12	0	12	2 to 17 June 2005	15
19	Rickshaw puller's	0	74	74	10 to 15 Sept. 2005	6
20	Banana Fiber Product design	18	0	18	13 to 18 June 2005	6
21	Biraha Choroeography	0	8	8	25 to 31 Dec. 2005	7
22	Pakaging box	2	6	8	13 to 22 Nov. 2005	10
23	Gender Equity	3	12	15	13 to 14 Dec. 2005	2
24	Advance Local Guide	3	14	17	16 to 22 Sept. 2005	7
25	Account and Management	0	14	14	8 to 10 May 2006	3
26	Follow up Training (Handicraft)	33	0	33	12 Sept. 2006	1
27	Follow up Training (Packaging)	2	3	5	11 to 12 Sept. 2006	2
28	Advanced Training (Sculpture Producing)	10	3	13	10-15 June 2007	5
	Total	197	403	600		

Source: TRPAP, 2007

the birthplace of Buddha. This sacred place has played a dynamic role to change and modernise the contemporary society.

After providing training, TRPAP has offered proper venture capital fund for the people of seven VDCs. Social Mobilisers of TRPAP have done research about their potentiality and finding their ability help them providing soft loan for proper jobs and business. Sustainable Tourism Development Committees (STDC) have been financed to develop infrastructure of their employment. Not only the TRPAP, but also other agencies have also launched various programmes to promote their economic status under the umbrella of Rupāndehi DDC. Community Organisations have been saving proper amount for their needs and promotion. Local people use this saving fund in order to solve their daily problems. One of the success stories of this sector is group install *Dhiki* pump. The members of Suryamukhi vegetable producers and Functional Group of Ekala-4 are proud to be in group following the imitation of TRPAP activities in their village. The group was contributed Rs. 20,000 for the installation of a *Dhiki* pump (water pump) for the members of the FG in the village. All these activities have been carried out focusing the birthplace of Lord Buddha and Buddhism by various agencies and organisations. Thus, all of these programmes are undoubtedly the consequence of Sacred Complex of Lumbinī.

TABLE 13.15 : Score of Development Wheel

Sl.No.	*Name of VDC*	*Score from Development Wheel*		
		APPA	*Re-APPA*	*Change (%)*
1	Bhagawanpur	39.5	55.5	16
2	Madhuwani	43.8	58.6	14.8
3	Ekala	51.57	79.52	27.95
4	Khudabagar	51.5	76.2	24.7
5	Ama	47.5	62	14.5
6	Lumbini Adarsha	33.07	44.32	11.25
7	Tenuhawa	40.33	61.05	20.72
	Total	307.27	437.19	129.92

Source: TRPAP, 2007

TRPAP has conducted various programmes to alleviate poverty at Lumbinī area during 2002 to 2007. Awareness programme, construction of public halls, infrastructures of tourism development, trainings, new technology of farming, etc. programmes was launched. Table No.13.15 presents appreciative participatory planning action, re-APPA chart and changing ratio at the lifestyle of the people. In total 129.92% is changed in 307.27. At Ekala 27.95% has changed and Lumbinī Adarsa is changed only 11.25. Khudabagar and Tenuhawa are changed in 24.7% and 20.725 respectively. Rural poverty alleviation program has also modified the daily life ways of the local people at Lumbinī area.

Cultural Aspect

Almost the Hindu and Muslim people reside in the outskirts of Lumbinī complex. Buddhists are also coming from various sites to reside in the monasteries and in their own houses. The atmosphere of Lumbinī area is favourable to create unity in diversity due to the tolerance of various sects, groups and communities. On the occasions of fair and festivals, local clubs and groups, generally entertain the pilgrims by organising traditional dance, music and drama. Dance and music are organised in Buddhist tradition based on *Jataka* stories. The mother tongue of the natives is Bhojapuri. Nowaday they use Nepāli, Hindi, English and Bhojapuri language due to the verbal communication among domestic and international visitors. The youths who work in the hotels, restaurant and monasteries speak Japanese, Chinese, Korean, Tibetan and Tamil languages in proper situation. Realizing the necessity and importance of the cultural elements, an organisation named 'Lumbinī Cultural Buddha *Biraha Geet Sadak Natak'* is established for the conservation, promotion and to show the visitors in proper time and situation.

Master Plan Area

Due to the modernisation of the area, many settlements have been populated in the vicinities of this sacred complex. Mayalawar, Padariya, Parsa, etc. residences have been changing their physical structures day by day. Modern buildings in the market area and important villages of the area have greatly altered the physical look of Lumbinī. In the three zonal areas of Master Plan, viz. Archaeological Garden, Monastic Zone and New Lumbinī village, many buildings have been built based on agreement with LDT. Re-storied Māyādevī temple has added superstructure component like a stūpa instead of *saptaratha* style, old temple. Foundation and structure of the original temple is preserved to show visitors and devotees. Puskarini pond has been cleaned and the artificial-mound on the south of Māyādevī temple, which was formed in course of excavation by Kaisher Shumsher Rana from 1933 to 1939, is also removed by cutting soil. Circular pond is going to be completed as mentioned in the Master Plan. Ring road is made of gravel on the bank of circular-pond.

On the east of Monastic Zone, Myanmar government has completed Lokamuni Pagoda Temple, vihar and guesthouses. International nuns Association and Maha Bodhi Society of India have completed their physical construction. Śri Lanka and Thāiland monasteries and vihars are also operating after their construction. On the north-east of Thai Royal Monastery, internal cemented road and bridge are constructed to adjoin Lumbinī Parsa road. Cambodian monastery is under construction. Central canal is also cleaned on the occasion of Buddha Jayanti and Lumbinī Day.

The eastern portion is known as Hinayān or Theravadi complex. Many stūpas, monasteries, guesthouses, temples and meditation centres have been constructing by various national and international agencies. Among these stūpa of Mananga Sewa Samaja, Chinese Temple, Tara Foundation of Germany and Korean guesthouses have completed and are operated. Vietnam temple, France, Japanese-Sokayo, Bhutan and Korean Temples are under construction. Lumbinī International Research Institute, Museum, Nipponzon Myohoji (World Peace Stūpa) and Hokke Hotel have been operating their proper duties. Hotel Mikasha is also completed. Śri Laṅkān pilgrimage house is also operating. Boundary wall is going to be complete. Local people have got opportunity for employment in physical constructions of all the unskilled, semi-skilled and skilled manpower in their proper sectors. Physical development of Lumbinī is not only changed the internal facing of Master Plan, but also the lifestyle and models of the people. Providing the sources of income, it has also played a vital role to modernise this area. Sacred functionaries and donor agencies have also done various activities in order to change and modernise the lifestyle of the people.

The monks and nuns of the Hinayān and Mahāyan schools are coming from the related countries. Their lifestyle, food and drinks, habits and social behaviours have also undergone changes. Old priest of Māyādevī Temple is also changing his lifestyle in Buddhist rules and regulations, who was Hindu at the beginning. Mixed-Buddhist culture and traditions have been practiced in this complex. Physical progress has brought a tremendous change and modernisation. In the process of modernisation, several kinds of changes have crept into social, economic, cultural life of the people of Lumbinī. The changes are not only in the lifestyle, but also in its physical development, food, drinks, dress, ornaments and aesthetic traditions. Almost the elements of changes and modernisations have depended in the process of development of Lumbinī.

CHAPTER **14**

Summary and Conclusions

The researcher has made an attempt in this research work to throw light on the sacred geography, history, Master Plan and development, art, architecture, pilgrims and pilgrimage, sacred performances, fair and festivals, sacred specialists, conservation and preservation, development of tourism and modernisation of sacred complex of Lumbinī. In course of this present study, Buddhist texts, Chinese accounts and field survey have been used. Sacred performances, specialists, fair and festivals, Master Plan, art, architecture and cultural contribution of Lumbinī are mentioned in brief. Methodologically, the study of Kashi, Ridi, Janakpur and Gaya has provided the first basic structure for such an apprasial of civilisation, the present study of Lumbinī the birthplace of Buddha provide the complete superstructure in its details.

The study area is located about 22 km west from Siddharthanagar, district headquarter of Rupāndehi district in the western Terai region of Nepāl. It is on the foot of Churia range, which is formed of the molasse deposit of the Siwālika group. Terai is composed of gravels and sands of the late Pleistocene to Holocene age. The river systems of Telār, Dāno, Harahawā, Koṭhī and Tināu have formed this area. During the Buddhist period this area, with hot and humid weather was covered with indigenous trees. At present, Lumbinī Development Trust (Committee) has planted hedge plantation, which is changed into a dense forest. Telār and Harahawā are the main rivers in the periphery of Lumbinī complex. Lumbinī was the ancient pilgrimage route from north to south, east to west, north to west and north to east during the period of the Śākyas.

Lumbinī have been occupied from the Mauryan period up to Modern times, we find remains of the human activities for all these periods. During the reign of the Śākya and Koliya many artistic activities had performed in the field of pottery, terracotta human and animal figurines, coins and architectural fragments. In the third century BC, Aśoka installed monolithic stone pillar in Lumbinī, which is inscribed in Brāhmi script. The pillar inscription of Lumbinī is the concrete evidence to identify the birthplace of Lord Buddha. Chinese pilgrims Fa-Hien, Hiuen-Tsiang and Shui-Ching-Chu had also mentioned the pilgrimage tradition and cultural details of Lumbinī. Their details throw light on the anthropological modes of the synchronous times. Khasa, Malla and Sen Dynasties had ruled here in the Medieval period. After the unification of this area by Gorkha a conflict arose between the British Government of India and Nepāl due to the possession of land of Butwal area, including Lumbinī area. This area was of Nepāl in course of Sugauli Treaty between East India Company and Nepāl.

To promote Lumbinī as the international pilgrimage site, an International Lumbinī Development Committee was formed in 1970 under the chairmanship of Nepāl. The Committee has the representive of 15 nations under the leadership of UNO. The renowned Japanese architect Prof. Kenzo Tange prepared the Master Plan of Lumbinī in 1978. With a total area of 25 sq. mile is used in master plan. New Lumbinī village, Monastic zone and Sacred garden area are divided one sq. mile area in each complex from north to south respectively. Asian Highway is also proposed from the north of New Lumbinī village. Foundations of school building, standard tourist Hokke Hotel and general basic infrastructures have been completed at this area.

Lumbinī International Research Institute and Lumbinī Museum have been operating at cultural complex. Theravadi and Mahāyani monastic zone, immediately south of Friendship bridge of Harahawā river, have been rapidly developed into Buddhist World. Thāi, Calcutta, Myanmar, Śri Lanka and International Nun's Association have built monasteries in their national styles and tradition in the eastern portion. Cambodia monastery is under construction. China, Korea, Vietnam, Japan, Bhutan, Mongolia,

Germany and Nepālese nations and institutes have been constructing and operating at present. Eternal Peace Flame is burning as the symbol of World Peace immediately south of central canal. Sacred garden consists Aśokan pillar, Māyādevī temple, Sacred tank, ruins of ancient stūpas, vihars and Royal vihar of Dharmodaya Committee. Administrative block of LDT and police station are also located to the south of Māyādevī temple. Master Plan has not completed even now.

Art is an effective medium as expressing the soul of human civilisation. It reflects the socio-culture, economic and religious modes and thoughts of a community. The Sacred Complex of Lumbinī yielded terracotta human and animal figurines, stone sculptures, coins, seals and sealing, beads, bangles and pottery from sixth century BC upto the Gupta-Pala periods. Finding of a 'Conglomerate Stone' in excavation of the complex has also provided a definite evidence to fix the exact birthplace of Lord Buddha. Panel of Buddha and Yasodhara in Royal bed, *Dharmacakra*, *Panchadhyani* Buddha, Bodhisattvas, Avalokiteswar in terracotta, Nativity sculpture of Buddha and stone fragments are unique pieces of art of this complex. Sunga tradition in terracotta figurines were made in the mould techniques. Kushāṇa figurines reflect that the artist did not use the mould and used inferior quality clay mixed with grit, husk and other impurities. In the Gupta period, moulding technique which was commonly practiced in the Sunga period was again revived. A bronze figure of Padampani Avalokiteswar, image of Ganesa and a figure of the devotee throw light on the metalwork and the tradition of Sena-Pala art tradition in the complex of Lumbinī. Different types of pottery from Lumbinī help us in understanding the cultural components of the various periods of human occupations.

Religious architecture of Buddhism, viz. monolithic stone pillar, railing, Stūpas, vihars and temple of Māyādevī as well as their construction periods from the Mauryan to Gupta periods have been exposed. Inscribed Aśokan pillar is the real evidence to identify the birthplace of Buddha. The shaft of the stone pillar is plain and circular in section, slightly tapering upwards. It is chisseled out of a single block of stone. Crowning figure on the abacus was horse as recorded by the Chinese accounts. Mauryan Stūpas were provided with hemispherical dome of brick works with *medhi* as the base. It was provided with a dome and umbrellas with square railing in solid. In later times, ostentatious stūpas of great height were built by filling the core with earth or rubble. Vihar, being a hostel of the Buddhist monks and nuns in ancient period has been developed as an organised educational institute and academic centre of Buddhist learning providing residence with many rooms for their use. The basement of the vihar was built on quadrangular plan consisting of a series of cells enclosed from three sides and the remaining side is left open as entrance gateway. The structural remains of the vihars have been discovered from Lumbinī. The ancient temple of Māyādevī was based on Nagar style. Restoried-Māyādevī temple is based on stūpa model on its superstructure. Remains of ancient temple are covered in the sanctum of the shrine. Ring-well had been constructed of precisely hewn slabs of bricks in the courtyard of the vihar complex. According to Master Plan, concerned nations as well as institutes have been constructed stūpa, vihar, monasteries and guesthouses based on their national architectural traditions and techniques. Wall paintings of the shrines are belonged to the lifestyles, teaching and events of Gautam Buddha. Fresco paintings of Royal vihar of Nepāl, Mustang-vihar and Lotus Stūpa of Tara foundation are remarkable elements of Modern art tradition.

Lumbinī is an important pilgrimage site for not only the Buddhist, but also human beings. It is playing a vital role in integrating the societies of this part of the World into one cognate order. The religious merits support and lead one to attain *Nirvana* in the end. Aśoka, Chinese visitors Fa-Hien, Hiuen-Tsiang, Shui-Chi-Chu and Ripu Malla, king of Karnali Pradesh, had visited in Lumbinī in ancient and medieval periods in course of their pilgrimage. After the exploration and excavation of A. Führer, P.C. Mukherji and Keshar Sumsher J.B.R., many VIP and VVIP, renowned persons, had also visited in Lumbinī. In 1967 U-Thant, the then General Secretary of the UNO, had visited Lumbinī. Late King Mahendra had shown keen interest to promote Lumbinī as a sacred complex for all the human beings. According to Master

Plan the various nations and institutes to promote pilgrims and pilgrimage tradition of Lumbinī have built stūpas, vihars, monasteries and rest houses. A large number of people since the Ancient period have continued to come here from China, India and other western countries. The pilgrims from Japan, South-Korea, Thāiland, Taiwan, China, India, British, France, etc. come here on the important days of festivals to offer their prayer and respect to Lord Buddha. In course of field study the ratio of the pilgrims has been categorised based on profession, literacy, age group, number of a team, modes of stay, number of national and international pilgrims. 26 and 22 per cent of peasants and students have visited Lumbinī respectively in the study period. 31 and 18 per cent literate and illiterate pilgrims have visited here respectively. Pilgrims between the age of 21 to 40 years are 34 per cent and 41 to 60 age group is only 28 per cent. 48 per cent of pilgrims visit in Lumbinī in-group. 35 per cent stay at hotel and lodges of Lumbinī. 26 per cent pilgrims stay at hotels of Bhairahawā. 40 per cent and 60 per cent pilgrims are domestic and foreign respectively.

Daily treatment of the shrines took the form of sacred performances. Various performances have been conducted with full preparation, devotion of mind, religious merits and sense of obligation. Daily and special performances have been conducted in the premises of the shrines. Daily performances of the vihar, monastery and stūpas have been conducting by the concerned authorities in the morning and evening, twice a day. Theravadi, Mahāyani and Vajrayāni chant their traditional *sutras* and *mantras* on daily worship in the shrines. Theravadi follow up Pali verses in hard and fastly. They do not like to change original *sutras*, i.e. triple gem, five, eight and ten precepts. Mahāyani and Vajrayāni play musical instruments in course of their prayer. Buddhist songs are charming and interesting to create peace and harmony in the mind of the devotees. Thāi, India, Myanmar, Sri Lanka and Nuns Association of Nepāl follow up Theravadi rules and monasteries in the western complex, viz. China, Korea, Vietnam, Germany, etc. follow up Mahāyani tradition. Mustang Vihar and Japanese Nipponzan Myohoji belong to Vajrayāni traditions. They follow up *tantrika* rule and regulations.

The fairs and festivals are an integral part of the culture, tradition, rite and rituals of the Buddhist as well as Hindu society. In course of conducting religious activities, people feel the entertainment by praying, singing, dancing and meeting with the people and feasting. Due to the mixed settlement of Hindu, Buddhist and Muslim people in the periphery of Lumbinī, Buddha Jayanti, Barsavassa, Dashain, Deepavali, Chhaṭa, Māghi, Śivarātri, Basanta Panchami, Holi Purnima, Rama Navami and Chaitra Purnima are celebrated by the local people. Buddha Jayanti, Barsavassa and Peace March are directly associated with Buddha and Buddhism in Lumbinī. LDT and other local agencies celebrate Buddha Jayanti in three day at Vaiśākha *sukla purnima*. On this occasion, the main functions are cleaning the sacred site and worshiping the shrines. Inter school oratory competition and inter campus essay writing competition on the topic belonging to Lumbinī have also organised on this occasion. At the last day of this occasion, the Chief Guest provide prizes, scholarship and certificates to the winner in various competitions. Barsavassa starts from *Shravana purnima* to *Kartika purnima* about three month to live at a site to the monk and nuns. Other special fair and festivals are celebrated by the local people based on their spiritual feelings.

Monk, nun, priest, musician, guard, gardener and barbers are directly and indirectly involved in daily performances of the shrines. The authority at the last of the nineteenth century had appointed functionaries of Māyādevī temple, priest and a guard. Dharmodaya Samittee of Lumbinī had also managed the performances of Māyādevī temple for some time. However, the LDT has left to conduct regular performances at Māyādevī temple due to Buddhist shrine. According to contract letter between LDT and concerned institutes, five Bhikshus and five their helpers, in total ten persons, are permitted to stay in each vihar, stūpa or monastery of Lumbinī area. Foreign Bhikshus has permission for a year-visa. Five years visa system is also providing by HMG of Nepāl for their facility. National and international monks, nuns and other functionaries are engaged in daily performances of Lumbinī complex.

In modern trend mass tourism, cultural tourism, pilgrimage tourism and nature tourism are very useful in the promotion of the local people as well as to generate national income as the holy site for the Buddhist. The ratio of foreign tourist is decreasing from 1997 to 2002. Its ratio is satisfactory in the years of 2002 and 2004. Due to the violence and unlawful activities in Nepāl, foreign tourists are not visiting in proper ratio. Śri Laṅkā, South Korea, Japan, China, Taiwan and Thāiland are potential for Lumbinī visit. TRPAP, Cross-Flow, IBS, DDC, etc. governmental and non-governmental organisations have also played a vital role to promote tourism and to alleviate poverty in this region. Concerned monasteries and institutes are completely responsible to preserve and conserve their shrines for ninety-nine years based on contract letter. Sacred Garden or archaeological monuments are under the supervision of LDT. It should be preserve and conserve under the criteria of UNESCO Heritage rule and regulations. Cemented-pavement, closed-ventilation of Māyādevī temple, superstructure based on Swayambhu stūpa model, etc. are not within the criteria of UNESCO. Chemical treatment is urgent to preserve monumental structures of this complex.

Several kinds of changes have slowly crept into the traditional beliefs, customs, food and drinks, dress and ornaments, position of family members, literacy rate, vocational training, organisation of functional groups, increasing the source of income and cultural activities due to the verbal communication and project works. Elements of modernisation is reflected in the management and maintenance of the lifestyle of the local people, monks, nuns, shop-keepers and labours who reside in Lumbinī area.

In the light of proper knowledge of art, architecture, culture pilgrimage, functionaries, fair and festivals, modernisation and changes of Lumbinī complex it will be possible for the governmental and non-governmental agencies to understand the modes of life and to prepare, projects for the development and modernisation of Lumbinī. The structure of the sacred performances is operative at all Buddhist shrines and hence all the places of Buddhist pilgrimage have the unity of beliefs and practices. However, the places of pilgrimage may be differentiated from one another also based on the sacred performances peculiar to them. There are varieties of rituals of Buddhist sects as well as specialists. Besides the specialists, i.e. monks and nuns who direct the rituals there are also some persons who assist at the time of performance. The florists, the musicians, the barbers, gardeners, guards and guides are the examples of ritual associates. The intrinsic relationship between sacred and secular is truly reflected in Lumbinī cultural complex in its settlement pattern, sacred performances and the professions involved in the sacred complex.

Man's final desire of enjoying beauty his sense of aesthetics is amply fulfilled in his sacred performances. All ritual performances are made with a perfect sense of aesthetics held with deep devotion. Sacred complex is an industry. A lot of population is dependent upon the pilgrim industry. Several thousands of people are employed in sacred total occupations of various kinds. It is hard to make a distinction between sacred and secular as far as the style of earning, the attitude towards earning and the professional ethics are concerned. It is also by this mechanism that Buddhist civilisation has been integrating through the ages of the geographical and cultural diversities of Nepāl. The civilisation boundaries cut across the national boundaries as described by M. Jha (1971).

It will further help to prepare plans for the conservation of important historical and archaeological monuments and the works of arts, which are decaying in the absence of proper care. The tourism industry is expected to respond to the challenges of times and help the country to forge ahead on the path of national development. Cultural tourism plays a major part in increasing national as well as international good well and understanding each other. Various activities of Lumbinī have been supported to change and modernise the lifestyle and status of the local people. A ring road should be constructed all around the Buddhist sites connecting Lumbinī. Five years plan of tourism of Rupāndehi district is proposed Buddhist Circuit Tour in this area. This plan will facilitate the pilgrimage tour and travel of Buddhist sites by bus or train. Lumbinī museum should be enriched with art, paintings and fragments of architecture belong to Buddha and Buddhism, especially of Lumbinī. All the development programmes of Lumbinī should be conducted based on mutual understanding between LDT and concerned party, who is interested to invest and develop of Lumbinī. More problems as well as suggestions are stated at the end of the concerned chapters properly, which will support for future planning and works.

Bibliography

Agrawala, V.S., *Studies in Indian Art;* First Edition, Varāṇasi: Vishwavidyalaya Prakashana, 1965.

Anderson, D. and Smith H. (ed.), *Sutta Nipata;* Reprinted; Oxford: Pal Text Society, 1990

Bandel, Lain Singh, *Prāchin Nepālī Mūrti Kalāko Itihāsa;* Kathmandu : Royal Nepal Academy, 2039.

Banerji, Arundhati, *Early Indian Terracotta Art;* New Delhi: Harman Publishing House, 1994.

Bapat, P.V. (ed.), *2500 Years of Buddhism;* New Delhi: Publication

Beal, Samuel (Trans.), *Si – Yu – Ki – Buddhist Records of the Western World;* Part II, Delhi: Motilal Banarashidas, 1994.

Bhatia, A.K., *Tourism Development Principles and Practices*; New Delhi: Sterling Publishers Private Limited, 2000.

Brown, P., *Indian Architecture*, '(Hindu and Buddhist period)', seventh print Bombay: D.B. Taraporevala sons and co. Private Ltd,1976.

Bidari, Basanta, 'Lumbinī: The Birth Place of Lord Buddha', *Ancient Ceylon:* Śri Laṅkā : No. 7, vol. II, (1990).

——, 'Forest and Trees Associated with Lord Buddha', *Ancient Nepal*; Kathmandu: DoA, No. 139, (June, 1996).

——, *Lumbinī: A Haven of Sacred Refuge;* Lumbini: The author, 2002.

——, *Kapilvastu: The World of Siddhartha;* Lumbini: The author, 2004.

Central Bureau of Statistics, *Population of Nepāl;* VDC, Municipalities wise-caste/ ethnicity/ mother tongue and religion, 2002.

Committee for the Development of Lumbinī, *Lumbinī: The Birth Place of Buddha;* New York: International Committee for Lumbinī, 1970.

Cowell, E.B. and Neil, R.A (eds.), *Divyavadana;* Cambridge, 1901.

Cunningham, A., *The Ancient Geography of India;* Reprinted, Delhi: Low Price Publishers, 1990.

Cuepper, Christoph, 'Lumbinī International Research Institute', *Souvenier;* Lumbinī; Liri:, 1996

Deo, S.B., *Archaeological Investigations in the Nepalese Terai, 1964;* Kathmandu: Department of Archaeology, H.M.G., 1968.

Development Associates for Rural and Regional Development (DEVA), *Lumbinī Visitors' Survey;* Submitted report to TRPAP, Kathmandu, 2004.

District Development Committee, *Participatory District Tourism Development and Management Plan, 2062-67*; Rupandehi: 2062.

Finland Government and HMG Nepāl, *Rural Water Supply and Sanitation Support Programme*; Annual Report, Fiscal Year 2002-03, 2003.

Forbes, Duncan,The Buddhist Pilgrimage; Delhi: Motilal Banarasidas Publishers, 1999.

Führer, A., *Pioneer;* Allhabad; 23rd December, 1896.

——, *Antiquities of the Buddha's Birth Place in the Nepālese Terai;* Reprinted, Delhi: Indologicol Book House,1972.

Giles, H.A. (Trans.), *The Travel of Fa– hsian* (399-414 A.D.) or The Records of Buddhist Kingdoms; Reprinted, America: Gereenword Press Publisher West Point C, 1981.

Giri, Gitu, *Cultural Touristic Sites of Lumbinī zone;* Siddharthangar: Lumbinī Youth Rural Development Forum, 2002.

——, *Art and Architecture Remains in the Western Terai Region of Nepāl;* Delhi: Adroit Publishers, 2003.

——, 'Devadaha', *Souvenir*; Devadaha: Bhawani High School, (2051), pp. 1-4.

——, 'Seal and Sealings at Kapilvastu and Lumbini', *Kshitija*; Siddharthanagar: Bhairahawa Multiple Campus, Tribhuwan University, No. 9, (2059), pp. 150-54.

——, 'Pilgrimage Tourism at Lumbinī and Siddharthanagar', *Siddhartha Special Issue*; Siddharthanagar: Industry and Commerce Council, (2061), pp. 39-44.

——, 'Pilgrims and Pilgrimage at Lumbinī', *Lumbinī*; Lumbinī: International Buddhist Society, Year 12, No. 16, (2006), pp. 9-16.

——, 'Fair and Festivals in Lumbini', Śānti Dīpa; Siddharthanagar: Lumbinī Academy; Year 1, No.1, (2063), pp. 6-11.

——, 'Lumbinī: Sacred Value and Environmental Challenges', *Lumbinī*; Lumbinī: International Buddhist Society, Year 13, No. 17, (2007), pp. 44-57.

Hagen, T., Nepāl: *The Kingdom in the Himālayas;* First Edition, Berne: Kummerly and Frey Geographical Publishers, 1961.

Hamilton, F.B., *An Account of the Kingdom of Nepāl;* Reprinted, New Delhi: Manjushree Publishing House, 1971.

Hashimoto, S. and et. al. (ed.), *Geography of the Nepāl Himālayas;* Tokyo: Saikan Publishing, 1973.

Horner, I. B. (Trans), *Cullavagga;* London: 1952.

International Buddhist Society, *Lumbinī*; Special Issue of Second World Buddhist Summit; Year 10, No.12, (2004).

Jha, Makhan, *The Sacred Complex in Janakpur;*Allhabad: United Publishers, 1971.

Khatry, Prem Kumar and Vaidhya, T.R., *Master Plan of Lumbinī and Its Implimentation*; (Unpublished paper presented on workshop conducted by Lumbinī Development Review Project, 28-29 Dec. 2002, Kathmandu, Proceeding to UNDP Local Office, 2003).

Lumbinī Development Committee, *Lumbinī Development Project Aide Memoir;* Kathmandu : LDC, 1975.

Lumbinī Development Trust, *LDT Newsletter*: vol.1, No.1 & 2, (2004).

Lumbinī Institues, 'Recommmendations for the Future Development of Lumbinī', *Lumbinī*; IBS, Year 10, No. 12, (2004).

Mishra, Tara Nanda, 'The Archaeological Activities in Lumbinī 1984-1985', *Ancient Nepāl*; Kathmandu: DoA, No. 139, (1996).

——, *The Location of Kapilvastu and Archaeological Excavation;* Kathmandu: Lumbinī Development Committee, n.d.

Mishra, Tirthprasada, '*Palpa ka Badahakima lai 1964 Salama Bhayako Saval'*, *Tribhuwan University Journal*; vol. XXII, No. 1, (June, 1999).

Mitra, Debala, *Buddhist Monuments;* Calcutta: Sahitya Samsad, 1971.

Mitra, Debala, *Excavation at Tilaurākoṭ, Kodan and Exploration in the Nepalese Terai;* Kathmandu: Department of Archaeology, 1972.

Mitra, R.C., *The Doctrine of Buddhism in India;* Calcutta: Bishwa Bharati, 1954.

Mukherji, P.C, *Antiquities of Kapilvastu Terai of Nepāl;* Reprinted, Delhi: Indological Book House, 1969.

National Museum of Nepāl, *Buddhist Collection of the National Museum of Nepāl;* Kathmandu; Department of Archaeology, 1998.

Nepal Rastra Bank, *A Report on Position and Possibility of Tourism in Lumbinī Zone*; Siddharthnagar: 2005.

Nepāl Tourism Board , *NTB Newsletter*; vol. 5, Issue 36 & 39, (2004).

Pandey, R.N., 'Archaeological Remains of Lumbinī', *Contributions to Nepalese Sudies*, Kathmandu: CNAs, T.U. vol. 12, No. 3, (1985).

——, *Sacred Complex of Ruru Ksetra;* Delhi: Adroit Publisher, 2000.

Petch, L., *Northern India According to the Shui-Ching-Chu;* Rome: Institute Italiano Peril Medio Ed. Estremo Oriento, 1950.

Pradhan, B.L., *Lumbinī Kapilvastu Devadaha;* Kathmandu: Tribhuwan University, Centre for Nepal and Asian Studies, 1979.

Regmi, J.C., *Nepalko Itihasika Bhugol;* Kathmandu: Tribhuvan University, Curriculum Development Centre, 1982.

Rhys Davids, T.W., *Buddhist India;* Reprinted, Delhi: Motilal Banarashidas Publisher Pvt. Ltd, 1971.

Rijal, B.K., 'Archaeological Activities in Lumbinī 1976-77', *Ancient Nepāl;* No. 30-39, (1975-77).

——, *Archaeological Remains of Kapilvastu, Lumbinī and Devadaha;* Kathmandu: Educational Enterprises, 1979.

——, *Archaeological Activities in Lumbinī, 1978-83*; Lumbinī: LDC, (1983).

——, *100 Years of Archaeological Research in Lumbinī, Kapilvastu and Devadaha;* Kathmandu: S.K. International Publishing House, 1996.

Rockhill, W.W., *Life of Buddha;* Reprinted, Varāṇasi: Orientalia India, 1972.

Rupandehi DDC, Decentrilized Local Goverance Support Programmes; NEP- 04/002, (Unpublished noted Report of DDC, 2005).

Sathe, shriram, *Dates of Buddha;* Hyderabad: Bharatiya Itihasa Sankalan Samiti, 1987.

Sharma, C.K., *River Systems of Nepāl;* Kathmandu: Sangeeta Sharma, 1977.

Sharma, R.C., *Buddhist Art;* New Delhi: Wiley Eastern Limited, 1995.

Singer, Milton, *Traditional India: Structure and change;* Journal of American Folklore, vol. 78, No. 281, (1958).

Somdet Phra Maha Samana Chao, *The Entrance to the Vinaya Vinamukha;* (vol. III), Bankok: Mahamakut Rajavidhyalay Press, 1983.

Srivastav, K.M., *Discovery of Kapilvastu;* New Delhi: Books and Books, 1986.

Srivastav, K.M., *New Horizons of Indian Archaeology;* New Delhi: Books and Books Publishers and Distributors, 1988.

Tange, Kenzo and Urtec, *Master Plan for the Development of Lumbinī Phase II*; Stage 2 Report, 1977.

TRPAP, *Village Tourism Newspaper*; Rupandehi: Year 2, No. 2, (2061).

Tucci, Giuseppe, *Stupa, Art and Architecture and Symbolism;* New Delhi: Aditya Prakashan, 1988.

Upadhya, B.S., *Buddha Kalina Bharataya Bhugol;* Prayag: Hindi Sahitya Sammelan, 2018.

Uesaka, S., *Achaeological Survey Record of Māyādevi Temple;* (Lumbinī: Japanese Buddhist Federation Unpublished Seminar Paper, 1997).

Vidyarthi, L.P., *The Sacred Compex in Hindu Gaya;* Bombay Asian Publishing House, 1961.

Vidyarthi, L.P., 'Social Anthropological Researches in India;, *Journal of Social Research,* vol. 9, No. 1, 1966.

Vidyarthi, L.P. and et al., *The Sacred Complex of Kashi;* Delhi: Concept Publishing Company, 1979.

Vimalananda, M., *Homage to Triple Gems*; Lumbinī; The author, 2043.

Warren, H.C., *The Life of The Buddha;* Reprinted, Delhi : Eastern Book Linkers, 1986.

Watters, Thomas, *On Yuan Chwang's Travels in India (A.D. 629-645);* II Part; New Delhi: Munshiram Manoharlal, 1961.

Yoshida, Mitsuo and Arita, Kazunari, 'On the Siwaliks Observed Along some Routes in the Central Nepāl', *Journal of Nepāl Geological Society*, vol. 2 Special Issue, 1982.

Appendices

Appendix-1
THE SACRED COMPLEX OF LUMBINĪ CITIZENS

Serial No. Code No. Date:

1. Name: House No. Own House / Rented House
   Age: Sex: Caste: Sect:
   Education:
   Period of stay in Lumbinī Ksetra: Profession:
   Total No. of family members:

2. I. **Sacred centres visited**
   Name of the sacred Centre purpose Frequency Remarks
   i) Māyādevī temple complex
   ii) Nepāl Vipasna Centre
   iii) International Viskchhuni Sangh
   iv) Myanmar Temple
   v) Śri Laṅkān Monastery
   vi) Mahabodhi Monastery
   vii) Thāi Monastery
   viii) Panditarama
   ix) Manang Sewa Samaj Monastery
   x) Chinese Temple
   xi) Korean Temple
   xii) Tara Foundation Duesseldrof , Germany
   xiii) Museum
   xiv) Lumbinī International Research Institute
   xv) Nipponzan Myohoji (World Peace Stūpa)
   xvi) Natural Scenes, i.e., saras, nilgai, bird watching .
   xvii) Any other place

   II. **Sacred performances**
   1. Name Frequency and Assistance of /Monk/Nuns

2. Purpose
3. Daily routine
(Specify activities related to sacred performances, distribution of time devoted to sacred / secular activities)

4. Conducted Programmes to change and modernise the lifestyle of the local people:

Name of the programme	Institute	Location	Remarks

5. Result of the programmes:

6. Proper suggestions to develop Lumbinī and lifestyle of the local people:

Appendix 2
SCHEDULE FOR STUDYING PILGRIMS

Serial No. Code No. Date:

1. Name of the pilgrim ....
Age : .... Sex ....Religion:Hindu/ Buddhist/..Caste : .... Ethnic group: ....
(In case of monks/nuns...................... sect)
Country: Profession: ......
Education: ....
Mother Tongue:........... Other language: ....
Local Address: ....

2. Pilgrimage to Lumbinī Ksetra
   i) Main purpose of
   ....
   ....
   ii) No. of his/her visit to this temple/shrine ......
   iii) Duration of stay in Lumbinī Ksetra ....
   iv) Stayed at a) Hotel/Lodge: b) Dharmashala c) Friends / Relatives: ....
   v) Visiting: a) Alongs
   b) With family members
   c) With friends/Relatives
   vi) Description of any special event, observation or happening by the informant (pilgrim) in Lumbinī Ksetra. Give details precisely.

3. Places/sacred centres, Vihar, Monastery, Stūpa, etc. visited or to be visited.

i) Māyādevī temple complex (Sacred garden)
ii) Nepāl Vipasna Centre
iii) International Viskchhuni Sangh
iv) Myanmar Temple
v) Śri Laṅkān Monastery
vi) Mahabodhi Monastery
vii) Thāi Monastery
viii) Panditarama
ix) Manang Sewa Samaj Monastery
x) Chinese Temple
xi) Korean Temple
xii) Tara Foundation Duesseldrof, Germany
xiii) Museum
xiv) Lumbinī International Research Institute
xv) Nipponzan Myohoji (World Peace Stūpa)
xvi) Natural Scenes, i.e., saras, nilgai, bird watching.
xvii) Any other place

4. Saced Performance (if any during your visit of Lumbinī Ksetra)
i) Simple darshan
ii) Any ritual a) Name:
b) Place:
c) Assistance of Priest, monk, nun or specialist, if any:
d) Frequency of performance:

5. Other Buddhist pilgrims sites visited by the informants in Nepāl/India/Else where
i) ....
ii) ....
iii) ....
iv) ....

6. Notes: (General description about how he or she was motivated to undertake the pilgrimage of Lumbinī. What knowledge about Buddhism has been added to him by the present visit. Also note the informant's knowledge of the sacred geography, history, pilgrim, etc. of Lumbinī Ksetra.

7. Suggestions to develop Lumbinī Complex:

Appendix- 3
THE SACRED COMPLEX OF LUMBINĪ
Life history

No. Date:
Name:
Age:
Sex:
Sect:
Education:
Occupation:
Birth and Early Childhood:
Sacraments of the Life:
Association with some temple or not
Religious Belief:
Any Association with Politics/Service:
Professonal Life and cultural knowledge:
Any Efficacy in Buddhism & dasavidya:
Tours, Travels and Pilgrimage:
Your View Regarding Wrld Peace:
Your social and Religious Activities:
Association with any Vihar, Monastery, Meditation Centre or Samiti:
Miscellaneous:

Appendix-4
THE SACRED COMPLEX OF LUMBINĪ
Pilgrimage (TIRTHAS)

Serial No. Code No. Date:

I. a) Name of the Shrine
   b) Location: East/West Zone; Plot No.
   c) Country and Institute:
   d) Contract date:

II. a) Structure of the shrine:

No. of monastery, vihar, guest house/other religious Shrines of establishments within the principle of the Tirtha:

   b) Name of the deity/deities enshrined:
   c) Principal deity:

III. Shrine functionaries: Total Nos.:
   Caste/group: Nature of appointment:

IV. a) Country name of the pilgrimage:

b) Average number of pilgrims visiting the shrine daily and on festive occasions:

V. Name of the sacred performances for which the shrine is popular:

VI. Notes:

(Please note the caste/liguistic/religious group inhabiting region where the shrine is located. Whether the shrine is managed by individual, a particular caste, or a linguistic or religious group? Whether the shrine is visited by both Hindus and Buddhist, Special offerings, special functions, such as dance, festivals, Jatras, etc. should also be recorded.)

Appendix- 5

THE SACRED COMPLEX OF LUMBINĪ

Questionnaire for the proper person and offices belonged to Lumbinī Area.

1. Office Name: Telephone No.

2. Respondent's Name:

3. Programmes:

Name Duration Aim Targeted population Achivement Remarks

4. Future plans:

5. Suggestions to promate the lifestyle of the local people:

Appendix 6

Life history

No. Date: 15 April 2005
Name: Bhikshus Maitri
Age: 51
Sex: Male
Sect: Theravada
Education: Diploma in Buddhist studies, Sri Lanka
Occupation: Buddhist Monk & social worker
Birth and Early Childhood: 28/12/1954 west no.1 Nuwakot, Trishuli.
Former Name: Kiran Chandra Kumar Shakya
Date of Birth: Dec. 28th, 1954 (Full moon day)

Place of Birth: Trishuli Bazar, Ward no. 1, Nuwakot District, Nepāl

Parent's name: Ravi Ratna Shakya & Shanti Shakya

Date of Ordination: November 4th, 1968 in Śri Laṅkā.

Date of High Ordination: June 30th, 1976 in Śri Laṅkā.

High School Education: Tribhuban Trishuli High School, Trishuli.

Higher Education: Śri Laṅkā Vidyalaya and University of Kelaniya, Śri Laṅkā

'Diploma in Buddhist Studies'

Sacraments of the Life: At the age of 5 ordained in Hiranya Varna Mahavihar, Patan as a Shakya boy. At the age of 13 ordained in Śri Laṅkā

Association with some temple or not

Associated Ananda Kuti vihar Swoyambhu, Kathmandu.

Religious Belief:

Belief on self, Do good, Be good.

Any Association with Politics/Service: Established IBS in Lumbinī.

Professonal Life and cultural knowledge: Social service in surrounding 6 Lumbinī.

Any Efficiency in Buddhism & dasavidya: We do inter-action between all religions.

Tours, Travels and Pilgrimage: US, Israel, Turkey, Italy, India, Thāiland, China, Japan, Korea, Canada, Śri Lakā, Germany, Vietnam, Cambodia, etc.

Your View Regarding World Peace: Everybody should have five precepts to have world peace.

Your social and Religious Activities: Drinkiy water supply, Drainage, Literacy & non-formal education, Free health service, Ambulance etc. in social & religious; Train young monks & send to Śri Laṅkā for further studies.

Association with any Vihar, Monastery, Meditation Centre or samittee: Associated with international Buddhist society, Lumbinī Development Trust, etc.

Miscellaneous: Main Aim is to make Lumbinī healthy, literate & clean.

Teachers: The Most Venerable Baddegama Wimala Wansa Anunayeke Mahathera. The Most Venerable Amritananda Mahanayeke Mahathera

Nepāli Programme Producer: Śri Laṅkā Broadcasting Corporation (1976-80)

Buddhist Programme Producer: Radio Nepāl and Nepāl Television (1981-93)

Teacher: Ananda Kuti Vidyapeeth, Swoyambhu, Kathmandu. (1981)

Founder: Sangharama Bhikkhu Training Centre, Nepāl Buddhist Scriptural Society International Buddhit Society, Lumbinī.

Member Secretary: Ananda Kuti Vihara Trust 1981-1991.

Founder and Secretary: Nepāl Buddhist Scriptural Society 1980-1990.

Manager: Ananda Bhoomi Buddhist Monthly 1981-1991

Superintedent: Lumbinī Sacred Garden 1999-2002

President: Nepāl Śri Laṅkā Friendship and Cultural Council 1981-1995

Chair Person: Kathmandu/Eugene Sister City Committee 1988-2002

Council Member: Lumbinī Development Trust

Executive Member: Ananda Kuti Vihar Trust, Society for Promotion of International Peace and Understanding

Advisor: Nepāl MSR Centre, Tibet Pragya Sangh, Nepāl Buddha Dharma Sewa Sangh.

Project Supervisor: R & K Project under World Terakoya Movement Literacy and Non-Formal Education Programme in Rupandehi and Kapilvastu District).

Founder Chairman: International Buddhist Society with the aim of Free Health Service Centre, Pur Drinking Water Supply, Sanitation, Drainage, Literacy and Non-Formal Education, Skill Training, Income Generating Programme in the surrounding VDCs of Lumbinī and Kapilvastu.

Produced Amritanjali Documentary on the life and deeds of the most Ven. Bhikkhu Amritananda Mahanayeke Mahathera in 1990, which was awarded by Sikha Sanjh Pali Nepāli Newari Dictionary.

Producing Lumbinī Magazine every six month based on World Culture Heritage. At the moment, we are running a free hospital in Lumbinī and a Bhikkhu training centre in Lumbinī. Sent 40 Sramaneras to Śri Laṅkā, among them 12 sramaneras from Lumbinī.

Appendix-7
Life History

No. Date: 17 April\2005

Name: Ven. Phra Nirandorn Sihanam

Age: 35

Sex: Male

Sect: Theravada Buddhist Monk

Education: M.A. (Linguistic, Delhi University)

Occupation: Buddhist Monk as the Dhammadupa Buddhist Missionary Monk.

Birth and Early Childhood: 27-10-1970 in 1983 became a novice (Samanera) in 1990 become a monk (continuely) Place of birth: Udonthani, Thāiland

Father's name:	Mr. Ken Sihanam
Mother's name:	Mrs. Yon Sihanam
Parent's occupation:	Farmer
Nationality:	Thāi
Religion:	Buddhism

ACADEMIC RECORD

Examination Passed	**Year**	**Institutions**
1. Pali 1-2	1989	Ministry of Education
2. Diploma of Teacher Training	1999	Mahachulalongkornrajar-vidyalaya University
3. Bachelor of Arts (English)	1996	Mahachulalongkornrajar-vidyalaya University, Bangkok, Thāiland
4. Master of Arts (Linguistics)	1998	University of Delhi, India (With second class honors)

Sacraments of the Life:

Buddham Saranam Gaccami- I go to the Buddha for refuge.

Dhammam Saranam Gaccami- I go to the Dhamma for refuge.

Sangham Saranam Gaccami- I go to the Sangha for refuge.

Association with some temple or not?

Yes, such as all international Buddhist Monasteries in Lumbinī.

Religious Belief: The three folold trainings (studies)

1. *Sila*: Morality- traing in higher morality.
2. *Samadhi*: Concentration/meditation- in higher mentality
3. *Panna*: Wisdom- and in higher wisdom.

Any Association with Politics/Service:

No, but for social activities is associated.

Professonal Life and cultural knowledge: Buddhist teacher and Buddhist philosophy.

Any Efficacy in Buddhism & dasavidya: Improving in the threefold studies.

WORKING EXPERIENCE

Place	Year	Institutions/ Organisations
1. Wat Thāikasinagar, India	1995	Department of Religious Affairs
2. Wat Bangplat, Bangkok	1999	Ministry of Education (Primary School)
3. Wat Dusitaram, Bangkok	1999	Ministry of Education (Secondary School)
4. Wat Pleng, Bangkok	1998-2000	Department of Religious Affairs (Buddhist School)

5. Royal Thāi Monastery Lumbinī 2000- Royal Thāi Government, Lumbinī, Nepāl.

Tours, Travels and Pilgrimage: Thāiland, Myanmar, Srilanka, India and Nepāl.

Your View Regarding World Peace: Calmness, tranquillity, reasonable in different religiouses and security all in the world.

Your social and Religious Activities: Buddhist missionary monk to Nepāl official)

- chairman, Pariyattidhamma study at Royal Thāi Monastery in Lumbinī. (Buddhist study)
- Secretary and member International Buddhist Monk in Lumbinī (Theravada) Association with any Vihar, Monastery, Meditation Centre or samiti:
- All international Buddhist Monasteries in Lumbinī Garden.
- Panditarama Meditation Centre in Lumbinī.
- Shree Shakya Singha Vihara at Lalitpur, Kathmandu.

Miscellaneous:

Also believe in Buddha Ovada: The three admonitions of exhortations of the Buddha

1. not to do any evil.
2. to do good, to cultivate good.
3. to purify the mind.

Appendix 8
Life history

No.

Name: THAY HUYEN DIEV (THE MOST VEN. LAM TRUNG)

Age: 60

Sex: Male

Sect: Vietnam Buddhism

Education: High Education

Occupation: Professor, President Founder Vietnam Phat Quue in Lumbinī, the first international Buddha monastery introduced in Lumbinī.

Birth and Early Childhood: x

Sacraments of the Life: Good environment and harmony of the life.

Association with some temple or not? President, International Buddhist Federation.

Religious Belief: Vietnami Buddhism.

Any Association with Politics/Service: No.

Professonal Life and cultural knowledge: Professor of History and International Relation.

Any Efficency in Buddhism & dasavidya: x

Tours, Travels and Pilgrimage: x

Your View Regarding World Peace: First the peace of mind must be practiced by every individul and then Peace will come to the world.

Your social and Religious Activities: To prompte and motivate people to do good things, understanding, live harmony with the people and the nature.

Association with any Vihar, Monastery, Meditation Centre or Samittee: Vietnam Phat Que, Lumbinī. Happy to contact and work with different organissations to this area.

Miscellaneous:

Lumbinī development was in so years.... for the plane, we have to interest the work and work hard in right situation. The pece and happyness will not come alone like a god, every body have work hard together and sincerly.

Appendix 9
Life history

No. Date: 10.5.2005.

Name: Ven. Vimalananda Mahasthavir

Age: 77

Sex: Male
Sect: Theravadi
Education: Buddhology - S.S.C.
Occupation: Monk

Birth and Early Childhood: birth-Tansen, Palpa on-5.6.1928. father-Motikaji Śākya and mother-Chandramaya Śākya. ordination-Anandakuti vihar,Kathmandu, on13.11.1951.Teacher-Ven. Kovida Mahasthavir.

Sacraments of the Life: Based on Theravadi tradition.

Association with some temple or not? Royal Buddha Vihar, Lumbinī.

Religious Belief: Theravadi Buddhism.

Any Association with Politics/Service: No.

Professonal Life and cultural knowledge: Head monk of Lumbinī, he knows life and teachings of Buddha and Buddhism.

Any Efficency in Buddhism & dasavidya:

Tours, Travels and Pilgrimage: Śri Laṅkā, Singapur, Thāiland, Verma, India, Japan, etc.

Your View Regarding World Peace:

Your social and Religious Activities: Human welfare activities are done.

Association with any Vihar, Monastery, Meditation Centre or Samittee: Śākyamuni Buddh Vihar, Lumbinī and Mahabodhi Vihar Tansen.

Miscellaneous:

Peace is not possible with out disarmment in present situation of Nepāl. Buddha's teachings should be borne in mind for peace and harmony.

Glossary

abhayamudrā	gesture made with raised right hand, palm turned towards the on looker, signifying protection
adhisthāna	pitha or foundation of temple
Adi Buddha	primordial Buddha
Agni	regent of southeast and God of fire
agni kunda	fire altar
ahimsa	without violence
akshamālā	rosary of beads.
āmalaka	ribbed-melon.
Amrita-ghāta	vessel containing the nectar of immorality.
anamela vivaha	very different in age between bride and bridge-groom.
ada	dome
ańgada	armlet.
*ań*jali	pose the palms of the hands are kept close to each other with folded hands in adoration.
ankuśa	a weapon with a sharp metal hook.
apatti	problem.
Aposthagarasālā	Buddhist resting site.
ārāmas	resting sites.
ārati	the worship of the deities performed by the priest in the morning by showing lighted lamp.
ardhaparyankasana	to sit with one leg crossed on the seat, the other hang on the pedestal.
arsanic	a kind of mineral in under ground water.
āsana	seat or seated posture.
asura	demon, enemies of gods.
Astamātrika	eight mothers worshiped by Hindus and Buddhists.
Āswinśukla navami	ninth full moon day of Āswin month, (Sept.-October)

Avalokiteśvar	Lord who gazes in all directions, Bodhisattva of compassion.
āvāsa	abode, apartment, habitation.
avatāra	incarnation.
āyudha	weapons.
Bālā *chaturdasi*	a festival celebrated remembering bala at Sivalaya.
Bazār	market.
Bhāgavata	sect pertaining to Vishṇu, devotees of Vishṇu.
Bhairava	terrible or anger position of Siva.
bhajana	singing of devotional songs in honours of the deities.
bhakala puja,	worship of the deities in lieu of the fulfilment of the promise on account of his grace.
Bhikshus	monks.
bhitrimadesha	inner Terai.
Bhodighara	a kind of Buddhist temple.
bhoga	sexual pleasure.
Bhūdevī	the earth Goddess.
Bhūmi	earth.
Bhūsparsa-mudrā	the posture of hand touching the earth by the fore-finger.
bighā	a measure of land, equal to about 5/8 acre.
bodhi	perfect knowledge, enlightenment.
Bodhisattva	a living being in the process of Enlightenment, brought to rest upon the thighs.
Buddha	awoken one, Enlightened One, specially the term refers to akyamuni Siddhartha, founder of Buddhism.
Buddha jayanti	Birth anniversary of Sakyamuni Buddha.
ceitiya	pagodas described by the Chinese pilgrims.
chaitya	a Buddhist temple, sanctuary.
chakra	discus, wheel, one of the Vishṇu's emblems.
Chāmunda	Goddess of dread, one of the mother Goddesses.
Chaturmukhi-liṅga	four-faced Śivaliṅga.
chautāri	a platform built of earth, plaster or brick for sitting.
chetiya-ghara	residence of the Buddhist monks and nuns.
chhatrāvali	wide spread parasol or shape of umbrella.
choten	Tibetan word for stupa.

churiā	range of low hills immediately to the north of the Terai
cire-perdue	lost wax method.
civilisation	Social structure of traditions, value system and cultural personality define civilisation.
consumers	Citizen and pilgrims, involved their routine, specifying their activities related to sacred performances, and the distribution of time devoted to sacred secular activities.
cyma	padma.
damaru	small drum in the form of an hour-glass,
Dānavas	sons of Kasyapa and Danu, enemies of the God.
danda	staff, siginifying power and sovernity.
dandadhara	rod (danda) bearer.
Daśāvatāra	ten incarnation of Vishṇu.
Dehī, Devi	Goddess.
Devatā	deity, God.
	Devī, always with them.
Dharma	moral, religious duty, universal law, order, custom.
Dharma chakra	propogation of Buddha; teaching, the wheel of the law.
dharmasālā	rest house for pilgrims.
Dharmaśāstra	scriptures, the law of science.
dharma-sūtra	of a short work of the religious categories.
dharmayātrā	piligrimage.
Dharmodayasabhā	a religious committee organised by the Buddhist.
dhotī	the lower garment, the drapery, unstitched cloth worn by men.
dhupikā-kuntala	hair-dressing in the style of deep curls.
dhvajā	banner.
dhyānamudrā	meditation pose.
duibhanga	to stand with double side-bends in the body.
Durgā	Hindu Goddess in destructive form.
galā	neck.
ganas	host of inferior deities attending on Śiva and others.
Gāndhakuti	a type of Buddhist temple.
ganta	bell.

garbha — the central room of a house or the room in a temple containing an idol, a sanctum; womb.
garbhagriha — the enclosed chamber.
Garuda — vehicle of Vishṇu, a kind of bird.
Gautam — clan name of the ancient Sakyas.
ghata — jar, vessel.
ghāta — burial or burning place.
ghata-shaped — vase shaped.
grām a — village.
Gumbaj style — semi-circular dome style.
guna — quality, three gunas: raja, sattva and tama.
Guru — spiritual teacher.

hāra — neck-ornament, necklace.
harmikā — four-sides of the stūpa indicated by eyes of Buddha
Hinayana — preliminary school of Buddhism, lesser vehicle.
homa — oblation to gods.

jangha — middle portion of the Hindu and Buddhist temples.
jā*nna* — spiritual knowledge.
janta-ghara-sālās — halls attached to bathrooms in the vihār.
jant-ghara — bathrooms in the vihār.
jatā — matted hair.
Jataka — birth story of Sakyamuni, especially reference of rules of action and rebirth.
jatāmukuta — a coil of matted and clotted hair.
jungle — forest.

*kachch*hā — loin cloth .
kachchi-kuti — a cottage made of mud, grass, bamboo and such perishable materials.
Kalaratri — night of astami at Dashain festival.
kalāsa — vase.
kamala — lotus.
kambarbandha — waist band.
Kami — a tribe of worker.
Kappiya-kutis — store house out side the vihārs.
karand-mukuta — karanda-shaped crown, short in height and small in size.
Karerikuti — Buddhist house as mentioned in *Vinayapitaka*.

karuna	compassion, embodied in male Buddhist deities.
kathina chivar	dress of monk and nuns.
Kathinadana	donation to monk and nuns.
katyavalambita	akimbo, to place the hand on the hip indicating a posture of ease.
kesabandha	hair tied in a knot.
kholā	river, rivulet.
kinnaras	heavenly musicians with human faces and the body of birds.
kiritamukuta	conical-shaped crown, face of glory, auspicious symbol.
Kolan tree	Nauclea Cordifolia tree.
Kosamba kuti	Buddhist house as mentioned in *Vinayapitaka.*
ksetra	a holy place, sacred area particularly for pilgrimage.
kumar	young boy, prince.
kuṇda	pit.
kuṇdal	ear-ring.
Kuśa-grass	a portic, kind of grass, *Poa Cynosuroides.*
Kusum tree	flower, a kind of fruit.
kutis	huts.
lalitāsana	a sitting posture, to sit with one leg crossed on the seat, the other one hanging down or placed below.
Lāmā	heads of the monasteries in Tibet, high dignitaries.
liṅga	representative of male, Śiva-linga, mark-sign.
Lokeśvara	Lord of the world, epither for Śiva and Avalokiteśvara.
Lumbinigāme	Lumbinī village.
Mahābhārat mountain	a range of hill from east to west below the mid hilly region and upto Churiā range.
Mahāparinirvāna	death event of the Lord Buddha.
Mahāpatha	road leading to the main gate.
Mahārājā	great king.
Mahāvana	great forest.

Mahāviniskramana	palace leaving event of Buddha.
Mahāviniskramana-dwār	palace leaving door of Buddha, eastern gateway of Kapilvastu.
Mahayana	one of the broad school of Buddhism in later than Hinayana, wide concept and practices.
Maitreya	friendly one; the future Buddha, whose appearance is a waited.
mandala	a circular diagram or design.
mandapas	halls in a vihār.
Mandir	temple.
Manjuśri	Bodhisattva of wisdom.
mantra	sacred incantation, mystical formula of invocation.
mantras	reciting sacred scriptures.
Manushi Buddha	human Buddha, of a former Buddha.
Māyā	mother of Buddha Sakyamuni.
medi	part of a stūpa raised on a basal cylinder.
mithuna	a couple of lovers, inter course, sex.
modernisation	sacred complex and sacred specialist's development leads in the process of modernisation and transmission.
mudrā	conventional hand-gesture, expressing feelings and thoughts.
mukuta	crown or coronet.
mundamālā	skull-garland , worn by Śiva or Devī.
mūrti	image.
nadi	river.
namaskār mudrā	Saluation or adoration mudrā, posture.
Nandi	bull, the mount of Śiva.
Nārāyan	the abode of man or moving on the water.
Nigrodharāma	a vihar at Kapilvastu in the ancient period.
Nirvāna	extinction, free from desire.
nritya mudrā	dancing posture.
Nyāgrodha tree	vatavriksha, fig tree, *Fiscus indica*.
Om mani padma hum,	Buddhist mantra, the mantra of Avalokiteśvara.
padam lotus. *padmāsāna*	lotus-seat, sitting posture in which two legs one

Padmpāni	lotus-handed; holding a lotus in the hand.
pādukā	footprint.
pale	watchman.
pancha sila,	five virtues–non killing, non stealing, non telling lies, non practice of adultery and non use of intoxicants.
Pañchāla coin	coin of ancient Pāñchala area.
Pañchamukha-linga	five-faced liṅga (phallus).
Pañchrātra	a cult grown around Bhāgvatism.
parda pratha	tradition in curtain, cover the face by the cloth.
Paribhogikā stūpa	erected over the objects used by Buddha.
parikrama	circumambulation of the temple by the devotee in the process of worship.
Parinirvāna	death of Buddha
Parinirvāna topes	stūpas erected after the death of Śākyamuni
pāśa	noose of ropes
pāthasālā	school, teaching houses.
patra-kundala	ear-rings, comprising of leaves.
pauwā	inn, public resting house on the road-sides, built by the devotees with arrangement of water-supply.
Phāguna krisṇa chaturadasi,	fourteenth day dark night in Feb.-March.
phulapati	flowers, leaves etc to offer the deities.
phulbāri	garden.
Pipal	*Ficus religiosa.*
pitha	stool, seat, pedestal or throne.
pokkharani	tank.
prabhāmandala	an aureole, a large halo or glory surrounding around the main figure.
pradakshināpatha	circumambulatory path.
Pradimokshavana	sacred Lumbinī garden.
Pragatishil	progressive.
prajnā	wisdom, embodied by Buddhist female deities.
Prithivi	earth.
priyadarsi	title of Emperor Asoka, good looking.
priyadarsi lāta	Aśokan pillar.
puja	worship.
R*āja-bhavan*	royal palace.
Rāja-mārga	ordinary street.

Rājā	king.
Rākshasa	demons, enemies of the god.
Rāma navami	birth day of Ram Chandra, Epic Hero.
rathayatra	chariot procession of the deities.
ratna-kuṇḍala	ear-rings of gems.
Ratnasambhava	jewel-born, one of five transcendental Buddhas.
Sa-ka-na-Sya	legend on a terracotta seal from Tilaurākot.
Sacred Complex	The sacred centres, the sacred performances and sacred specialists of a Buddhist place of pilgrimage reflects the level of continuity, compromise and combination of the traditions.
Sacred specialist	Performance great tradition, to the rural population by popularising certain texts, by organising pilgrimage and by officiating as the ritual and monastic priests.
sāgar	water tank
Śaiva	sect pertaining to Śiva , worshipper of Śiva.
Śākta	sect pertaning to Devī, devotees to Devī.
Śākyamuni	one of the mortal Buddhas, son of Suddhodhana and Mayadevi of ancient Kapilvastu, who was born in Lumbinī.
sāl tree	*robusta*.
sālālghara	a kind of Buddhist house as mentioned in
samabhanga	to stand straight without any bent in the body.
samapādasthānaka	standing without bent.
samkrānti	the first day of the month.
samskārs	sacraments.
sangarāma	monastery.
sangha	Buddhist monastic committee.
sangharāmas	Buddhist monastery resting houses.
sanghāti	scarf.
sankha	conch-shell one of the emblems of Vishnu.
saptaratha	pedestal of a building divided in to seven sections, seven chariot.
Saririka stūpa	erected over the corporal relics of Buddha.
Sikhara	the spire, tower model shrine.
Śiva-rātri	birth-night of Śiva, (February-March), anniversary of Śiva.
Siwalika	Churia range, low hill range immediately north of terai region.

snāna	bath.
Śramaṇa	ascetic, monk.
stambha	a pillar.
sthān	place.
sthānaka	standing pose, to stand.
sukhāsana	sitting at ease, any comfortable sitting position.
s*ūtra*	verses of scriptures.
tāl	tank.
tāntrika	a class of work teaching magical or mystical.
tapas	penances, austerities.
tapo-bhumi	land of meditation.
tathagata	Thus-Gone-One, arrival at perfect knowledge.
Tathāgata	Śākyamuni Buddha.
Telār-nadi	oil river.
terabhuvan	thirteen-steps on the stūpa upto the *harmika*.
tika	mark made on the forehead of a person.
tirtha	a holy place of pilgrimage.
tirthasthala	holy site that provides salvation.
torana	arched gateway.
tribhańga	standing pose in which the body has three side way bends; the first from feet to hip, second from hip to shoulder and the third from shoulder to crown.
triśula	trident.
Uddesikā	commemorative stupa of the Buddha's life.
upavita	sacred thread.
uppatana-sālās	service halls.
ushisha	a hair-knot bound at the top with a protuberance.
vahāna	a mount or seat of the deity.
vaijantimālā	garland of vaijayanti flowers worn by Vishnu.
vairāgya	renunciation.
Vaishnava	sect relating to Vishnu, devotes of Vishnu.
Vajra	thunderbolt.
vali	sacrifice.
vamsa	generation.
vāna	arrow.
vana	forest.
varadamudrā	hand-gesture bestowing boons.

Vāyupuraka	circular component of a spire (*gajur*) at the top of the shrine.
vidhyarambha	start to study.
vihār(s)	dewelling rooms of the monks and nuns, rest houses.
viṇā	a musical instrument.
votive stūpa	built by devotees and small in size.
vrata	act of keeping fast on the day of religious festival.
yajña	sacrific offered to the gods.
yantra	geometric drawings used in Hindu and Buddhist rituals.
yasthi	a part of a crowned umbrella in the stūpa.
yoga mudra	meditation posture.
yogi	saint, mendicant.
yojana	a measurement of length as mentioned by Rhys Davids one yojana corresponds to 7.5 miles.
yupa	inner part of a dome in the stūpa.

Illustrations

1. Peace Stūpa, Japan

2. Birth Panel of Buddha of Peace Stūpa

3. Enlightenment Panel of Buddha of Peace Stūpa

4. First Sermons of Buddha of Peace Stūpa

5. *Mahaparinirvana* Panel of Buddha of Peace Stūpa

6. Sanctum and Sanctorum of Nippanzan Myohoji

7. Lumbinī Museum

8. Lumbinī International Research Institute

9. Friendship Bridge of Harahawa River

10. Peace Flame and central canal

11. Stupa of International Nun's Association

12. Lokamuni Golden Stūpa of Myanmār

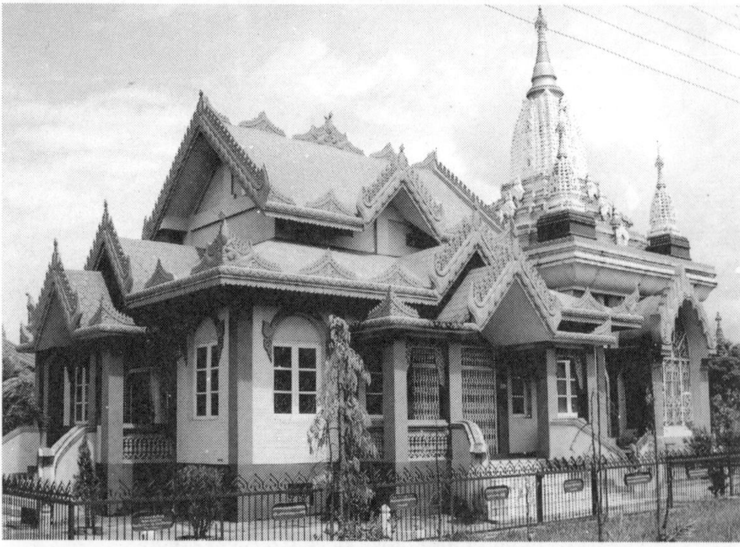

13. Pagoda of Myanmār

14. Monastery of Mahabodhi Society, India

15. Śri Laṇkan Monastery

16. Facing of Thai Monastery

17. Thai Monastery

18. Stūpa of Mananga Sewa Samaja

19. Lama Gumba

20. Chinese Pagoda

21. Lotus Stūpa of Tara Foundation

22. Tympanum of Royal Vihar

23. Wall Painting of Lotus Stūpa, Tara Foundation

24. Wall Painting of Royal Vihar

25. Coins of Lakshmipur

26. Eastern Face of Mayadevī Temple

27. South Face of Mayadevī Temple

28. Aśokan Pillar

29. Structural Remains of Māyādevī Temple

30. Stūpa and Ring-well

31. Sacred Puskarini Tank

32. Group of Stūpas

33. Root of Sacred *Pipal Tree*

34. Pilgrims of Lumbinī

35. Pilgrims of Lumbinī

36. Performances of Nipponzan Myohoji

37. Full Moon Day Performances

38. Chaitra Purnima Melā

39. Chaitra Purnima Melā Dancing

40. Festival-Scene

41. Buddha Jayanti Melā

42. Buddha Jayanti Melā

43. Sacred Specialist of Thai Monastery
(Named Ven. Phra Nirandorn Sihanam)

44. Sacred Specialist's Cottage of Vietnam (Named THAY HUYEN DIEV (THE MOST VEN. LAM TRUNG)

45. Sacred Specialist of International Buddhist Society
(Named Bhikshus Maitri)

46. Sacred Specialist of Royal Vihar
(Late Ven. Vimalananda Mahasthavir)

47. TRPAP Productions by Local People

48. TRPAP Productions by Local People and Exhibition at Lumbinī.

Index